LECTURE NOTES ON
INTERNATIONAL TRADE THEORY AND POLICY

LECTURE NOTES ON
INTERNATIONAL TRADE THEORY AND POLICY

Richard Pomfret

University of Adelaide, Australia

Wp World Scientific

NEW JERSEY • LONDON • SINGAPORE • BEIJING • SHANGHAI • HONG KONG • TAIPEI • CHENNAI

Published by

World Scientific Publishing Co. Pte. Ltd.

5 Toh Tuck Link, Singapore 596224

USA office: 27 Warren Street, Suite 401-402, Hackensack, NJ 07601

UK office: 57 Shelton Street, Covent Garden, London WC2H 9HE

Library of Congress Cataloging-in-Publication Data
Pomfret, Richard W. T.
    Lecture notes on international trade theory and policy / Richard Pomfret.
    p. cm.
    Includes bibliographical references.
    ISBN-13: 978-981-281-443-2 (wood-free paper)
    ISBN-10: 981-281-443-4 (wood-free paper)
    1. International trade. 2. Commercial policy. I. Title.
    HF1379.P663 2008
    382.01—dc22

                         2008030256

British Library Cataloguing-in-Publication Data
A catalogue record for this book is available from the British Library.

Typeset by Stallion Press
Email: enquiries@stallionpress.com

Printed in Singapore.

Preface

These lecture notes are intended for students with some background in economics (at a minimum an Economics Principles course, preferably an intermediate course in Microeconomics). They formed the basis for courses taught in 2006-8 to third-year Economics undergraduates at the University of Adelaide and to students studying for the MA in International Studies at the Johns Hopkins University Bologna Center in Italy.

The lecture notes provide an integrated account of trade theory and policy that can be read straight through, and they can be treated as either a substitute for or as a complement to the standard international economics textbooks. The textbooks for these courses were in 2006-7 Paul Krugman and Maurice Obstfeld *International Economics* (7th Edition) and in 2008 the first edition of Robert Feenstra and Alan Taylor *International Economics*, which are both useful for their exposition, the problem sets and other ancillary material. The footnotes to the lecture notes provide caveats, extensions and entry points for further reading, and can be ignored without loss of continuity or essential content. For readers wanting to move to a higher technical level, the advanced textbook by Feenstra (2004) is recommended.

Part Two provides an analysis of trade policies. While it aims to relate to current issues and policy debates, it does not pretend to provide an authoritative account of actual trade policies. Good overviews of trade policies are for the USA Pearson (2003) and Devreux, Lawrence and Watkins (2006) and for the EU Messerlin (2001). Annual reviews of developments in international trade and investment can be found in the WTO's *World Trade Report* (available at www.wto.org) and UNCTAD's *World Investment Report* (at www.unctad.org). The WTO's World Trade Profiles first published in 2006 and available at www.wto.org provides a useful summary of national tariff policies.

Much of the material in these lecture notes draws consciously or unconsciously on my 1991 book *International Trade: Theory and Policy* (Oxford, UK and Cambridge, MA: Basil Blackwell), which went out of print during the 1990s and was reissued as print-on-demand through Lightning Print in 1999. I am grateful to Basil Blackwell for their release of copyright claims over the contents of that book.

Contents

List of Figures

Part I
Theory

Chapter 1

Introduction

Trade theory has long been at the heart of economics. Adam Smith, the father of modern economics, identified the *division of labour* as the key to *The Wealth of Nations*. This is true at any level; an individual can have much higher material living standards by specialising than by being self-sufficient. If one person produces cloth and another produces the necessary pins and needles and a third sews the garment, more clothing can be made than if each person tries to do all the tasks. In the opening chapter of his book Smith goes a step further, describing a pin factory in which different specialists make the various components and join them together. Such manufacturing was at the heart of the industrial revolution going on around him in Scotland in 1776.

Such specialisation only works if each producer can find people with whom to exchange his or her services, and this requires an institutional framework. Secure property rights so that when a good is exchanged the recipient is confident of owning it, and enforceable contracts, so that artisans could specialise in manufacturing with some confidence that they would receive food in return, were early examples of basic institutions required for specialisation and exchange. The more that transactions and transport costs are reduced, the more willing each person will be to specialise within a larger and larger market area. For Adam Smith the main constraint on economic growth was the extent of the market.

International trade has the same basis. A country can enjoy a greater total of goods and services through specialisation and trade than if it tries to be self-sufficient. This truth is illustrated by the falling behind, throughout history, of countries that tried to shut themselves off from trade and by the absence of such countries today — even North Korea trades.

What do countries trade? To some extent they trade for things that they cannot produce themselves, e.g. Italy sells olive oil and imports furs. This sort of trade is, however, a small and declining portion of world trade; in the early 21st century agricultural goods and minerals accounted for less than a fifth of world trade. In practice, short of oil, some minerals and a very limited number of agricultural products, there are few goods that cannot be produced, at a cost, in most countries. Most of the world's merchandise trade is in manufactured goods and the fastest growing sector is trade in services, both things that can be produced in almost any geographical setting.

The great contribution of David Ricardo, in the first half of Chapter 7 'On Foreign Trade' in *The Principles of Political Economy and Taxation*, was to establish **comparative advantage** as the basis for mutually beneficial exchange. The gains from trade do not depend upon one country being absolutely better at producing one good and a second country being absolutely better at producing another good, but on comparative differences. It is not true that, when one country is more efficient than another in all activities, there are no gains from trade. Thus, Thailand may be more efficient than

Laos in producing both clocks and cabbages, but if it is relatively more efficient at producing one good then there are potential gains from trade.

Comparative advantage is most simply illustrated with a numerical example and a single input. Suppose in Thailand a worker can make five clocks or produce 100 cabbages in a month, while in Laos a worker can produce two clocks or 50 cabbages. Thai workers have an absolute advantage in both activities, but have a comparative advantage in making clocks. Suppose now that a Thai farmer stops growing cabbages and makes clocks instead, and that two Laotian clockmakers start growing cabbages. As a result of this specialisation, joint production is increased: cabbage output is unchanged (100 less in Thailand, 100 more in Laos), but clock production is higher (five more in Thailand, four less in Laos).

The key to the increase in total output is the existence of differences in opportunity costs. Although Thai workers are more efficient in both activities, the opportunity cost of producing cabbages (i.e. the amount of clocks foregone) is higher than in Laos. This is a very powerful argument for trade because for any pair of countries it is inconceivable that opportunity costs will be identical for every pair of goods and services, and thus that a country does not have a comparative advantage in some activity.

Specialisation by comparative advantage creates a potential win-win situation. Several popular misconceptions about trade are simply incorrect as generalisations. It is not true that the more productive country must lose because it will be undercut, nor is it true that the less productive country will lose from trade because it cannot compete. Finally, it is logically impossible for a country to have a comparative advantage in all goods. The location of comparative advantage may not be obvious to policymakers, but if in bilateral trade one country has a comparative advantage in a good, then the other country must, definitionally, have a comparative advantage in some other good, because opportunity cost is a relative concept.

The potential gain from specialisation by comparative advantage is as true at the individual level as at the national level. Suppose two people agree to run a brain surgery and one is a better surgeon and a better manager than the other. There are still gains from specialisation; if she is relatively better at brain surgery, then she should specialise in surgery and the other person should specialise in managing the business. Of course, people can change their comparative advantage by training and education, and in the international trade context we will come to that dynamic story later. In the short-run, it may still be better to specialise by current comparative advantage while devoting resources to increasing productivity; that is why we see future brain surgeons working as waiters as they pass through their early university years in medicine.

This is not to say that comparative advantage always leads to trade. High transactions costs make trade impractical. One way to view economic development over the centuries, emphasised by Nobel laureate Douglass North, is that falling transactions costs have led to ever increasing specialisation, trade and wealth. Prehistoric trade was largely (but not entirely) barter, but having to find somebody wanting to exchange something you want for what they have to offer at a mutually convenient time is restricting. Arms-length trade in monetized economies requires institutions to ensure at a minimum that exporters receive payment and importers have recourse if a good they have paid for is not delivered. From the basic letter of credit to sophisticated instruments for hedging against exchange rate risk, such "institutions" have emerged and are constantly being refined. Innovations such as the container revolution or reduced telecommunications costs underlie the rapid growth of trade in the last half century, but causality runs both ways and such innovations were in part responses to the potential but unrealised gains from trade.

Governments may also place obstacles to international trade, perhaps because they dislike some of the outcomes from specialisation by comparative advantage. In past decades, some governments resisted a situation which led to them specialising in primary products but with booming energy and minerals prices in the early 21st century countries like Canada and Australia were happy to see their commodity exports boom.

More difficult to assess are situations where trade exposes societies to drastic change. After the arrival of Columbus in 1492, the opportunities for exchange between Europe and the Americas were massive. Half a millennium later both sides of the Atlantic have been transformed. Transatlantic trade has been an important source of higher living standards on both sides of the ocean, but the distribution of the gains from trade has been highly unequal and includes huge costs. Today's native peoples of the Americas may be better off than their ancestors were before European contact, but for the many who died from diseases, guns or alcohol trade was of dubious benefit. The population of Mexico fell 90% in the century after 1519, and it took over 350 years for the population to regain its 1519 size; similar human devastation occurred throughout the Americas.[1] The millions of Africans transported to slavery in the Americas suffered from high mortality rates en route and awful work conditions when they reached their destination. The British occupation of Australia in the late 1700s also involved unwilling settlers (convicts) and a high death toll among the native peoples; the population of Tasmania was callously and completely eliminated.

---

[1]In many respects Aztec society in present-day Mexico was no less developed than Europe; the capital city, with about a quarter of a million people in 1500, was larger than any European city, reflecting a sophisticated division of labour (Grennes, 2007). However, inferior military technology and the absence of horses exposed them to military conquest. The absence of domestic animals, apart from dogs and llamas, contributed to the low resistance of Americans to European diseases. Horses, cattle, pigs, sheep, wheat and bananas were unknown in the Americas, and potatoes, tobacco, tomatoes, maize and cocoa beans were unknown in Europe. Without the 'Columbian Exchange' there would be no tomato sauce in Italy, no potatoes in Ireland, no Belgian chocolate, no tacos or refried beans in Mexico and no hamburgers in North America.

Chapter 2

The Ricardian Model

The benefits from specialisation according to comparative advantage can be powerfully illustrated by a numerical example, as with the cabbage growers and cuckoo clock makers in Chapter 1. A more general approach to illustrating the potential gains from trade is to represent all the production possibilities in both countries. For a pair of goods we can do this in a two-dimensional diagram showing the *production possibility frontiers* (PPFs).

The simplest application to trade, often called the classical trade model or Ricardian model, assumes two goods, two countries and one input. The primary input, e.g. labour, is fixed in each country, but is mobile between the two activities. The productivity of labour is constant in each activity, but labour productivities differ between countries. These are simplifying assumptions which yield a parsimonious model whose results concerning the gains from trade are powerful and general.

Table 2.1.　Alternative output combinations in two Ricardian economies.

Europe						
Grain	48	40	32	24	16	8	0
Cloth	0	4	8	12	16	20	24
America						
Grain	60	45	30	15	0		
Cloth	0	5	10	15	20		

The data for the PPFs in two Ricardian economies are provided in Table 2.1. America has four workers each of whom can produce 15 kilos of grain or 5 metres of cloth, while Europe has six workers each of whom can produce 8 kilos of grain or 4 metres of cloth. This can be represented diagrammatically by the PPFs in Figure 2.1. If labour is perfectly mobile between the two activities and is divisible (i.e. a worker can work part-time in both activities without altering productivity per hour), then the frontiers are linear. Without trade, consumption of the two goods in each country cannot be at a point beyond the frontier.

Figure 2.1 indicates that America has an absolute advantage in the production of both cloth and grain, but America's comparative advantage is in grain. The American production possibility frontier (PPF) is flatter because the opportunity cost, in terms of foregone cloth, of producing grain is less in America than in Europe. The slope of the PPF is equal to the opportunity cost of producing an additional unit of the good measured on the vertical axis. In this case the slope is constant and equal to one third (1/3) in America and one half (1/2) in Europe. The difference in slope of the PPFs determines the specialisation patterns which can yield gains from trade.

The gains from trade implicit in Figure 2.1 can be made explicit by constructing a box out of the two PPFs. This is done in Figure 2.2 by aligning the output levels which result from specialisation according to comparative advantage, in this case with America producing only grain and Europe producing only cloth. The rectangular box

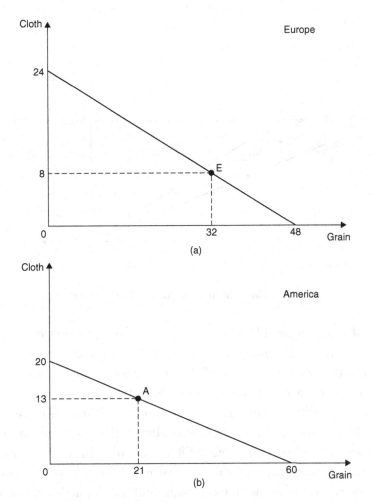

Figure 2.1.   Production possibility frontiers: (a) Europe; (b) America.

enclosed by the two axes contains all of the possible consumption
points in the two countries given a joint output of 60 kilos of grain
and 24 metres of cloth, and assuming no transport costs. Specifically,
both of the autarchic consumption points, *A* and *E*, lie within the
box. However, if either country were to consume at its autarchic point
after trade took place, then the other country would consume more
of both goods than it did before trade. Any other consumption point

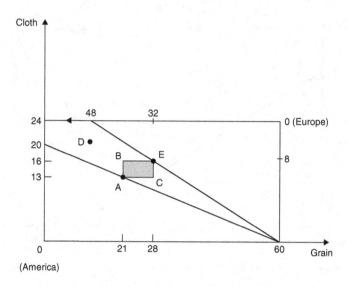

Figure 2.2.   Gains from trade in the classical model.

within the rectangle *ABEC* involves added consumption of one or both goods in both countries. Since any point in the rectangle leaves both countries clearly better off, the existence of such a rectangle proves the existence of potential gains from trade.

The generality of the gains from trade is clear in Figure 2.2. The only requirement for a rectangle like *ABEC* to exist is that the slopes of the two PPFs must differ over some range. The linear PPFs are a special case of this general conclusion; they are not a likely description of an actual situation, and few countries specialise completely. Nevertheless, the same analysis applies as long as there is any difference between opportunity costs in the neighbourhood of *A* and *E*; the two PPFs can be aligned at points other than the origins, and a wedge containing superior with-trade outcomes will exist.[1]

---

[1]The analysis can be generalised to many goods. Representing the opportunity costs by pre-trade price ratios, the price ratios can be ordered in a chain to determine where comparative advantage is greatest in each country; each country will specialise in goods starting from different ends of the chain (Haberler, 1936; Deardorff, 1979).

The Ricardian model with a single input, labour, and fixed relationships between the input is a supply-side theory of international trade. Without introducing demand-side considerations, the consumption points are exogenously determined and, although we can identify a set of superior consumption points with trade, there is no way of identifying which will actually exist. The actual outcome in Figure 2.2 could be anywhere in the wedge between the two PPFs, i.e. a combination of consumption points that was unattainable without trade, but we do not really know whether the country which produces less of one good and more of another good is actually better off. The distribution of gains from trade within the country may be such that rich clock buyers are better off and poor cabbage eaters worse off, or perhaps everybody is better off; within this framework we cannot address this kind of question.

Another reason for moving beyond the single-input fixed-coefficient classical model is that, for a supply-driven model, the technology is remarkably simple. Our next step is to introduce a second input, which also introduces the possibility of diminishing marginal productivity of labour as the country specialises. It will normally rule out complete specialisation, and also allow us to say something about the distributional consequences of trade. This will be done in Chapter 4, where we also introduce demand elements to close the model. Later, in Chapter 9, the introduction of increasing returns to scale will enhance the gains from trade but may again lead to complete specialisation; in the extreme case there will be a single global producer.

In sum, the simplifying assumptions of the Ricardian model make it inappropriate for answering many questions about international trade. That should not, however, distract from the fundamental conclusion that potential gains from trade exist wherever opportunity costs differ. Another major implication of the Ricardian model is that trade patterns are determined by differences in labour productivity. This has strong empirical support, dating back to a pioneering

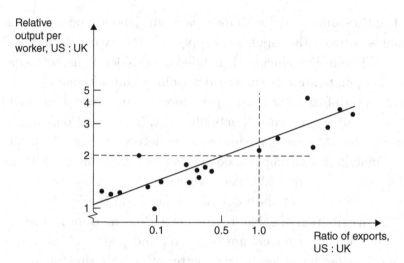

Figure 2.3.   McDougall's results.
Source: Adapted from McDougall (1951).

1951 paper by G.D.A. McDougall, who examined the relative performance of US and UK exporters in manufacturing industries. US
workers were more productive in all 20 industries studied, but the
ratio of US to UK exports was highest where the productivity differences were greatest and lowest where the US advantage was smallest
(Figure 2.3). A similar result has been found in many subsequent
empirical studies. In the period when McDougall was writing, US
wages were roughly double those in the UK, and his evidence indicated that the point at which UK exports were larger than US exports
coincided with where US labour productivity was twice that of the
UK; in industries where US firms were more than twice as productive
as US firms US exports exceeded UK exports, but in industries where
the gap was less than double UK exports exceeded US exports.

Before turning to extensions of the core trade model, the next
chapter addresses the question of why analysis of international trade
is any different from analysis of trade between individuals or between
regions within the same country.

Chapter 3

Why International Trade?

The analysis in previous chapters is very general and could apply equally to individuals or any group of individuals as to countries. The clocks and cabbages example could have involved Teddy and Larry instead of Thailand and Laos. What then is the reason for focussing so much on the nation as the unit of analysis?

Most nation states do have some sense of identity, as a result of which tastes may differ or other cultural breaks may occur at the border. If this influences attitudes towards residence, people may be less willing to move across national borders than to move within countries. A distinguishing feature of the standard neoclassical trade model in the next chapter is the assumption that goods are perfectly mobile across borders, but factor endowments are fixed. This is a reasonable assumption for land, but much less so for other inputs such as capital which clearly does cross borders, while labour is in an intermediate position.

A stronger argument for focussing on the nation state is that national borders represent breaks in regulatory control. National governments have the power to regulate trade at their borders, by erecting barriers to imports, subsidising or restricting exports. They may also have idiosyncratic regulations that make it more difficult for foreigners to compete in their markets, for example by requiring complex labelling in the national language. The existence of separate national currencies also introduces an added cost to trading across borders.

These are valid arguments, but a legitimate question is how important are they? Is it so much more difficult for a Thai farm to sell their products in Laos rather than in Thailand, or for a South Australian firm to sell in New Zealand rather than in Western Australia? This is a fundamental, but also typical, example of where the empirical evidence matters. Many commentators look at the fall in import duties and other trade barriers and see the emergence of a global economy in which the nation state is no longer a useful unit of analysis, but whether this is in fact true is testable.

The Gravity Model

Economics is an applied social science in which empirical studies play two important roles: hypothesis testing and measurement. The first role was seen in the previous chapter in McDougall's test of whether theories that trade patterns are determined by relative productivities stood up to real world evidence in the form of US and UK exports. This is important because economic theorists are good at devising logically sound theories, but when several competing theories claim to explain the same phenomena the usual test is to see which theory best explains the known facts about the phenomenon. A common process in economics is for somebody to produce a new theory, which upon testing helps to explain a phenomenon but is revealed to have some inconsistencies with reality which require refinement of the theory — a process described, for example, in Chapter 7. In sum, empirical testing indicates which theories provide better explanations and highlights where more thought is required to refine the theories.

A second role of empirical work is to measure the size of predicted effects. This is important in the analysis of trade policy. Theory may show that a trade policy change will benefit some people and hurt others, but policymakers will want to know whether the gainers benefit more than the losers lose, and if the latter are to be compensated what is an appropriate amount.

Another area where empirical work has been important in recent years has been in the analysis of the importance of distance and national borders. The most successful model for analysing bilateral trade patterns is the gravity model, which explains trade between two countries by the size of their economies and the distance between them. This is a very simple model; after all, larger economies have more to sell than smaller economies and larger economies generate more demand than smaller economies and it is obvious that, other things equal, transport costs are negatively associated with distance.

In its simplest form, the gravity model is estimated econometrically as:

$$T_{i,j} = f(Y_i, Y_j, D_{i,j})$$

Where the subscripts i and j refer to a pair of countries, $T_{i,j}$ is the bilateral trade between i and j, Y_i and Y_j represent the incomes of the two countries, and $D_{i,j}$ is the distance between them. The model was originally developed by Linnemann and Tinbergen in the 1950s and 1960s and proved successful in explaining bilateral trade patterns, but occupied a small place in the trade literature because the results seemed obvious and unexciting.

The gravity model has enjoyed a renaissance since the mid-1990s as people have focussed less on the basic model and more on understanding deviations from the basic model. Among the reasons why trade between a pair of countries may deviate from the general pattern described by the simple model are cultural affinity (a common language or shared history has a positive impact), geography (coastal nations trade more and landlocked countries trade less), and borders.

A very influential 1995 study by John McCallum examined US–Canada trade. The two countries had a free trade agreement, simple border crossing procedures, a common language and other features which might be expected to make the border virtually meaningless for trade. Yet when McCallum examined bilateral trade flows among the 48 contiguous US states and ten Canadian provinces he found that the simple gravity model worked well for the 58 units and for within-country trade, but there were substantial differences when a trade flow was between a state and a province than when it was between two states or two provinces. For example, British Columbia and California are roughly equidistant from Ontario and the Californian economy was roughly ten times the size of that of British Columbia and yet Ontario traded three times as much with BC than with California.

McCallum's results have been replicated in several subsequent studies using data for more recent periods and variations in method, and they have proven to be robust. It remains unclear why there is such a strong border effect, but an important point is that if the US–Canada border represents a substantial break in the ease of trade then other borders are likely to be much more significant. Thus, this result gives support for the continued study of international trade even in an era when formal trade barriers have been much reduced.[1]

---

[1]The existence of a border effect, in the sense of a downward impact of national boundaries on the volume of trade, has been found in other parts of the world. Head and Mayer (2000) show that even after the elimination of tariffs on intra-EU trade and the reduction in non-tariff barriers in the EC92 Single Market Programme, a significant border effect remained. Carolyn Evans (2003) argues that the border effect may have minor welfare implications if they are due to minor inconveniences and reflect small price differentials. This does not overturn the conclusion that borders matter for trade flows and Engel and Rogers (1996) have shown that, for a given distance apart, prices are more closely related between pairs of US and pairs of Canadian cities than between a US and a Canadian city.

One candidate for why within-country trade is easier than between-country trade is that almost all countries have a single domestic currency and few countries share a common currency — at least until eleven European countries adopted the euro around the turn of the century. In a much-cited 2000 paper Andrew Rose ran a gravity model of bilateral trade which included a dummy variable to indicate whether the two countries had a common currency. His striking result was that countries with a common currency traded about three times as much with one another as a similar pair of countries which used different currencies. This result was criticised in part because the common currency countries in his study tended to be either dependencies or microstates and hence atypical, but the positive relationship between common currency and bilateral trade appears to be robust to other specifications even if the size of the effect is less than in Rose's initial study.

Another finding from recent applications of the gravity model has been that the negative effect of distance on trade, while continuing to be significant, has grown smaller over time. This is in principle a way of measuring increased globalisation, and is consistent with observing the continuous reductions in the costs of doing trade over recent decades. However, it is an imprecise way of capturing the extent of the increase in globalisation because the results are sensitive to the specification of the gravity model (for example, how income and distance are measured and which other factors are incorporated into the estimation). Moreover, over the longer-run political factors such as wars can have a larger impact than technical innovations in transport and communications, so that the continuous increase in globalisation is far from inevitable; the establishment of a global economy in the century before 1914 was substantially reversed between 1914 and 1945, and even after the process resumed it took decades to reattain the degree of globalisation that had existed in 1913.[2]

---

[2]Measured by the share of trade in GDP, the dominant economy in the early 2000s, the USA, had a lower level of international economic involvement than the United Kingdom had had in 1913.

The gravity model has become a workhorse for studying many aspects of international trade. However, the common use of dummy variables to track the importance of particular features must be done with care. Trade between the English-speaking Caribbean countries may be especially high because they have a free trade agreement but it may also be because they share a common language or because islands tend to trade more than other countries. In other words, dummy variables are a simple construct and may be picking up more than their creator bargains for. Also, the use of gravity models has become more frequent because large bilateral trade datasets have become readily accessible and computing power has mushroomed so that it is easy to run regressions. With many thousands of observations standard errors are low and significance tests often satisfied, even when the economic significance of the variable in question may be dubious. This is not to question the usefulness of the gravity model, but rather, as with any econometric results, to caution against drawing economic conclusions without due care.[3]

---

[3]Richard Baldwin and Daria Taglioni (2006) provide an introduction to the gravity model for dummies, and assess the use of dummies in gravity models.

Chapter 4

The Neoclassical Model

The Ricardian model is a simple and powerful tool for showing the gains from trade in a very general way. It also captures the empirically supported result that comparative advantage reflects productivity differences. However, the simple Ricardian model has weaknesses, most apparent in its implication of complete specialisation and the absence of demand-side analysis, but also in its reliance on unexplained differences in productivity to explain trade.

This chapter introduces a model with two substitutable inputs and with demand. It is often known as the neoclassical model because it applies mainstream microeconomic theory, as developed in the late 19th century, to international trade. It is also known as the Heckscher–Ohlin model after two Swedish economists who pioneered the explanation of trade flows in terms of factor proportions, which is one of the key results from the model. In its standard form the model owes much to Paul Samuelson, the US economist whose book *The Foundations of Economic Analysis* set out the formal structure of neoclassical economics in terms of constrained maximisers (given technology and tastes, producers maximise profits and consumers maximise utility subject to budget constraints), and to James Meade, who not only wrote an influential international economics textbook, but also at LSE in the mid-1950s was the focus for a posse of young economists who developed the core propositions of trade theory (including Bhagwati, Corden, Lancaster, Lipsey, Mundell and Rybcynski).[1] The core propositions were established by the mid-1960s, when Ron Jones (1965) provided a neat synthesis of the model's structure.

Several assumptions from the Ricardian model in Chapter 2 are retained. Markets operate competitively. Goods flow freely across borders. Factor inputs are fixed, and while mobile across sectors factors are not internationally mobile. Transactions costs are ignored. The new assumptions are, firstly, that there is more than one factor input and producers combine inputs to maximise profits, and, secondly, consumers purchase goods in a combination that maximises their utility subject to their budget constraint. The technology that defines how inputs can be combined and the preference functions that define how consumers assess utility are both "well-behaved", in the sense of being continuous and differentiable.[2] In contrast to the Ricardian model, there is no assumption that producers in one

---

[1]Meade's textbook appeared as two volumes (1951, 1955) and was supplemented by a 1952 handbook on the geometry of international trade. Harry Johnson, probably the most influential trade economist between the late 1950s and his death in 1977 aged 57, was at the University of Manchester until 1959 and also associated with these young economists.

[2]In calculus terminology, the first derivatives are positive and second derivatives negative. Thus, increasing any input leads to a higher output but at a diminishing rate, or increased consumption of any good leads to higher utility but at a diminishing rate. Marginal productivity or marginal utility can be negative (e.g. as more and more workers are combined with a fixed piece of land, or as a consumer eats more and more doughnuts) but these situations are ignored because rational producers and consumers should not enter the zone of negative marginal contributions to output or utility.

country are inherently better at certain activities or that technology differs across countries.

Many of these assumptions will be relaxed in later chapters when we examine the implications of imperfect competition or international factor mobility. We will also try to mediate between the extreme assumptions of perfectly immobile or perfectly mobile technology, neither of which seems fully appropriate to a world in which knowledge transfer is widespread but not costless and not universal. Meanwhile, the Heckscher–Ohlin theorem provides the important insight that, even with identical production functions, gains from trade are possible.

The Closed Economy Neoclassical Model

A *production function* indicates the relationship between inputs and outputs given the state of technology. It can be interpreted as either the minimum quantity of inputs needed to produce an output or the maximum output that can be produced with given input quantities. One way to represent the production function is as an *isoquant map*. In Figure 4.1 each isoquant represents an output level and traces out the combination of inputs (labour and capital) needed to produce this amount. Any combinations of the inputs to the northeast of an isoquant are feasible but inefficient, while combinations to the southwest are inadequate to produce this output. In neoclassical models the isoquants are smooth, assuming continuous substitutability of the two inputs, and curved, because the marginal rate of technical substitution diminishes (e.g. the more labour is used relative to capital then the less capital has to be substituted for a unit of labour in order to maintain a constant output).

For a given output level, the actual combination of inputs used depends upon the relative price of inputs. Suppose that $100 is to be spent in producing the good and the prices of capital and labour are $20 and $10 per unit. In Figure 4.2 the input combinations

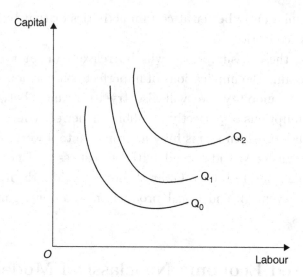

Figure 4.1.   An isoquant map.

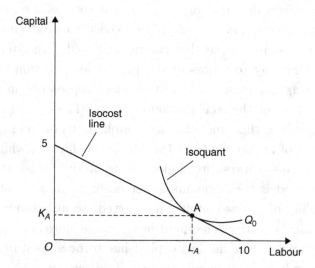

Figure 4.2.   The optimal combination of inputs.

Note: K_A and L_A represents the least-cost combination of inputs to produce output Q_0 when $P_K = \$20$ and $P_L = \$10$. With these input prices Q_0 is the maximum output with can be produced with an outlay of $100.

that can be used given the budget constraint are indicated by the triangle which is defined by the intercepts 5 units of capital and 10 labour units and the origin; this is a right-angled triangle, whose slope is P_L/P_K, or one half. Given the shape of the isoquant, the maximum output is produced with the combination of labour and capital at point A; L_A combined with K_A is the cost-minimising way of producing quantity Q_0 and the output-maximising use of \$100 worth of inputs. At the tangency point A, the slopes of the isocost line and the isoquant are equal, i.e. the marginal rate of technical substitution (MRTS) is equal to the factor price ratio (in this numerical example the MRTS of labour for capital is 2).

Different goods have different production functions, and thus for any budget constraint they will have differing efficient input combinations. In the **Lerner diagram** (Figure 4.3) with the same cost of inputs, good Y is produced at tangency point B, which involves more capital and less labour than production of good X, which is at point B. Define Y as the capital-intensive good and X as the labour-intensive good; as long as the isoquants only intersect once, this ranking by *factor intensity* holds for all sets of input prices.[3]

If X and Y are the only two goods to be produced, then the output mix depends upon factor supplies and relative factor prices. The **Edgeworth Box** combines the isoquant maps for X and Y in a rectangle whose dimensions are the total amount of labour and capital in the economy. In Figure 4.4 the isoquant map for X is drawn from the origin O_x and the isoquant map for Y is drawn from the origin O_y. A point like Z is a feasible allocation of capital and

---

[3]If the isoquants intersect twice, then two factor price lines can be drawn, each of which has a tangency point with both isoquants; for one factor price line X will be the labour-intensive good and for the other factor price line Y will be the labour-intensive good. The possibility of **factor intensity reversals**, i.e. that factor intensities are not invariant to input prices, is discussed in the context of the Leontief Paradox in Chapter 7. The original contribution by Lerner (1952) is discussed in greater detail by Feenstra (2004, 10–13 and 26–9).

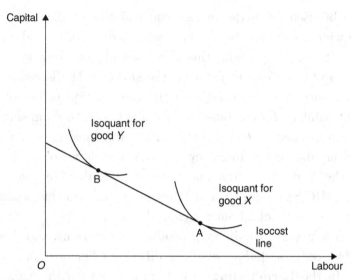

Figure 4.3.   Comparing factor intensity of two goods.
Note: X is the labour-intensive good because the capital: labour ratio at A is lower than that at B. Y is the capital-intensive good because, faced with the same factor prices as producers of X, its producers adopt a higher capital : labour ratio.

labour between the two activities, but it is inefficient[4]; from point Z transferring capital into Y-production and labour into X-production to attain point Q increases the output of Y without reducing the output of X, i.e. Q is on the same X-isoquant as Z but on a higher Y-isoquant. Similarly, point S is superior to Z because reallocating capital and labour can increase output of X without reducing output of Y. Efficient allocation of inputs implies being at a tangency point such as Q, S or V, where $MRTS_x = MRTS_y$.

The locus of these tangency points is the ***contract curve***. The contract curve bulges downwards (i.e. is below the diagonal in

---

[4]At point Z, $O_x L_x^z$ units of labour and $O_x K_x^z$ units of capital are used in production of good x and $O_y L_y^z$ units of labour and $O_y K_y^z$ units of capital are used in production of good Y. All capital and labour in the economy is employed, but the MRTS differs in the two activities, so that price signals will show that capital can be more productive in Y production ($MP_K/MP_L > r/w$) and labour can be better used in X production, where $MP_L/MP_K > w/r$.

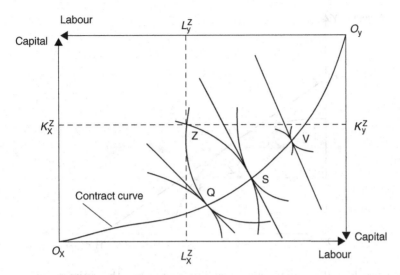

Figure 4.4. Allocation of inputs between activities (the Edgeworth Box).
Note: Each point in the Edgeworth Box represents an allocation of the economy's labour and capital between the two activities X and Y. For example, at Z activity Y employs L_y^z and K_y^z, while activity X employs L_x^z and K_x^z. The dimensions of the box are set by the total availability of each factor, that is, the total labour force is $L_x^z + L_y^z$ and the total capital stock is $K_x^z + K_y^z$.

Figure 4.4) because X is the labour-intensive good and labour is on the horizontal axis.[5] Which point on the contract curve represents the most efficient allocation of resources depends upon relative factor prices, because for any set of factor prices only one point will satisfy the optimising condition $MRTS = P_L/P_K$. In sum, given the production functions and factor supplies, for any factor price ratio there is a single optimum output mix, or for any output mix there is a single equilibrium factor-price ratio.

Each point on the contract curve corresponds to a point on the production possibility frontier, and vice versa. Thus, for point Q in Figure 4.4 the output values of X and Y can be read from the

---

[5] At any set of factor prices, the capital/labour ratio is smaller in X. A ray from the origin, O_x, to any point on the contract curve will be flatter than a ray from O_y to the same point.

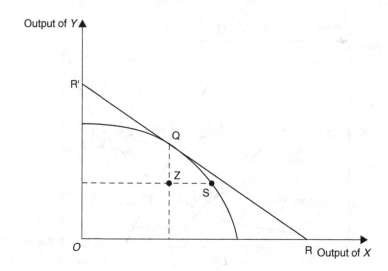

Figure 4.5.   The production possibility frontier and the optimum mix.

isoquants and plotted in goods space. Doing the same for S, V and all other points on the contract curve traces out the PPF, with the intercepts in Figure 4.5 corresponding to the origin points of the Edgeworth Box. The PPF is convex to the origin because of diminishing MRTS. As greater quantities of the labour-intensive good, X, are produced, this places more and more demand on the limited labour resources, raising the opportunity cost, in terms of foregone Y, of producing an extra unit of X.[6]

The point on the PPF at which profit-maximising producers will operate depends upon relative goods prices. With a price line $R'R$, whose slope is P_x/P_y, production occurs at Q; at any other point the value of output could be increased by changing the output mix, e.g. from point S produce more Y and less X. The intercepts of $R'R$ provide a measure of total output at current prices in terms of

---

[6]The degree of convexity is greater if there are diminishing returns to scale in an activity, but this is not a necessary condition. Increasing returns to scale in an activity may, however, offset the factor substitution effect and produce a concave PPF at least over some range; this possibility is ignored here but will be returned to in Chapter 9 (Figure 9.1).

X or Y, corresponding to gross domestic product in national income accounting.

Since any goods price ratio implies a single optimum output mix, given the PPF, then it also implies a unique optimum point on the contract curve and a single equilibrium factor price ratio. Similarly any factor price ratio can only be associated with one equilibrium goods price ratio. Thus, although in Figures 4.4 and 4.5 the relevant price ratio was introduced exogenously, only one price ratio can be determined independently. The model will now be closed by showing how relative goods prices are determined by the interaction of demand and supply.

The underlying forces on the demand side are consumer preferences, which are represented by indifference curves. Individual indifference curves are smooth, because goods are assumed to be substitutable in consumption, and concave, due to diminishing marginal rates of substitution. In Figure 4.6 higher indifference curves represent higher utility levels because consumers prefer more to less. The **community indifference curve** (CIC) is a summation

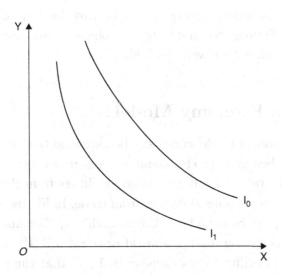

Figure 4.6. Community indifference curves.

of all individual indifference curves and is assumed to retain the same properties. This is a controversial step because, if individual preferences differ, then the community indifference curve may aggregate gainers and losers from a change and hence implicitly makes interpersonal utility comparisons in determining whether the community is better or worse off. Because trade and trade policies do have implications for income distribution this is a serious shortcoming, and in the next chapter the analysis is repeated with demand and supply curves; this produces the same general conclusions but highlights different features.

Within a closed economy production and consumption of each good must match. The highest attainable utility level is where a community indifference curve is tangent to the production possibility frontier. At this point there is no more efficient use of the country's endowment of inputs and no superior output mix. The tangency point can be supported by a sole equilibrium price ratio, tangent to both the PPF and the CIC, and corresponding to this goods market outcome is a single equilibrium factor price ratio and allocation of factors between activities. As first demonstrated by Arrow and Debreu in the 1950s, competitive markets will lead to this Pareto optimum outcome with many goods and factors as long as production functions and utility functions are well-behaved.

The Open Economy Model

The closed economy model can easily be extended to show the gains from trade. When an autarchic country opens up to trade, as long as the world price ratio for any pair of goods differs from the domestic price ratio, there are potential gains from trade. In Figure 4.7, $R'R$ is the pre-trade price ratio and C is the autarchic equilibrium described in the previous section. Facing a world price ratio $W'W$ the country can increase its utility by specialising in Y, so that the production point shifts from C to G, and consuming at J, which is on a higher community indifference curve than C.

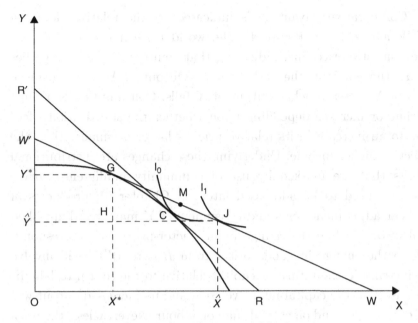

Figure 4.7.   The gains from trade with given world prices.
Note: At world prices the country produces OX^* and OY^* and consumes $O\hat{X}$ and $O\hat{Y}$.

It is unnecessary to draw community indifference curves to show that gains from trade exist. Specialising and trading allow consumption to be at a point like M in Figure 4.7, with greater consumption of both goods. The only necessary condition for potential gains from trade is that the world price line has a different slope to the pre-trade domestic price line, i.e. that there is some difference between the two countries in factor endowments or tastes; the wedge between $R'R$ and $W'W$ has similar implications to the wedge in Figure 2.2, but without assuming differences in technology the neoclassical model adds greater generality to the Ricardian model's emphasis on differing labour productivities as the basis for trade. The community indifference curves are helpful in identifying at which point on $W'W$ consumption actually takes place, but they are not essential for showing the gains from trade.

Comparative advantage is indicated by the relative slopes of
$W'W$ and $R'R$. In Figure 4.7 the world price line is flatter than
the domestic price line, indicating that comparative advantage lies
in Y, the good on the vertical axis. Output of Y and consumption of X increase, while output of X falls. Consumption of Y may
decline or increase depending upon whether the substitution effect
due to an increase in its relative price is larger or smaller than the
effect of higher income. Underlying these changes are distributional
effects that are masked by use of community indifference curves
and will need to be addressed later (in Chapter 6); producers of
X bear adjustment costs and consumers of Y may face diminished
real income, while the change in the factor-price ratio corresponding to the change in goods prices from $R'R$ to $W'W$ will involve
an increase in the return to capital relative to the return to labour,
because Y is the capital-intensive good and its increased output will
place more demand on capital than on labour. Nevertheless, the presence of distributional effects does not undermine the basic conclusion
about the potential gains from trade; at a point like M the country
is unambiguously better off, and as long as the extra goods can be
redistributed it is possible for all individuals to gain.

In a two country model, world prices are endogenous because each
country's exports must be equal to the other country's imports. In
Figure 4.7 with a price line $W'W$ the country exports GH units of Y
and imports HJ units of X. For $W'W$ to be the equilibrium world
price ratio, the **trade triangle** GHJ must be equal to the other
country's trade triangle, where GH is the other country's imports
of Y and HJ its exports of X. Such an outcome is illustrated in
Figure 4.8, where triangles GHJ and VST are equal, with slope,
$W'W$, and $ST = HJ$ and $GH = VS$.

The difference between the two economies could lie in their PPFs
or in their CICs, but neoclassical trade theory has tended to ignore
differences in tastes and emphasise differences in PPFs. The PPF in
country I is flatter than the PPF of country II, because the former

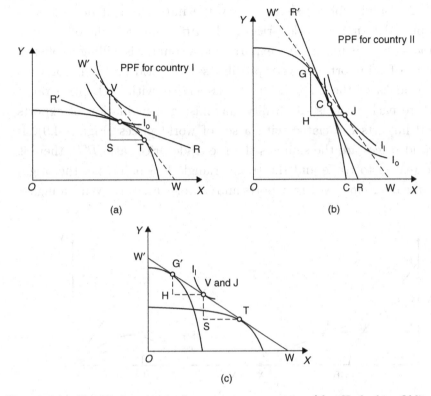

Figure 4.8. Equilibrium trade between two countries (the Heckscher–Ohlin theorem).
Note: (a) PPF for country I; (b) PPF for country II; (c) both countries' PPFs together. Note that in (c) it is assumed that both countries are of the same size (that is, both have a post-trade GNP equal to OW units of X); this is not necessary for the Heckscher–Ohlin theorem. In a two-country world the trade triangles must be equal: $GHJ = VST$.

is more poorly endowed with capital and hence less well placed to produce the capital-intensive good, Y. The capital-abundant country, II, is less well placed to produce the labour-intensive good X. The factor proportions explanation of trade, **the Heckscher–Ohlin theorem**, states that a country will have a comparative advantage in producing the good using its abundant factor relatively intensively, and will export this good in return for imports of the good that uses its scarce factor relatively intensively.

A useful tool for showing how the interaction of demand and supply determines world prices is the ***offer curve***. The offer curve traces out how much of its export good a country is willing to offer in return for imports at every possible set of world prices; it connects the peaks of the trade triangles associated with each price ratio, where each peak is the utility-maximising combination of exports and imports associated with a set of world prices (Figure 4.9). If world prices are the same as the pre-trade price ratio $R'R$, there is no reason to trade and the trade triangle is a point, i.e. the origin of the offer curve where exports and imports are zero. With a higher

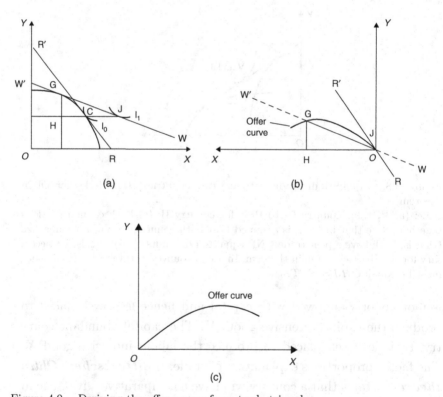

Figure 4.9. Deriving the offer curve; from trade triangles.
Note: (a) deriving a trade triangle (Figure 4.7); (b) tracing out the offer curve; (c) redrawing the offer curve in positive space. Note that the offer curve always bends toward the axis of the import good (X in this example).

relative price of Y the trade triangles have progressively longer bases (i.e. more and more X is imported).[7] Corresponding to Figure 4.7, one trade triangle has a base OH and its point on the offer curve is G; more favourable **terms of trade** (i.e. higher prices for the export relative to the import) are associated with points to the left of G and less favourable terms of trade by points to the right of G. Thus, moving along the offer curve from the origin is associated with improved terms of trade, more trade and increasing welfare. There is a comparable offer curve in the southeast quadrant of Figure 4.9(b), i.e. to the right of the origin and below the horizontal axis, and this represents the trade combinations when the relative price of X is higher than $R'R$ and the country is an X-exporter, without knowledge of the trading partner we cannot say where comparative advantage lies, but once that information is known it is more convenient to focus just on the relevant quadrant.

The two-country situation is shown in Figure 4.10, where the ray OP is the equilibrium world price ratio and point E represents the equilibrium level of trade. The world price ratio is such that OO_a units of Y exchange for OO_b units of X. It is the equilibrium because if the price of Y were higher country A would want to trade more but country B would want to trade less, and if the price of X were higher country B would want to trade more but country A would want to trade less. By contrast, at any level of trade involving less

---

[7]The offer curve may bend backwards beyond some point. This occurs if the higher real incomes associated with more trade stimulate greater domestic demand for the export good to the extent that the country can only be induced to import more if the terms of trade are so favourable that it needs to export fewer units of the export good, i.e. the income effect outweighs the substitution effect so that domestic demand for the export increases despite a higher relative price. The inelastic portion of the offer curve can be the source of paradoxical results (e.g. multiple equilibria or the immiserising-growth outcome described in Chapter 8), but it is rarely observed in a multi-country world. The condition for a stable equilibrium, i.e. the absolute values of the import demand elasticities in the two countries must sum to at least one, is known as the **Marshall–Lerner condition**.

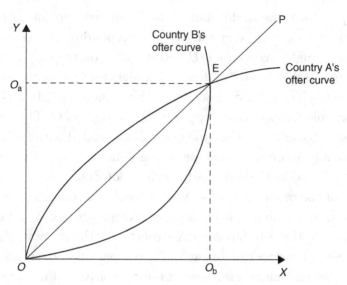

Figure 4.10. Equilibrium in a two-country model.
Note: In equilibrium, country A exports O_a units of Y and imports O_b units of X.
Given the production functions and consumer preferences in the two countries,
no other level of trade could be supported by a price equating demand and supply
for both goods.

than OO_a units of Y and OO_b units of X, i.e. points within the
lozenge between O and E, both countries are willing to trade more.

In the two-country setting, each country is exposed to fallout
from any shift in preferences or the production function of its trading
partner. This illustrates the important point that the well-being of
people in an open economy can be influenced by events elsewhere,
whether it is the increase in the efficiency with which China produces
toys or a bad harvest in the USA. This danger is, however, exagger-
ated in a two-country diagram; in a world with many trading nations,
few countries are large enough for their domestic changes to shift
world prices. Moreover, being part of a trading system can reduce
economic fluctuations, because some negative domestic shocks, such
as a bad harvest or other production shortfall, can be mitigated by
exporting other goods and importing the good in short supply.

Chapter 5

A Partial Equilibrium Model of International Trade

The standard trade model is a general equilibrium model, which highlights the way in which goods and factor markets are interconnected. The fundamental drivers, the production possibility frontier and community indifference curves are difficult to construct, and in a world of many goods and factors tracking all of the general equilibrium interconnections may be overwhelming. For analysing trade in a good which does not form a large part of total trade, and hence has limited impact on the rest of the economy, it is useful to adopt a partial equilibrium approach, with the more familiar and operational constructs of demand and supply curves in a single market.

Panels (a) and (b) in Figure 5.1 contain the domestic demand and supply curves for the good X in two countries, A and B. In

Price of good A

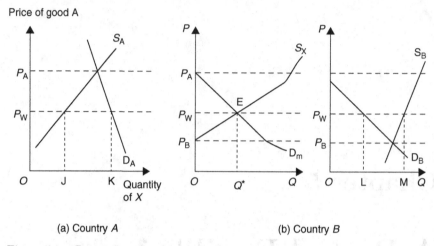

(a) Country *A*   (b) Country *B*

Figure 5.1.   Determination of world price.
Note: At point E the equilibrium price is P_W and the amount traded is OQ^*, which is the amount imported by country A (quantity JK) and the amount exported by country B (quantity LM). Note that at prices above P_A both countries would be exporters and at prices below P_B importers — these price are outside the relevant range if B is the rest of the world.

autarchy the price of X, in terms of all other goods or in terms of a measuring rod such as 'dollars' or 'pesos', is higher in country A than in country B, so that with trade B exports the good in return for a bundle of imports from A. In a two-country setting, the world demand for imports of X is given by the excess demand in A. The import demand curve D_m is traced out in the middle panel of Figure 5.1; the intercept is A's autarchy price and at prices below P_A world import demand is the horizontal distance between A's domestic demand and supply curves. The world export supply of good X is equally to the excess supply in B, and can be plotted in Figure 5.1 for all prices above B's pre-trade price. At point E world demand equal world supply, and the corresponding price, P_W, is a stable equilibrium.

The important special case of a country too small to affect world prices by its trade in international markets can be defined in terms of the partial equilibrium approach. A "small" country faces a perfectly

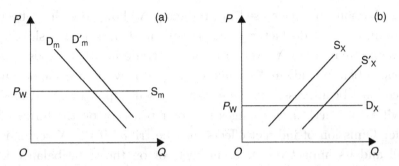

Figure 5.2.   Demand and supply curves for (a) imports and (b) exports of a small
country.
Note: In a small country a change in the demand for imports (for example, from
D_m to D'_m) or in the supply of exports (for example, from S_x to S'_x) has no effect
on price.

elastic import supply curve and a perfectly elastic export demand
curve (Figure 5.2). From here on, the term small country will be
used in this precise sense and without quotation marks. The economic
significance of the **small country assumption** is much clearer in
Figure 5.2 than in the general equilibrium model, where a small country is one facing a linear rest-of-the-world offer curve. A two-country
model tends to highlight situations where both countries influence
prices, but in a world of about two hundred countries the small country assumption is useful because in most markets most countries are
small in this technical sense.[1]

A drawback of the partial equilibrium approach is that we do not
know what underlies the demand and supply curves, which makes it
difficult to predict shifts in the curves due to fundamental changes.
More importantly, they ignore indirect effects of goods price changes.
For example, in Figure 5.1(a); what happens to country A's factors

---

[1]In 2007 the United Nations had 192 members, but not all trading units are members of the UN (e.g. Hong Kong and Taiwan are not UN members but are distinct
units for customs purposes, while breakaway provinces such as Transdniester in
Moldova or Abkhazia in Georgia may act as distinct entities for trade). On the
other hand, some UN members are part of a common unit for trade purposes,
e.g. the European Union represents its member states in trade negotiations.

of production no longer used in producing X, how does that affect factor prices and do factor price changes feed back into a shift in the supply curve for X? If the country's trade in other goods was balanced before trade in X began, country A now has a trade deficit which must be addressed in some way. How will export or non-traded activities be affected by changes in factor prices or on the terms of trade? Omission of indirect effects may be trivial if the X sector is small and its impact on factor markets or on the trade balance is minimal, but general equilibrium effects will always exist.

One advantage of the partial equilibrium approach is that it sheds light on the distribution of the gains from trade within countries. In Figure 5.1, both consumers and producers in the importing country feel the impact of a lower price of X. Consumers of X pay less for the quantity that they were buying in autarchy, and in addition they may now buy more units at the lower price; these gains can be represented by the change in the area between the price line and the domestic demand curve, i.e. an increase in *consumer surplus*. Producers of X receive less revenue for each unit sold and will cut back output because for marginal units the costs of production are now higher than the price; these effects can be represented by the reduction in the area between the price line and the domestic supply curve, i.e. a reduction in *producer surplus*.

Figure 5.3 provides an alternative way of showing the fundamental conclusions about gains from trade. Because of the inevitable distributional consequences, any judgment about the benefits from trade depends upon interpersonal utility comparisons or the possibility of lump-sum compensation. In Figure 5.3 gains from trade exist if each unit is granted equal weight, in which case the increase in consumer surplus exceeds the reduction in producer surplus. Consumer surplus is increased by the areas $a + b + c$ while producer surplus is reduced by the area a, with a net gain of $b + c$. As in the general equilibrium model, the net gain consists of two parts. First, the benefit from specialising in production and importing those units of

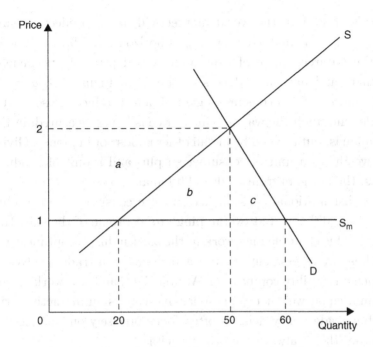

Figure 5.3.   Welfare effects of trade on consumers and producers.

the good for which the world price is less than domestic marginal cost, measured by triangle b. Second, the benefit from being able to consume units of the import good which consumers value at more than the world price but less than the pre-trade domestic price, measured by triangle c.

A major advantage of the partial equilibrium approach is that the welfare effects described in the previous two paragraphs can be measured if the pre-trade price and output, P_A and Q_A, the world price, P_W, and the elasticities of demand and supply are known. These data requirements are not very onerous, and this technique has been frequently used to estimate the welfare gains from freer trade. Figure 5.3 presents a simple numerical example. Suppose that without trade, a shirt sells for two bananas, 50 shirts are produced and consumed, the elasticity of demand is -0.4 and the elasticity of supply is 1.2. The world price is one banana per shirt and the country's entry into the world market will have no effect on shirt prices, i.e. it is a small country (S_m is horizontal). The fall in price from the autarchy price of two to the world price of one benefits consumers and harms producers of shirts. In Figure 5.3, $a = 35$, $b = 15$ and $c = 5$, so consumers gain 55 and producers lose 35; the units depend upon the way in which price is being measured, in this case bananas, but it could be in "all other goods" or in money. Giving equal weight to a unit of consumer surplus and a unit of producer surplus, the net gain from trade is 20 bananas.

The distributional consequences involve consumers and producers, who are different but overlapping groups; some of the shirt consumers in this example may work in the shirt industry, but most will not. Thus any assessment of the net benefits from trade involves an inter-personal utility comparison. At first sight, and as a working rule of thumb, equal weight or one-dollar-one-vote is an attractive principle, but trade policy debates often focus precisely on the question of whether this is always the best principle.

There are other distributional aspects of trade. In the previous chapter, the offer curve analysis highlighted the zero–sum nature of the determination of relative world prices, so conflicts over the distribution of the gains from trade between countries are possible. The next chapter analyses the functional distribution of income, i.e. the distribution of the gains from trade between owners of factors of production such as workers, capitalists and landowners.

Chapter 6

International Trade and the Distribution of Income

In the general equilibrium neoclassical model the one-to-one correspondence between goods market equilibrium and factor market equilibrium means that any change in goods prices will affect the functional distribution of income. Thus, opening up to trade or any changes in world prices will affect the relative returns to the owners of different factors of production. In the examples in Chapter 4 where the export good is capital-intensive, opening up to trade is associated with a movement along the contract curve to a new equilibrium associated with a higher price of capital relative to the price of labour.

This is, of course, not a new conclusion and income distribution consequences have been at the heart of many political disputes over trade policy. When Ricardo was writing in the years after 1815, the policy debate in Britain over the adoption of free trade pitted landowners against capitalists, with the owners of the relatively scarce factor, land, clearly understanding that they would be the losers from trade liberalisation. In the 1800s in the USA, where land was plentiful and capital scarce, landowners in the south and west favoured free trade while capital-owners in the northeast lobbied for trade restrictions. Similarly, it does not require economics training for the owners of capital in poor countries or workers with skills specific to an uncompetitive industry in a high-income country to realise that they may be threatened by trade liberalisation.

Nevertheless, there may be some ambiguity. Suppose, for example, that the export good is capital-intensive. As producers the owners of capital benefit from the opening up of trade, but what if they disproportionately consume the now higher-priced export good: could they lose more as consumers than they gain as producers, and end up worse off? The ***Stolper–Samuelson theorem*** provides an unequivocal answer: the real return of the factor used relatively intensively in the good whose price has risen will unambiguously increase. There is a magnification effect that ensures that the price of the abundant factor increases relative to the price of either good and the price of the scarce factor decreases relative to the price of either good.

The Stolper–Samuelson theorem can be illustrated numerically with any relative price movement. Suppose the price of good Y increases by 10% while the price of good X is unchanged. The increase in the price of Y can be divided into the higher costs of labour and capital used in Y production, but these costs cannot have increased equally because we know from Chapter 4 that the factor-price ratio P_K/P_L has increased. Both P_K and P_L cannot have increased by more than 10% or by less than 10% (otherwise the change in P_y would have to have been greater or less than 10%), so the increase in P_K must be greater than 10% and the increase in P_L must be less than 10%. A similar argument with respect to P_x established that the increase in P_K must be greater than zero and the increase in P_L must be less than zero. Thus there is a strict ranking:

$$\uparrow P_K >\uparrow P_y >\uparrow P_x >\uparrow P_L$$

This is the magnification effect incorporated in the Stolper–Samuelson theorem. With more than two factors, the same method could be used to show that one factor price must increase by over 10% and one factor price must increase by less than zero, i.e. one factor's real return must increase and one factor's real return must fall.

The Stolper–Samuelson theorem can also be illustrated in an Edgeworth Box diagram. Suppose that an autarchic capital-abundant country is operating at point A on its contract curve (Figure 6.1). Opening up the economy and responding to a higher relative price of Y, the capital-intensive good, shifts the equilibrium point from A to B, where more resources are devoted to producing Y and less to X. The flatter factor price line, with slope P_L/P_K indicates that the relative price of capital has increased. Since the capital/labour ratio is now lower in both activities, the productivity

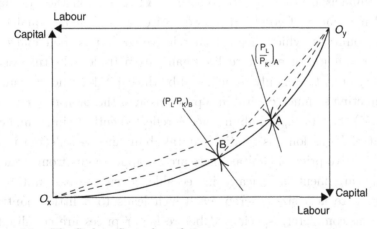

Figure 6.1. The Stolper–Samuelson theorem.
Note: Point A is the pre-trade equilibrium and point B the post-trade equilibrium. At B the price of capital relative to that of labour is higher (indicated by the flatter factor price line) and the capital: labour ratio is lower in both activities (indicated by the flatter dotted lines from O_x and O_y) than at A.

of capital has also increased, so that the real return to capital is higher.

The Stolper–Samuelson theorem is robust and powerful. It is robust because it does not rest on a large number of assumptions; there is no presumption that production functions are the same or about preferences in the rest of the world or whether international markets are perfectly competitive. It is powerful because the message that there are gains from trade, but that some groups inevitably lose out, is clear and important.

In the two-country general equilibrium model, opening up trade will cause a change in factor prices in both countries. The increase in the real return to capital in the country just analysed will be accompanied by an increase in the real return to labour in the labour-abundant country. How long will this process continue? With identical production functions and consumer preferences, and in the absence of transport costs or other obstacles to trading, the process will continue until factor prices are identical in the two countries.

The *factor price equalisation theorem* was first proved by Paul Samuelson (1948; 1949). With no restrictions on the international movement of goods, the goods price ratio must be equalised across countries, which means that relative costs must be equalised across countries, or else unrealised gains from trade will still exist. Equality of costs can only be achieved by the capital-abundant country directing so much capital into production of the capital-intensive good (Y) that its capital-abundance is reflected entirely in its higher output of Y; as long as relative capital-abundance is reflected in a lower relative price of capital, there are untapped gains from trade.

The argument is logically impeccable, given the assumptions; unless there is a size discrepancy which leads to a little country becoming completely specialised before factor prices are equalised. The factor price equalisation theorem follows from the point, made in Chapter 4, that in the neoclassical model there is only one degree of freedom; once one set of relative prices or outputs is fixed, the rest are determined endogenously. Robert Mundell (1957) proved the corollary: if factors could move freely across borders so that relative factor prices were the same everywhere, then there would be a process of goods price equalisation even in the absence of trade in goods. In the neoclassical general equilibrium model with no deviations from perfect competition other than the inability of either goods or factors to cross borders, there are both goods price equalisation and factor price equalisation.

The factor price equalisation theorem is less robust than the Stolper–Samuelson theorem because it requires a more restrictive set of assumptions. In the presence of any differences in production functions or barriers to the movements of goods, the factor price equalisation theorem will not hold. Mundell observed that the real world outcome would be convergence rather than equalisation. Convergence is likely to be greater in some goods markets (e.g. homogeneous goods with low weight-to-value ratios such as gold or diamonds) than others (e.g. differentiated products whose prices are hard to compare). Despite its failure to explain international differences in factor rewards, especially the wide disparities in incomes between rich and poor countries, the factor price equalisation theorem may be useful as a pointer to long-term tendencies. Anne Krueger (1968) argued that international differences in per capita incomes reflect differences in resource endowments, especially human capital, implying that investment in human capital in low-income countries would lead to convergence in per capita incomes. The rapidly rising incomes in the high-performing and open East Asian economies also suggest that trade is a path to convergence, although the evidence from cross-country growth studies is that convergence is conditional on many things, especially good institutions.

The Specific Factors Model

In the partial equilibrium model of the previous chapter producers of the import-competing good and consumers of the export good are the losers from trade. How can this emphasis on sectors be reconciled with the above emphasis on factors in analysing the distributional impact of trade? The answer depends upon the degree of factor mobility between sectors within a country.

In the **specific factors model** developed by Paul Samuelson (1971) and Ron Jones (1971) some factors are assumed to be sector-specific. Suppose that the production of food requires labour and land and the production of cloth requires labour and capital. Land and capital are specific factors and labour is mobile. The mobile factor will be allocated between sectors so that the value of its marginal product is the same in each sector, and equal to the wage rate. Figure 6.2 shows the labour demand curves in the cloth and food sectors (VMP_c and VMP_f), with the origins chosen so that the length of the horizontal axis, $O_c O_f$, is equal to the total labour supply. The intersection of VMP_c and VMP_f determines the wage rate (W_1) and the allocation of labour between the two sectors, $O_c L_1$ in cloth and $O_f L_1$ in food.

Now, suppose that the price of cloth increases, represented by an upward shift in the VMP_c curve. The equilibrium wage rate increases

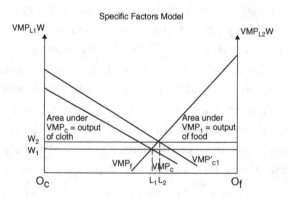

Figure 6.2.   Labour allocation in the specific factors model.
Note: At the original prices of cloth and food, the equilibrium wage rate is W_1 and $O_c L_1$ units of labour produce cloth and the rest, $O_f L_1$, produce food. When the price of cloth increases, the value of the marginal product increases by the size of the price increase (from VMP_{c1} to VMP_{c2}), more workers are employed in cloth production and the wage increases from W_1 to W_2.

from W_1 to W_2 as $L_1 L_2$ units of labour are reallocated from food to cloth production. The effect on real wages is uncertain, because the increase in W is less than the increase in the price of cloth (i.e. the vertical distance from W_1 to W_2 is less than that from VMP_c to VMP'_c) but greater than the zero change in the price of food. Capitalists are, however, unambiguously better off because they produce more and receive more per unit produced; their return per unit sold is the difference between the price and the wage cost. Conversely, landowners are unambiguously worse off because they produce less and their costs per unit sold have increased while the price of their output is unchanged.

The specific factors model, like the Stolper–Samuelson theorem, yields a strict ranking of factor returns and price changes:

$$\uparrow \text{returns to capital} > \uparrow P_c > \uparrow W > \uparrow P_f > \uparrow \text{returns to land}$$

with the conclusion that the factor specific to the increasing-relative-price activity is better off and the factor specific to the decreasing-relative-price activity is worse off, while the real return to the mobile factor (W/P in this case) is ambiguous. Thus, trade benefits factors specific to the export sector and hurts factors specific to the import-competing sector, while the impact on mobile factors is unclear.

The specific factors model captures an important truth when dealing with owners of natural resources, and explains the opposition of landowners to trade liberalisation in 19th century England just as well as the Stolper–Samuelson theorem. For most factors, however, mobility is a matter of degree. Workers may have skills that are specific to their current job, but they can move to another job and acquire new skills. The specific factors model may, thus, be best at picking up short-run distributional impacts of relative price changes. When an industry is threatened by import competition, both workers and owners often unite in demanding protection because both have some degree of sector specificity irrespective of whether the sector is

labour- or capital-intensive. From a national perspective, there may
be a time-inconsistency problem; adjustment costs are lower if the
economy is sheltered from world price changes, but the long-term
benefits may be greater if factors move between sectors in response
to price signals from world markets.

The policy implication of the analysis in this and the previous
chapter is that governments may need to intervene to realise the gains
from trade. In the analysis of Figure 5.3 the net gains from trade arise
from the difference between consumers' gains and producers' losses.
If it were possible to compensate the losers by a non-distortionary
measure, such as a lump-sum transfer from consumers equal to the
loss in producer surplus (area *a* in Figure 5.3), then the post-trade
situation would be Pareto superior, i.e. some people are better off
and nobody is worse off. Similarly, the specific factors model highlights the adjustment costs of trade when some people have capital or skills specific to their current occupation; compensation for
the reduced value of the specific equipment or skills is necessary to
achieve a Pareto superior outcome. We will return to these issues in
the discussion of trade policy, but the difficulties should be apparent; consumers may not want to be taxed to compensate producers
and producers may not want to risk losing their producer surplus in
return for a political promise of compensation which may be reneged
upon. Similar caution may apply to owners of specific factors, and in
all cases losers have an incentive to overstate the magnitude of compensation required and to use political power rather than economic
analysis to push their case.

Over the longer term, when all inputs are mobile, the Stolper–
Samuelson theorem comes into its own. For the 19th century,
O'Rourke and Williamson (1999) show that the evolution of the
Atlantic economy was driven by responses to factor price differences. Elsewhere, opening up to international trade led to income
distribution changes consistent with the Stolper–Samuelson theorem. In Thailand export of rice, a labour-intensive good, benefited

small-scale farmers, and in Japan export of silk and tea benefited low-income households, although a land tax changed their after-tax situation.[1] In 19th century Chile nitrates were the dominant export, and capitalists, mainly American and British investors, were the chief beneficiaries from trade. This last example illustrates how, in interpreting actual circumstances, institutions or the nature of the multifactor production function are important, e.g. foreign capitalists may be important in mining or pharmaceutical activities which require not only capital but also skills or proprietary knowledge. Incorporating technology and imperfect competition are among the tasks in the next two chapters.

---

[1]By the 1880s Thailand and Japan were the two East Asian economies with the highest import penetration. Daniel Bernhofen and John Brown (2005) claim that Japan provides a natural experiment of the impact of a market economy opening up to trade, because it moved from almost complete autarchy in 1858 to almost complete free trade by 1865 after two centuries of isolation (1639–1853); they see it as confirming the predictions of the standard neoclassical trade model, with gains from trade that added about 8–9% to the value of total output. The price of the main export good, raw silk, had been stable, but had a structural break in 1859 and a strongly rising trend in the 1860s.

Chapter 7

The Leontief Paradox and Technology–Based Trade Theories

Although the Heckscher–Ohlin theorem has been at the centre of standard trade theory since the middle of the 20th century, its empirical relevance has been challenged for almost as long. In perhaps the most famous empirical study in international economics, Wassily Leontief (1953) aggregated US industries into 50 sectors, of which 38 were directly involved in international trade, and depending on the sign of their trade balance he divided the latter into import-competing and export industries. The capital/labour ratio for the export industries was \$14,010 per man–year and for the import-competing industries \$18,180 per man–year. Since the USA was clearly the world's most capital-rich country at that time, the finding that US exports were relatively labour-intensive and US imports relatively capital-intensive directly contradicted the Heckscher–Ohlin theorem and became known as the **Leontief Paradox**.

Following Leontief's study a large number of other researchers conducted tests on later US data or on other countries' trade and many found similarly paradoxical results. One response was to question whether factor intensities could be ranked or whether factor intensity reversals undermined the Heckscher–Ohlin theorem. India's agriculture is labour-intensive but India was a net grain importer in the 1960s. The trade pattern might be explained by the fact that in the USA wheat production is capital-intensive, but this explanation leaves the Heckscher–Ohlin theorem in limbo; a theorem which could equally well explain why the USA exported grain to India or why India exported grain to the USA is of no use in explaining which outcome is actually observed. Although factor intensity reversals exist, they are uncommon and seem insufficient to explain much of the Leontief Paradox. Similarly, differences in tastes could explain trade patterns, perhaps outweighing differences in factor endowments, but the international evidence is that, at least for broad categories such as 'food' or 'meat', household expenditure patterns for given income levels do not vary greatly between countries.

A more plausible way of reconciling Leontief's results with the Heckscher–Ohlin theorem is to recognise that the two-factor version of the factor proportions model is a simplification. With more than two factors there is no simple ranking of goods by factor intensity. Several researchers have allowed for the existence of additional factors. Jaroslav Vanek (1959) observed that the USA was a net importer of resource-intensive goods, such as oil, coal, copper, chrome and other minerals, many of which can only be efficiently produced by highly capital-intensive techniques. Thus, while it may look as though the USA was importing capital-intensive goods, it was really importing resource-intensive goods that happened to be capital-intensive due to production complementarities. Subsequent research by Ed Leamer and others which identified more factors (e.g. a dozen types of labour, land and capital in Leamer, 1984, or Bowen, Leamer and Sveikauskas, 1987) found that predictions based on relative factor abundance explained about two-thirds of international trade. Some commentators see this as a poor performance by the factor proportions model, which confirms the Leontief paradox, although Leamer's own interpretation was that with a properly specified list of factors there was no paradox.[1]

The Heckscher–Ohlin theorem is more successful in explaining trade between rich and poor countries. The rapid growth of exports since the 1960s from the new industrialised economies of East Asia was overwhelmingly based on labour-intensive goods, which reflected these economies' relative abundance of unskilled labour. However, Daniel Trefler (1995) has argued that even here the Heckscher–Ohlin theorem comes up short, because trade between rich and poor countries is much less than might be expected on the basis of their differences in factor endowments. US imports of labour-intensive goods or Chinese exports of labour-intensive goods are far less than would be expected. One explanation, much in the way that we explained the empirical shortfall of the factor price equalisation theorem, is that trade costs limit both price equalisation and realisation of the quantity of trade that factor endowment differences might justify if trade were frictionless. An alternative resolution of the 'Case of the Missing Trade' proposed by Trefler is that labour in high-income countries may be much more efficient than labour in poor countries; he calculated that the technological differences implied by the missing trade are very large.

Trefler's argument is similar to Leontief's explanation of his paradox, which Leontief thought was in some way related to US labour

---

[1]Krugman and Obstfeld (7th ed., 2006, 74) observe that "This result confirms the Leontief paradox on a broader level: Trade often does not run in the direction that the Heckscher–Ohlin theory predicts," while Leamer states that "There is no paradox if the conceptually correct calculations are made". The differing views of whether two-thirds is a poor or a good success rate illustrate the importance of interpreting empirical findings.

being more efficient than labour elsewhere. During the 1960s the most successful empirical approaches to reconciling the Leontief paradox and the Heckscher–Ohlin theorem were studies that questioned the homogeneity of labour or capital. Dividing capital into physical and human capital suggested that the relative resource abundance of the USA was in human capital even more than in physical capital. Although labour skills are not easy to measure on aggregate, proxies such as educational qualifications or high skill grades tended to be positively correlated with exports of US industries. Studies using R&D expenditure, which requires skilled labour, also found that this was a reasonably good explanator of net exports.

Technology Gaps and the Product Cycle

During the 1960s the most popular new trade theories assumed the existence of a technological gap, which gave innovating firms a temporary monopoly at home and advantage in foreign markets. The USA as the global technology leader at the time was a particularly successful product innovator, and that could explain US trade patterns irrespective of capital/labour ratios. Moreover, if innovations tend to be in response to domestic demand conditions, then new-goods exports would be most successful in the markets of similar countries, which helps to explain the phenomenon that trade is more intense among high-income countries than between countries at differing income levels.

The most influential of these trade theories was the *product cycle model* developed by Raymond Vernon (1966). Innovations, improvements in a new product and marketing all require highly skilled labour, so innovative activity and production of new goods are most likely to be located in the skill-abundant country. As the product matures, its demands for skilled labour in production and marketing become less pronounced, and comparative advantage shifts to another country. For a mature good, the production location may

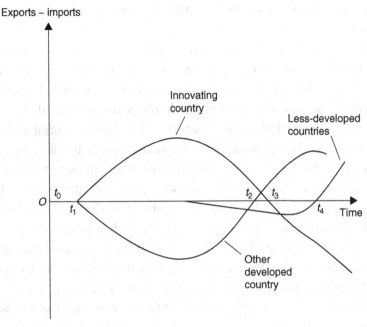

Figure 7.1.   The product cycle.
Note: The diagram represents trade in a single product; that is, world net exports sum to zero.

be determined by other considerations, perhaps the factor endowments emphasised by the Heckscher–Ohlin theorem.

Figure 7.1 illustrates a possible evolution of international trade balances over the product cycle. The horizontal axis measures time, with the origin, t_0, the date when the new product is first produced. At time t_1, the innovating country starts to export the good to other high-income countries. Over time, the importing countries begin to produce the good themselves, reducing their demand for imports, and demand emerges in lower-income countries, which may be supplied by the innovating country or perhaps increasingly by other high-income countries. At point t_2 the second-generation producers become net exporters of the no longer new good, and the innovating country may become a net importer (e.g. at time t_3 in Figure 7.1). Later still, at time t_4 low-income countries become net exporters of the standardised product.

Cotton textiles provide a long-term example of the product cycle. In the industrial revolution of the 18th century these products became Britain's leading export. As knowledge of the mechanical production which had provided Britain's technological edge spread through western Europe and the north-eastern USA, domestic producers in those countries began to displace imported cotton textiles. Britain continued to be the dominant supplier of other markets until after Japan adopted by now the standardised technology at the end of the 19th century, with far lower labour costs than European or North American producers. Japan expanded her cotton textile exports in the first half of the 20th century, and Britain lost export markets. One reaction in western Europe and North America was to erect trade barriers to restrict Japanese access to their markets, or those of their colonies. The second half of the 20th century was characterised by further cycles as Japanese exporters were displaced by textile producers in the new industrialised economies of Hong Kong, South Korea and Taiwan, and then in the 1980s these countries lost markets to second-generation new industrialised economies with lower labour costs, notably China. The cotton textiles story indicates the common phenomenon that the raw materials producers are rarely involved in the product cycle; neither Britain, the north-eastern United States, nor Japan was a significant grower of cotton, and later when synthetic fibres or petrochemicals were developed this did not happen on any meaningful scale in wood-pulp producers such as Canada or Sweden or in oil-producing countries.

Many other examples of the product cycle could be described. For some goods, scale economies, the importance of brand loyalty, after sales service networks, or other barriers to entry limit the process. In automobiles, for example, where the USA developed mass production technology and marketing techniques in the 1920s and became the dominant exporter, the rise of European producers in the

1950s and 1960s did not pose a great challenge, and it was only when Japanese producers made large investments not only in production facilities but also in dealer and after-sales networks that a major new net exporter emerged in the 1970s. In this industry product cycle phenomena were apparent, but scale effects limited the number of actively participating countries.

A single product might pass through a series of product cycles if repeated innovations occur. Figure 7.2 is a stylised picture of US and Japanese trade in radios starting in the 1940s. Initially, the technological gap in vacuum tube radios favoured the USA, but as the product matured Japan emerged as a major supplier and US net exports declined. The USA reversed this decline by developing a new technology based on transistors, US net exports revived and Japan's net exports declined as its old-technology radios lost market share. The second product cycle mirrored the first one, as Japanese producers adopted the new technology and began to outsell the US innovators, but this too was reversed by a technological innovation

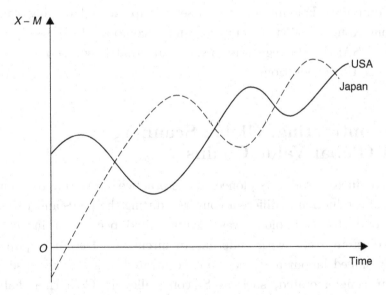

Figure 7.2. Stylised product cycles for radios since the late 1940s.

in the USA, the silicon chip. In this example it is difficult to test any theory of trade patterns, because at a point in time the USA and Japan might both be exporting 'radios'; when they represent different technological vintages the radios could be better characterised as different products, but that is unlikely to be picked up in the trade data, which will report simultaneous import and export of radios (e.g. Japan was importing hi-tech transistor radios from the USA at the same time as it was exporting low-tech low-price vacuum radios) or intra-industry trade rather than the inter-industry trade predicted by standard trade theory.

A pattern like that in Figure 7.2 had an obvious message for US producers. Since the Japanese upswings reflected lower Japanese wages and high US labour costs, why not lower costs by shifting assembly activities to low-wage countries? When Japanese firms began to produce and export transistors in the late 1950s, two US firms pursued different reactive strategies. Philco invested in automated production technologies to offset high US labour costs, and suffered disastrous losses due to the rapid obsolescence of their expensive equipment. Fairchild reacted by setting up a manufacturing plant in Hong Kong in 1961 to assemble US-made components for re-export to the USA; the strategy was so successful that it was soon copied by other US corporations.

Subcontracting, Global Scanning, and Global Value Chains

Semiconductor producers pioneered the practice of locating different steps of production in different countries during the 1960s and 1970s. Semiconductor technology was ideally suited because it involved four discrete steps with differing requirements. Design required highly skilled labour and became concentrated in areas where such labour conglomerated, such as Silicon Valley in California. Fabrication is capital-intensive, requiring state of the art machinery.

Assembly can also be automated (as Philco did), but seldom is, because of rapid obsolescence; manual assembly is often extremely labour-intensive — an estimated 54 years of labour were required per million dollars of semiconductor output in 1976, compared to 35 years in apparel. Testing requires expensive equipment. American firms, following Fairchild's example, located design and fabrication in the USA, sent the components to Mexico or Asia for assembly, and returned the finished product to the USA for testing and marketing. This was facilitated by the high value/weight ratio of silicon chips (and hence low transport costs) and by tariff reform, which exempted the US-made components from import duties when the assembled product was imported into the USA. Competition forced all producers to follow this model, and to search for the least-cost reliable assembly locations and to move more steps offshore as skills were developed; some design and testing activities were moved to Hong Kong and Singapore, which also became regional marketing centres for the finished products.

The process could be conducted within a firm through direct foreign investment in production facilities overseas or it could be done by subcontracting to local producers. The choice depends upon the trade-offs between retaining control over things like proprietary technology and quality control and the extent to which a local firm or joint-venture partner may be better able to deal with local labour regulations or relations with governments.[2] Whether via subsidiaries or by subcontracting, the separation of production steps quickly spread to other branches of the electronics industry and to other industries. Initially this largely involved sewing, whether using copper wire in electronic equipment, making garments, travel goods or baseballs.

---

[2]Producers in the follower countries also had choices. Mathews and Cho (2000) analyse the evolution of the semiconductor industry in Korea, Taiwan, Singapore and Malaysia, emphasising how local firms acquired experience and knowledge through a mix of strategies which included joint ventures, licensing of technologies, and original equipment manufacturing (OEM).

Athletic shoes are assembled in many low-wage countries for famous brands.

These activities, not just the last, are often referred to as foot-loose industries because the principal may relocate production in response to changes in relative wage rates, economic stability or any-thing else considered important for minimising costs. When the pro-cess started to flourish during the 1970s many host countries were sceptical about their vulnerability, fearing that a powerful multina-tional enterprise would reap all the gains from subcontracting and would leave at the first sign of erosion in its bargaining power. In practice, however, multinational enterprises often have few truly pre-ferred locations and once they have built up relations with officials, subcontractors and workers in one location there are costs to relo-cating — although if they are big enough they may locate similar subsidiaries or have similar subcontractors in several countries as insurance against political or economic instability in any one coun-try. When processes are relocated it is most often as part of a general change in the host country's output mix. Thus, as wages and skill lev-els rose, Hong Kong and Singapore became unattractive locations for unskilled-labour-intensive activities, but more attractive locations for activities involving skilled labour. Such quality upgrading is a normal and desirable process, which subcontracting can help by developing skills needed in a modern economy.

Subcontracting was consistent with the product cycle model, although the cycle began to speed up as the innovators sought out the least-cost location for each production step from an early stage in new product development. When products like the disposable razor or digital quartz watches were developed in the 1970s, they were soon assembled in low-wage locations and marketed globally. Vernon him-self conceded that, although the product cycle might have explained much international trade in the 1950s, this was no longer true by the 1980s because transnational corporations had increased global scan-ning capacity. In a study of 181 US-based and 135 European-based corporations, Vernon (1979) found that whereas 254 of the 316 firms had subsidiaries in less than six countries in 1950 only 40 did in 1975, and whereas only three operated in more than twenty countries in 1950, 73 had subsidiaries in more than twenty countries in 1975.

The internationalisation of production almost certainly represents a strengthening of factor endowments as the basis for international trade. Whereas the Heckscher–Ohlin theorem focuses on specialising according to relative factor endowments as the basis for gains from trade, the neoclassical model underlying the theorem also indicates that specialisation according to factor endowments is a way to minimise costs. Multinational enterprises and their subcontracting arrangements have evolved as institutional devices to minimise costs and to overcome some market imperfections, especially for knowledge and intangible property rights such as secret formulae, trademarks and so forth which would not be protected in arms-length business, or to reduce monitoring costs where quality is important. If firms do not locate activities according to relative factor prices, then presumably there is some market imperfection which they cannot (yet) overcome.

The fragmentation of production is not limited to simple subcontracting arrangements or vertical integration of multinational enterprises across borders. Any step in the value-added of a product can in principle be separated and carried out at the least-cost location, as long as the cost-savings are greater than the transactions costs.[3] The leaders in the development of *global value chains* vary from activity to activity. In fresh fruits and vegetables and to some extent in

---

[3]The income distribution consequences of global value chains, and especially of the offshoring or outsourcing of jobs, are debated. Critics in high-income countries focus on the impact on low-wage workers who suffer from reduced demand for their labour and through relative price effects (Stolper–Samuelson theorem). On the other hand, Grossman and Rossi–Hansberg (2006) argue that global value chains are a source of technical change that can augment the productivity of all factors of production sufficiently to outweigh the labour market or relative price effects.

processed or packaged foods large retailers such as Carrefour or Tesco have taken the lead, opening direct links to growers or processors worldwide who can reliably meet large orders at the right time and price and with the right quality. In manufactured goods the end-producer may take the lead, but often a first-tier supplier whose name is virtually unknown to the final consumers plays this role, with the brandname company focusing on design and marketing. For Levi jeans, Li & Fung of Hong Kong coordinate a global value chain in which Korean yarn is woven and dyed in Taiwan, cut in Bangladesh, sewn in Cambodia, where Japanese zippers are inserted, and dispatched into Levi's marketing network. Singapore-based Flexitronics plays a similar role for Ericsson and Visteon for Ford Motors or Denso for Toyota, organising the supply chain by a mix of subcontracting, subsidiaries and direct purchases from worldwide sources.

The fragmentation of value-added has been facilitated by dramatic decline in transport and communication costs over the last half century. Some of these changes have been endogenous, as firms trying to develop ever more efficient global value chains have pioneered means to reduce their costs. Reduced inventories through just-in-time deliveries are one striking example; the more the value chain is split up the more vulnerable it is to hold-ups, but keeping many days' worth of inventories at every step is expensive, so with the increased complexity of value chains a wider range of delivery modes emerged with real-time tracking systems that were increasingly sophisticated and reliable.[4] Other logistical advances such as improvements in intermodal transport have put pressure on governments to deregulate trucking, rail freight, shipping and air transport

---

[4]The rapid expansion of FedEx, DHL, UPS, etc. indicated the latent demand for such services. Their growth put pressure in institutions such as postal services' monopolies and regulated air freight services. Important externalities accrued to individuals wanting to use courier services and to macroeconomic policymakers whose job was made easier because smaller and more stable inventories tamed one of the most volatile elements of aggregate demand.

so that users have flexibility to determine the best means of combining and operating their transportation needs.

Trade policy has also been endogenous. Countries adopted amendments to their tariff codes, which exempted imports from duty on the part of their costs represented by domestic components. More generally, corporations involved in global value changes became increasingly vociferous proponents of trade liberalisation and trade facilitation, because any delays at a border reduce the efficiency of the value chain. Trade policy debates have become clouded with uncertainties, such as which are domestic products when value chains stretch over many borders and which firms are domestic producers when a majority of production or sales occur outside their "home" country and ownership is changed by takeovers or characterised by shareholders of many nationalities.[5]

---

[5]China complains that US estimates of its bilateral trade deficit with China are inflated by recording nationality according to the final stage of assembly, e.g. Mattel's Barbie Dolls which sell in the USA for $10 are marked 'Made in China' even though less than a dollar of their value-added accrues in China (raw materials for the plastic body comes from Saudi Arabia via Taiwan and for the nylon hair from Japan and other inputs are sourced from a large number of countries depending on the model). When Miller breweries export beer brewed in Milwaukee, it is a US product, but the owner is South African Breweries (SABMiller) whose primary listing is on the London Stock Exchange in England.

Chapter 8

Growth and Trade

A frequent criticism of the neoclassical trade theory in Chapters 4 and 5 is that it is static. To some extent the product cycle model was intended to capture a dynamic element of trade patterns missing from the standard theory. There was also a strong sense that trade theory was inapplicable to the policy debate in developing countries whose governments were concerned about increasing incomes rather than about efficient allocation of resources — an attitude that led to many policy missteps in the third quarter of the 20th century. Yet, growth can easily be introduced into the neoclassical trade model, and the consequences of growth for trade are readily analysable. The reverse relationship between trade and growth, and the policy implications for countries seeking to promote growth and development, will be dealt with in Chapter 16.

Economic growth can be represented by an outward shift in the production possibility frontier; more combinations of goods can be produced now than before. For a small open economy, this increases

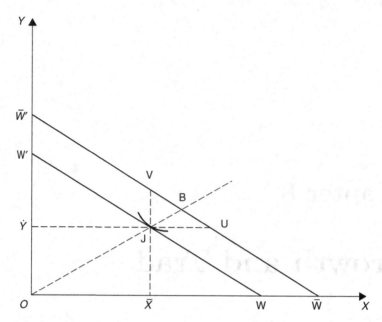

Figure 8.1.   Growth and trade in a small economy.

Note: Because of an outward shift in the production possibility frontier (not drawn) the economy can consume on a higher world price line ($\bar{W}'\bar{W}$ instead of $W'W$); that is, GNP measured at world prices has increased from OW to $O\bar{W}$ units of X. If consumption is to the right of point B, the share of the export good Y in gross national expenditure has fallen (there is a pro-trade bias) and if it is to the right of U there is an absolute fall in domestic consumption of Y (an ultra-pro-trade bias).

welfare because the economy now produces on a higher world price line. In Figure 8.1, if the share of X and Y in total consumption is unchanged with growth, then consumption will increase from J to B and the country is clearly better off. At any point between U and V on the new world price line more of both goods is consumed, and even at points outside this range total consumption has increased whether measured in units of X (total consumption, and GDP, increases from W to W-bar) or units of Y (total consumption, and GDP, increases from W' to W'-bar). This conclusion does not depend upon the social indifference curves, although we need some measure of demand to tell precisely where on the new world price line consumption takes place.

Growth increases welfare for a small open economy, but its impact on the level of trade is ambiguous. If post-growth consumption in Figure 8.1 is at point B, then the country's demand for imports and supply of exports increase proportionately to the growth in output. Otherwise, trade may grow by more or by less than output. Consumption bundles to the right of B, such as U, reflect a greater increase in consumption of X than in consumption of Y; hence, if X is the import good, as in Figure 4.7, there is a ***pro-trade bias*** because consumption of the import good has increased by more than the level of output. If consumption is at a point to the left of B, such as V, with a greater increase in consumption of Y than in consumption of X, then if Y is the export good there is an ***anti-trade bias***; a smaller share of Y output is exported, and relative to total output and income a smaller amount of X is imported. In the extreme cases to the left of V where consumption of the imported good falls absolutely, then growth leads to an increase in self-sufficiency; this outcome only occurs if the import is an inferior good, demand for which declines with income.

A similar taxonomy of pro- and anti-trade biased growth arises from the nature of the outward shift in the production possibility frontier. If the PPF shift is uniform, in the sense that along any ray from the origin the percentage change in possible output is the same, then there is no trade bias. If, however, the shift is not uniform because growth is due to technical change which is more capital-saving or more labour-saving or because growth is due to unbalanced increase in factor supplies, then growth can be either pro-trade-biased or anti-trade-biased.

When growth is due to increased supply of a single factor of production, then a strong result about the trade bias holds. In the 2×2 model, growth in one factor leads, *ceteris paribus*, to a decline in the output of the good using the other factor relatively intensively. This result, the ***Rybczynski Theorem***, is analytically closely related to the Stolper–Samuelson theorem; the latter refers to prices and the former to quantities, but both results involve a magnification effect and a similar proof can be used. Suppose that the labour force grows by ten percent, with no change in the capital stock. Output of both goods cannot increase by more than ten percent because that would require more capital as well as ten percent more labour, nor can output of both goods increase by less than ten percent because that would leave labour unemployed. Thus, one good's output must increase by more than ten percent, and that must be the labour-intensive good (X in Chapter 4). Expansion of X production must draw capital away from Y production, and since the capital/labour ratio is unchanged (because, for a small country with constant goods prices, factor prices cannot change) output of Y must fall:

$$\uparrow Q_X > \uparrow Q_L > \uparrow Q_K > \uparrow Q_Y$$

Figure 8.2 illustrates the Rybczynski Theorem with an Edgeworth Box diagram. An increased labour supply expands the box in one direction. With constant factor prices the capital/labour ratio in each activity, represented by a ray from the origin, remains unchanged.

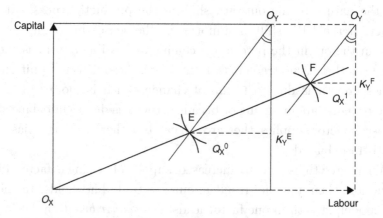

Figure 8.2. The Rybczynski Theorem.
Note: After an increase in the labour force, output of the labour-intensive good X increases; that is, isoquant Q_x^1 represents a higher output level than Q_x^0. Since the amount of capital allocated to Y production has fallen, from K_y^E to K_y^F, and the capital : labour ratio is unchanged, output of the capital-intensive good Y must fall.

The equilibrium points on the old and new contract curves, E and F, are the intersection points of the relevant rays; with less of both inputs used in Y production, F must be associated with a smaller Y output than at point E.

The Rybczynski Theorem is, like the Stolper–Samuelson theorem, reasonably robust because it does not depend upon assumptions about countries outside the one being analysed. The conclusion that the output mix must change by more than the factor endowment mix changes holds irrespective of whether technology and preferences differ across countries. However, the applicability of the Rybczynski Theorem is limited because we seldom observe a pure case of growth being due to increased supply of one factor with no change in technology or other factor supplies. One case where the theorem may be indicative concerns labour-abundant countries with rapid growth in their labour supply; if such a country is open to trade, then growth will be pro-trade biased with exports increasing faster than output.[1]

Growth and Trade in a Large Country

For a country that can affect world prices, the impact of growth on the terms of trade depends upon the trade bias of growth.[2] Anti-trade bias shifts the growing country's offer curve closer to its import-good axis, so that less is demanded and the terms of trade shift in the

---

[1]The increase in labour force could be due to rapid population growth (as in Bangladesh) or to a falling birth rate which drives increased labour force participation rates as in the high-performing east Asian countries (the demographic dividend reaped, for example, by Korea and Taiwan in the 1960s and 1970s and by Thailand and Indonesia in the 1980s and 1990s).

[2]A similar conclusion applies to a large demand shift. Although large changes in demand are uncommon, a famous example was the requirement for Germany to pay reparations after World War I. Keynes argued that this was a double punishment because supplying the added exports to pay the reparations would worsen Germany's terms of trade. Ohlin, rightly, pointed out that the overall impact of the transfer also depended upon the composition of demand. A modern example of the *transfer problem* could arise if an aid recipient found that its increased demand for imports using the aid money pushed up the price of imports.

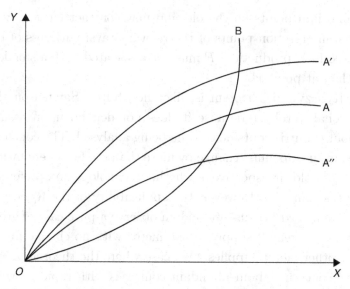

Figure 8.3.   Growth and the offer curve.
Note: Anti-trade biased growth shifts country A's offer curve OA to OA''; less of
its export good Y is offered at any set of world pieces, so that the relative price
of Y increases and the rest of the world moves to a lower utility point on its offer
curve OB. Otherwise, growth has the opposite effect, with A's offer curve shifting
from OA to OA'.

country's favour, as in the shift from OA to OA'' in Figure 8.3. If
conditions in the rest of the world are unchanged (i.e. its offer curve
does not move), then the growing country enjoys a double benefit
from economic growth: its output is greater and it pays less for its
imports.

Pro-trade biased growth shifts the offer curve in the opposite
direction, from OA to OA' in Figure 8.3. Now, because the country
wants to trade more, it suffers deterioration in its terms of trade,
which offsets some of the benefits of growth. In an extreme case,
the negative terms of trade effect may more than offset the benefits from increased output, leading to the case of ***immiserising
growth*** (Bhagwati, 1958). In Figure 8.4 expansion of the factor used
relatively intensively in the production of the export good, Y, is
associated with a larger trade triangle at the old world prices, i.e.

growth is pro-trade biased (consistent with the Rybczynski Theorem). The offer curve will shift as from OA to OA' in Figure 8.3,
and the world price line becomes steeper so that utility is reduced
from that associated with point J on the indifference curve I_3 reached
after growth at the old world prices. Just how much steeper the world
price line becomes in Figure 8.4 depends upon the various elasticities of demand and supply, but it could end up like VV' where even
the pre-growth consumption point, C, is not attainable. At point M,
growth has been immiserising because the country is worse off than
it was before growth; indifference curve I_1 is below the pre-growth
indifference curve I_2.

How likely is immiserising growth? Three major conditions must
hold. Growth must be pro-trade biased. Foreign demand for the

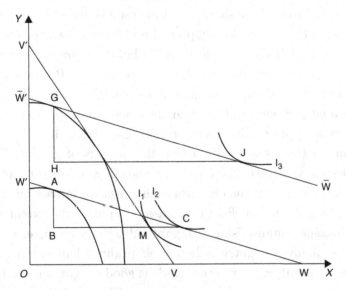

Figure 8.4.   Immiserising growth.
Note: Here, economic growth is pro-trade biased; at constant world prices the
trade triangle becomes GHJ instead of ABC. For a large country, the relative
price of the export good Y will fall; that is, the world price line becomes steeper.
If the price of Y falls far enough, for example as indicated by $V'V$, then post-
growth consumption, M, may be on a lower indifference curve than pre-growth
consumption; that is, economic growth has left the country worse off.

export must be priced inelastic, so that increasing the amount of Y being offered leads to a substantial reduction in its price. The growing country must be heavily trade dependent.

Brazilian coffee-based growth in the 1930s is a frequently cited example of immiserising growth, although this interpretation is debated because there were many other reasons for the country's poor economic performance during the 1930s. The phenomenon depends upon the existence of imperfect competition, in the sense that an individual country can affect world prices, although the immiserising outcome implies that the country as a unit does not use its market power, rather that the uncoordinated actions of its producers may inadvertently hurt them all.[3] Although many have seized on the possibility of immiserising growth as a justification for developing countries to beware of international trade, it is an unlikely outcome for a poor country whose share of world trade is likely to be small.

Although the models in Chapters 4 and 5 are static, the conclusions about the gains from trade generally hold in a growing economy. For a small open economy the share of trade in GDP may change but the welfare implications of growth are straightforward and positive. For a large economy, if the combined changes in the output mix and the consumption mix create an anti-trade bias, then the positive terms of trade effect will add to the benefits of growth. With pro-trade-biased growth, the terms of trade effect offsets some of the benefits of growth, but the case where the negative impact on world prices outweighs the benefits of increased output to the extent that growth becomes immiserising is highly unlikely. In practice, with a growing economy a country is better off trading than not trading. The reverse causality, i.e. whether trade is good for growth, has been more controversial and will be addressed in Chapter 16.

---

[3]It is an example of the theory of the second-best, that states that if one of the conditions for a welfare optimum is absent then changes which would be welfare-improving in the unconstrained general equilibrium model need not necessarily be so. In the absence of perfectly competitive markets, paradoxical outcomes are possible.

Chapter 9

Economies of Scale and Imperfect Competition

Economies of large-scale production can increase the potential gains from specialisation and trade. They did not play a major role in the development of neoclassical trade theory, in part because if scale economies alone are important then the pattern of trade may be arbitrary. This was clearly recognised by, for example, Ohlin (1933, Chapter 3), who argued that factor proportions determined trade patterns and scale economies might offer additional scope for gains from trade. A second problem is that when scale economies are internal to the firm, they are incompatible with perfectly competitive markets.

To separate out the market structure and scale economy issues, let us start by considering economies of scale that are independent of the size of the firm. *External economies of scale* occur when the cost per unit of output depends upon the size of the industry. They

can arise from the establishment of suppliers of specialised equipment
or services, labour pooling which reduces the search costs of finding
appropriate employees, and knowledge spillovers. In the film industry
Hollywood in Los Angeles and Bollywood in Mumbai are magnets for
a large range of specialised skills, not just actors and directors, which
make it difficult to imagine US or Indian movie companies at another
location. External economies of scale are consistent with competitive
markets. Agriculture, for example, may consist of many small farms
operating in perfect competition, but a larger agricultural sector may
have lower costs because specialised tractor agencies or vet services
and examples of new seeds or techniques being used under local conditions are all more likely.

In a two-good world with strong economies of scale, the production function will become concave, i.e. bowed into the origin, rather
than convex, because the more that is produced of one good the lower
the opportunity cost of producing an additional unit of that good.
In Figure 9.1 two identical countries have the same production possibility frontier and consume at point A. By each country completely

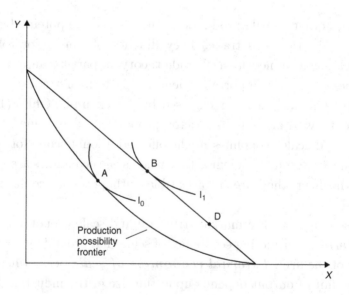

Figure 9.1.   International trade with economies of scale.

specialising in one of the goods they can both consume at point B, which is on a higher indifference curve than A. This simple example illustrates two general propositions:

1. Scale economies are an independent reason for trade, because they are a source of gains from specialisation.
2. The pattern of trade based on scale economies alone is arbitrary; in Figure 9.1 it is a matter of chance which country produces X and which country produces Y.

Chance is an unsatisfactory explanation for trade patterns, which explains why Ohlin relegated scale economies to being a subsidiary cause behind factor endowments, but in some cases it may be correct. Seagrams became the best-selling whiskey in North America because in 1933 when the USA repealed Prohibition (the prevention by law of the manufacture or sale of alcohol which had been in effect since 1920) the Canadian manufacturer had stocks of aged whiskey, denied to legitimate US producers.

An alternative way of characterising the trade patterns associated with economies of scale is to consider the advantage of being the first mover. In Figure 9.2 the downward-sloping average cost curve of the Swiss watchmaking industry indicates that it could supply the world market, represented by demand curve D, at a price of P_1. An Asian country may be potentially a lower cost supplier, but the first firm to start producing would have an average cost of C_0, which is above the world price, so the industry never takes off. The incumbent will only lose market share when the cost gap becomes large enough that $C_0 < P_1$ or the new entrant has enough resources to start on a large scale. With the mechanisation of agriculture in the second half of the 19th century, John Deere supplied farm machinery to farmers in the American Midwest, but as an established producer it had an advantage over potential producers in newly mechanising agricultural areas and remains a major exporter today even though the source of its locational advantage is no longer obvious. Similarly, the position

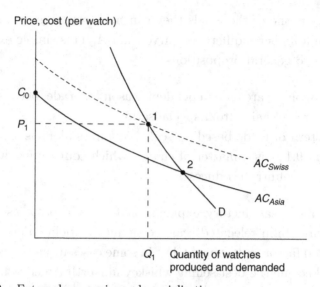

Figure 9.2.   External economies and specialisation.
Note: The average cost curve for Asia, AC_{Asia} lies below the average cost curve for
Switzerland, AC_{Swiss}. Thus Asia could potentially supply the world market more
cheaply than Switzerland. If the Swiss industry gets established first, however, it
may be able to sell watches at the price P_1 which is below the cost C_0 that an
individual Asia firm would face if it began production on its own. So a pattern
of specialisation established by historical accident may persist even when new
producers could potentially have lower costs.

of London or Luxembourg as European financial centres is rooted in
long ago events, but in the presence of strong external economies of
scale their advantage has become fossilised.

Murray Kemp (1964, 110–31) developed the offer curve analysis
of two countries whose economies are characterised by economies of
scale. In Figure 9.3(a), which corresponds to the production possibility frontier analysis in Figure 9.1, at world prices TT' a small country
may specialise in producing Y (point H) or in producing X (point
J) or remain in autarchy (the origin, O). If the country is large, the
two-country international equilibrium in Figure 9.3(b) may involve
complete specialisation in Y production (point L), complete specialisation in X (point N), incomplete specialisation in X (point M), or
no trade (point O). In sum, almost any outcome is possible, and the

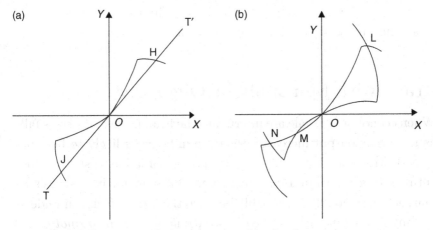

Figure 9.3.   Offer curve analysis with economies of scale.
Note: (a) the offer curve corresponding to Figure 9.1: at world prices $T'T$ the country may specialise completely in Y (point H) or in X (point J) or remain in autarchy (point O, corresponding to A in Figure 9.1); (b) international equilibrium: at L both countries are completely specialised, at M neither country is and at N one is completely specialised and the other is not. Assuming that producers rather than consumers respond first to domestic disequilibrium, points L and N are stable equilibria and M is unstable.

welfare implications may be very different, e.g. the terms of trade are different at L and N and welfare will differ depending upon which good the country specialises in. In Figure 9.1 for any consumption points which do not exactly divide the specialised outputs, the gains from trade will be unequally distributed; at point D, for example, excess demand for X will bid up the price of X and the country fortunate enough to have specialised in X will receive most of the gains from trade, perhaps to the extent that the country specialising in Y ends up worse off than in autarchy (i.e. if the price line becomes so steep that coming out of the Y intercept of the PPF it passes to the left of A).

These depressingly ambiguous conclusions are fortunately not very applicable to the real world. Countries' aggregate production functions are not characterised by economies of scale, and countries' ranking by per capita income bears no relation to size. Even at

the industry level, it is hard to think of an industry in which scale
economies are so strong that a country has a monopoly.

Trade with Monopoly or Oligopoly

When economies of scale are internal to the firm, i.e. average costs fall
as the firm's output increases, then the industry is likely to become
imperfectly competitive. In the extreme case of falling costs over the
entire relevant output range (e.g. domestic demand in a sheltered
market), a monopoly is probable because the largest firm can undercut any rivals. Once established, a profit-maximising *monopoly* sets
marginal revenue equal to marginal cost. In Figure 9.4 the shaded

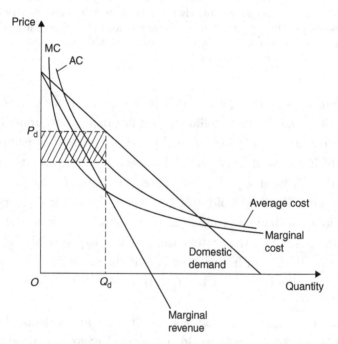

Figure 9.4.   Price and output decision of a profit-maximising monopoly.
Note: To maximise profits the monopolist produces output level Q_d, where
$MR = MC$. Profits are equal to the shaded area.

area represents monopoly profits, i.e. returns to capital over and above the returns to capital in competitive parts of the economy.

The monopolist's profit-maximising output level is not a socially optimal outcome because some consumers are willing to pay more for additional units of the good than the cost of producing those additional units. In an analysis similar to that in Chapter 5, if prices capture social costs and benefits, then the monopoly profit is always less than the loss of consumer surplus associated with a price above average cost. There is a net social gain from having the industry produce more and sell at a lower price than that which the unregulated monopoly will charge, and many countries have laws restricting the use of monopoly power. One example of a welfare-improving monopoly policy is a price ceiling; in Figure 9.4 any price ceiling below P_d, down to the price where the average cost curve cuts the demand curve (i.e. where excess profits equal zero), increases consumer surplus by more than it reduces monopoly profits, while still providing an incentive for the firm to operate. Implementation is, however, imperfect because firms have an incentive to understate their market power or their profits, or large firms may have sufficient political influence to avoid constraints on their behaviour.

An important gain from trade arises when an import-competing industry is a monopoly. There is not only the usual gain from specialisation, but if the price of competing imports is less than the pre-trade price charged by the domestic monopoly then there is also the benefit of reducing the social costs of monopoly. This is not such an unusual case; many autarchic countries have small domestic markets, so that economies of scale may still exist in a firm supplying the entire domestic market. Given the impartiality of market pressures and their relative immunity to corruption, it is often said that trade is the best anti-monopoly policy. In Figure 9.4, as long as the price of imports in the domestic market is below P_d, then there are gains from increased consumer surplus which outweighs loss of monopoly profits.

When we turn to global markets, the pure monopoly analysis is less helpful because it is difficult to find any world market with a single supplier. De Beers influence over the diamond market is sometimes cited, but there are many producers of diamonds and there are incentives not to use de Beers central selling organisation. Microsoft may appear to have a strong hold over computer operating systems and it has been the subject of anti-monopoly actions in the USA and EU, but it has competitors.

Imperfect competition is difficult to analyse in a systematic manner. With a small number of firms, but more than one, analysis becomes more complex, because we need to consider strategic interaction and market segmentation. These are addressed in national competition policies because oligopolistic firms are likely to earn excess returns and their profits may be increased by collusion or price discrimination, at the expense of consumers and with negative net welfare effects. Such behaviours and policies to counteract them impinge on international trade in several ways:

1. national competition policies may affect the international competitiveness of firms from differing countries,
2. governments may be able to use so-called 'strategic trade policies' to shift monopoly profits from foreign to home firms by influencing the firms' strategic interaction,
3. discriminatory pricing may be used to boost monopoly profits, and 'dumping' may be perceived as unfair or anti-competitive.

These policy-oriented arguments, including the influential Brander–Spencer duopoly model, will be analysed in Chapter 11.

An analytically tractable and empirically plausible approach to imperfect competition is to assume that firms produce differentiated products and have market power in that demand is not perfectly price-elastic, but free entry and exit limit opportunities for excess profits. Monopolistic competition is analysed below, but first it is useful to look at the empirical literature which stimulated interest in incorporating imperfect competition into trade theory.

Intra-Industry Trade

Second only to the Leontief Paradox as a challenge to neoclassical trade theory and the Heckscher–Ohlin theorem was the finding by Herbert Grubel and Peter Lloyd (1975) that almost half of trade among high-income countries was within industries rather than between industries. Is this inconsistent with the conclusion that an industry will either be an export or import-competing activity depending upon the relative factor-intensity of its output and the factor endowments of the country in which it is located? *Intra-industry trade* may be a phenomenon of global production as, for example, electronics firms ship components among factories in different countries, driven by factor endowments. Intra-industry trade may reflect that the definition of industry in trade statistics is not that of the neoclassical model (where industries are defined by differing factor proportions). Both of these suggest that intra-industry trade may be an aggregation issue, although we can also explain intra-industry trade in terms of imperfect competition.

Grubel and Lloyd measured intra-industry trade as the difference between total exports and imports of a good $(X + M)$ and the absolute value of net imports or net exports (the lines around $|X - M|$ indicate that the sign of this expression is to be ignored). The share of intra-industry trade in total trade of an industry is:

$$B = \frac{X + M - |X - M|}{X + M}$$

where the value of B varies between one, when $X = M$ and all trade is intra-industry, and zero, when X or M is zero and all trade is inter-industry.

Using data for three-digit Standard International Trade Classification (SITC) groups for ten industrialised countries, Grubel and Lloyd found that intra-industry trade accounted for almost half of these countries' international trade.[1] This suggests that studies like Leontief's which analyse a country's net exports or net imports of each industry's goods are only dealing with half of international trade. The high level of intra-industry trade posed a new challenge for standard trade theories which explain trade patterns in terms of an industry having either a comparative advantage or a comparative disadvantage.

Some intra-industry can be related to transport costs; e.g. if British Columbia exports coal to Washington state and Pennsylvania exports coal to Ontario this will enter into Canadian and US trade statistics as intra-industry trade. There is also seasonal trade due to high storage costs, e.g. a northern hemisphere country may export fruits during the summer that it imports from the southern hemisphere during the northern winter. These are fairly obvious but also quite a minor part of international trade. They represent an aggregation problem which would disappear if we divided trade statistics by region or by month. A more general, and more controversial, aggregation problem surrounds the definition of 'industry'. Grubel and Lloyd chose the three-digit aggregation level on the grounds that it most closely corresponds to what people think of as an industry, e.g. SITC 781 (passenger motor vehicles except buses) is an industry with readily observable intra-industry trade. On the other hand, a group such as SITC 793 (ships and boats) is more heterogeneous and it would be no surprise if a country exported supertankers and imported kayaks.

---

[1] In the original study European countries were heavily represented. In part that was because the phenomenon had first been highlighted after the establishment of the western European customs union; it was anticipated that trade would be between industries, e.g. German cars exchanging for French wheat, but the expansion of trade was within industries as Germany exported cars to France and France exported cars to Germany. Subsequent studies have found that, at the level of aggregation used by Grubel and Lloyd, intra-industry trade is a global phenomenon, higher in high-income countries but increasing everywhere.

At finer aggregation levels the share of intra-industry trade is lower, e.g. using the six-digit level which contains about 2,000 categories instead of the 182 three-digit groups intra-industry trade was generally less than ten percent. Of course, if we disaggregate down to individual transactions, every transaction would involve a different good; there would be no intra-industry trade, but this would be a meaningless definition of an 'industry.'

In sum, it is difficult to know where to draw the line and to what degree intra-industry trade is a substantive phenomenon. Even if intra-industry exists it may be compatible with the Heckscher–Ohlin theorem if what is being observed are different parts of the global value chain in a single industry. The observation that measured intra-industry trade is increasing over time may be capturing the phenomenon of locating different stages of production within an industry in different countries as trade costs and trade barriers decline. Intra-industry trade may simply be picking up increased division of labour in the expanding global economy, without posing any challenge to trade theory and would largely disappear if it were measured at the appropriate level of aggregation (Pomfret, 1986a).

Monopolistic Competition

As with the Leontief Paradox literature, the intra-industry trade literature stimulated an important rethinking of trade theory. Grubel and Lloyd highlighted some industries where intra-industry trade clearly seemed to be a substantive phenomenon, e.g. cars and cigarettes in Europe, and suggested that the reason was a mixture of scale economies and taste diversity. Thus, if there are economies of scale in car manufacturing, then there will only be a few producers in any country and they will cater to the majority tastes. If tastes differ across countries, then consumers with minority tastes may import; if Germans prefer larger cars and Germany produces Mercedes while Italian preference is for smaller cars and Italy produces Fiats, then German consumers wanting small cars might import Fiats and Italian consumers wanting large cars might import Mercedes. Similarly if the cigarette industry is characterised by economies of scale, each country may produce a limited range of styles; English smokers might import Gauloises, while French smokers import Benson and Hedges.

Paul Krugman (1979; 1980) combined scale economies and product differentiation by assuming that industries are monopolistically competitive. Under **monopolistic competition** each firm produces a differentiated product and thus has some monopoly power; firms act like monopolists, equating marginal revenue and marginal cost, but they do not earn monopoly profits because there is free entry and exit into the industry. In equilibrium (Figure 9.5), a firm produces an output level where price is equal to average cost, because if price were below average cost the firm would make losses and go out of business and if price were above average cost the monopoly profits would induce firms to enter the industry, driving down prices and profits. Because the firm's demand curve is downward-sloping, the firm must be producing on the downward-sloping part of its average cost curve, i.e. there are economies of scale.

To model monopolistic competition, Krugman assumed equal-sised firms and no strategic interaction, i.e. each firm ignores the impact that changes in its own price will have on competitors. The representative firm will sell more the larger the industry's total sales and the higher the prices charged by its rivals, and it will sell less the larger the number of firms in the industry and the higher its own price. For any overall market size, the larger the number of firms and the greater the competition, the lower the price each firm can charge. At the same time, the greater the number of firms, the higher the average cost of each producer; because they are producing on the downward-sloping part of their average cost curve, a smaller market share translates into higher costs. At some number of firms, n, the equilibrium price, which decreases in n, matches the average cost, which increases in n. This is the equilibrium number of firms, because when price equals average costs there are zero excess profits and there is no incentive for firms to enter or exit the industry.

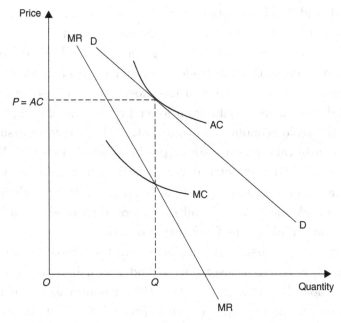

Figure 9.5. Price and output decision of the representative firm under monopolistic competition.
Note: DD is the demand curve facing the individual firm. If all firms are identical then in equilibrium total demand is equal to nQ, where n is the number of firms in the industry (that is, the number of firms is equal to the total market size divided by Q).

Opening up to trade increases the market size. Trade flattens each firm's demand curve because there are more competing varieties, and for each firm the new equilibrium is at a lower average cost, lower price and higher output. Suppose trade is between two similar economies; demand has doubled, the number of firms in the joint market has doubled to $2n$, but each firm is larger. The post-trade equilibrium requires that some firms go out of business, but with the number of surviving firms somewhere between n and $2n$, the total number of varieties available to consumers increases because they can now buy either domestically produced or imported varieties. The monopolistic competition model predicts intra-industry trade, as in the European car or tobacco examples highlighted by Grubel and Lloyd, and this is associated with new gains from trade through greater variety and lower costs. The increased variety is an added source of increased consumer well-being not captured in models with homogeneous goods. Because trade is associated with a smaller number of firms, each remaining firm has moved down its average cost curve, and consumers benefit from lower prices. The ensuing trade also has the scale economies feature that, without further assumptions, it is arbitrary which country produces which varieties. With identical firms and symmetrical varieties, it is unimportant which varieties a country produces, but, if demand for some varieties is more income-elastic than demand for others, then production location may have implications for future prosperity.

It is difficult to assess the significance of the simple monopolistic competition of trade insofar as a model with identical firms is an abstraction. Nevertheless, as with the extreme cases of perfect competition and monopoly, the results from an abstract model can provide insights into situations where the model's assumptions do not fully apply. Moreover, monopolistic competition may provide a better source of insight into global than domestic markets. Imperfectly competitive domestic markets are often oligopolies where a few suppliers hide behind barriers to entry, whereas in imperfectly competitive global markets firms are more numerous and entry is less regulated or hampered by other barriers. The car industry, which was long portrayed in US economics textbooks as a three-firm oligopoly, has at least ten major producers in the world market and, although entry barriers are substantial, new entrants like Toyota and Nissan in the 1960s and 1970s, and Hyundai in the 1980s have established themselves and it is likely that new global marques will emerge from China in the coming years. This example highlights, however, the shortcoming of a model that assumes symmetrical firms, and during the 1980s and 1990s monopolistic competition was often viewed as an interesting theoretical model but of limited applicability because of its unrealistic assumption. Bernard and Jensen (1995) were the first to work with non-identical firms, although this was primarily an empirical paper.

In the most exciting recent development in trade theory, writers such as Marc Melitz (2003) and Andrew Bernard, Bradford Jensen and Peter Schott (2006) have taken the theoretical analysis a step further, disaggregating to the individual producer, which is a differentiated firm in an imperfectly competitive industry.[2] With the opening up to trade or reductions in trade costs, the price of factors used intensively in the export industry increase, and the most efficient firms become competitive exporters, while the least efficient firms go out of business (or perhaps maintain an established niche in the domestic market).[3] Empirical studies with firm–level data confirm that there is a high degree of *firm heterogeneity*, and most firms do not export at all. There is almost universal support for the hypothesis that firms which export have higher productivity, and less strong support for the hypothesis that exporting leads to faster productivity growth.[4] In a heterogeneous firm setting exporters may sort by quality as well as by efficiency, with some high-cost firms

---

[2]Recent contributions by the same authors to the heterogeneous firms literature include Bernard, Redding, and Schott (2007) and Helpman, Melitz, and Rubinstein (2007). Baldwin and Robert-Nicoud (2008) explore the trade-growth relationship, and in their opening section survey the heterogeneous firm trade literature.

[3]A striking feature of firm–level data is that in the large established economies even at the finest level of disaggregation all activities are represented. Even as China's exports have moved into new lines, so that the share of all possible products represented in China's export bundle has increased dramatically (from 9% to 85% according to Schott, 2008), US imports from high-income countries continue to include goods from every industry.

[4]Wagner (2007) summarises the findings of 54 empirical studies using firm data from 34 countries from the decade following the pioneering study by Bernard and Jensen (1995). The source of exporters' greater efficiency is unclear. Greenaway, Guariglia and Kneller (2007) find that among British firms exporters exhibit better financial health than non-exporters, but the relationship does not hold for new exporters, who have low liquidity and high leverage. This suggests that the decision to export is a risky one, but being an established exporter is a source of strength. Eaton, Eslava, Kugler and Tybout (2007) reach a similar conclusion for Colombia; using data for 1996–2005 they find that out of each year's cohort of new exporters, a few expand rapidly to join the small number of firms which dominate the country's export earnings.

exporting if high costs are associated with high quality (Baldwin and Harrigan, 2007), which could explain the finding that quality increases with the distance to the export destination (Hallak, 2006; Schott, 2004) because transport costs are relatively less of an obstacle to high-cost high-quality exports.

As firm–level data, and the software and computing power to use it, have become more plentiful in recent years, more rigorous testing of the gains from trade has become feasible. Reviewing the empirical evidence on trade in imperfectly competitive industries, Robert Feenstra (2006) concludes that the early theoretical emphasis on the benefits from realising economies of scale and passing on lower prices to consumers obtains, at best, mixed support. On the other hand, the benefits from increased variety and from increased firm–level efficiency due to expansion of the most efficient firms, as predicted by heterogeneous-firm models, are substantial.[5]

When Krugman and others introduced imperfect competition into international trade theory in the late 1970s and 1980s, the new trade theories were presented as a major challenge to established trade theory. This was because imperfect competition could lead to new arguments for interventionist trade policies; theoretical paradoxes can inevitably be found because imperfect competition is a second-best situation, but their practical significance was hotly debated and the extent to which such theories are good guides to policymaking will be assessed in Chapter 11. In terms of explaining the patterns of international trade, the new trade theories' impact was less dramatic; they supplement rather than displace older theories. In particular, by adding further sources of gain (scale economies, output

---

[5]Feenstra's conclusion about product variety rests especially on the work by Broda and Weinstein (2006) who, using highly disaggregated US trade data for 2001, estimated that the gains from trade to the USA due to increased varieties amounted to 2.6% of GDP, which as a recurring increment is a large amount. On the expansion of efficient firms, Feenstra's conclusion draws on Trefler's (2004) study of Canadian firms' response to free trade with the USA and on the study of French trade by Eaton, Kortum and Kramarz (2004).

variety, and firm selection), they reinforce the conclusion that potential gains from trade are pervasive. The applicability of the factor endowment explanation of trade patterns is reduced by the arbitrariness of industrial location when scale economies are important and by the heterogeneity of a country's firms in any industry. Finally, when trade is intra- rather than inter-industry the distributional impact of price changes may be less serious, because adjustment costs are likely to be lower if workers have an opportunity to relocate within an industry instead of having to shift to another industry.

Chapter 10

Factor Flows

Just as differences in goods prices provide an incentive for trade, differences in factor returns provide an incentive for international factor flows. The effects can be analysed in a similar way to the effects of inter-sectoral labour migration in the specific factors model. Assuming a factor of production is internationally mobile in response to differences in factor rewards, then joint output in two countries will be maximised when the return to the mobile factor is equalised in the two countries, but there will be gainers and losers.

With competitive markets and diminishing marginal product, a factor will be employed up to the point where its price is equal to the value of its marginal product. In Figure 10.1, the supply of labour is OQ, the demand for labour depends upon the value of its marginal product, and the market-clearing wage rate is W_A. If labour is internationally mobile and the wage rates in country A and country B differ, then labour migration from the low-wage country to the high-wage country (from A to B in Figure 10.2) will lead to increasing

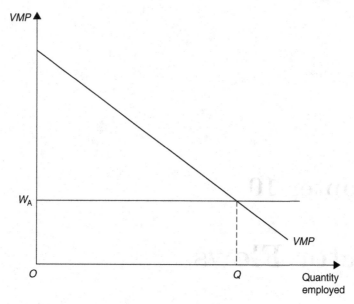

Figure 10.1.   Wage rate determination.
Note: With competitive labour markets, the wage rate will be equal to the value
of the marginal product of the last worker to be employed. Note the similarity to
Figure 6.2. The area under the *VMP* between *O* and *Q* measures the total output
of these workers.

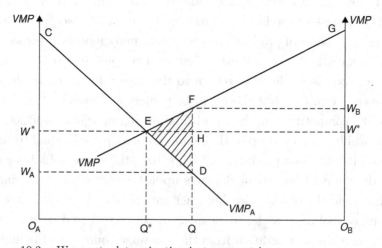

Figure 10.2.   Wage rate determination in two countries.
Note: The horizontal axis measures the quantity of labour, with $O_A O_B$ being the
total labour force in the two countries.

wages in A and declining wages in B. If there are no other considerations affecting labour mobility, then migration will continue until
both countries have a wage rate W^*.

The sum of the marginal product of every worker is equal to
total output. Total output in a country is measured by the area
under the *VMP* curve to the point where the least productive worker
is employed. In Figure 10.2, where $O_A Q$ workers are employed in
country A, the total output in that country is the area $O_A QDC$.
Of this output the rectangle $O_A QDW_A$ measures the total wage bill
and the triangle $W_A DC$ measures the total return to other factors of
production. Similarly in country B, where the labour force is equal
to $O_B Q$, total output is area $O_B QFG$, of which $O_B QFW_B$ accrues
to labour and GFW_B accrues to other factors of production. Global
output with immobile labour is equal to area $O_A QDC$ plus area
$O_B QFG$.

With international labour mobility and wage equalisation, $Q^* Q$
workers move from A to B. Global output increases from $O_A QDC +
O_B QFG$ to $O_A Q^* EC + O_B Q^* EG$. The increase in output is captured
by the gap between the two *VMP* curves. The shaded area DEF
represents the net increase in output due to workers moving to where
their productivity is higher.

The distributional consequences of labour migration are that the
migrants and the workers remaining in their sending country benefit and workers in the receiving country lose wage income, while
owners of other factors of production lose in the sending country
and gain in the labour-receiving country. In Figure 10.2 the migrant
workers receive a higher wage, which is why they migrate, and also
the OQ^* workers remaining in country A receive higher wages, while
the return to other factors falls from $W_A DC$ to $W^* EC$. There is
a net gain to citizens of A, equal to triangle DHE, because the
benefit to workers $W_A DHW^*$ is greater than the loss of income to
other factors, $W_A DEW^*$. In country B, the indigenous workers suffer from increased competition from immigrants and their income

falls by FW_BW^*H, but the owners of other factors of production are better off because they pay less for labour; the gain to other factors, FW_BW^*E, exceeds the loss to workers by the area FEH. In sum, both countries are net beneficiaries from the migration; $DHE + FEH$ equals the global net gain, DEF.

Figure 10.2 is called the **Beaker Diagram** because of the cup-shaped equilibrium value of marginal product, CEG. It captures a large part of the story of major international migrations, such as the millions of people who emigrated from Europe to work in North America, Australia or Argentina before 1914. Wages in major sending countries such as Italy, Norway, Sweden and Ireland were between half and a quarter of those in the destination countries. The migrants sometimes took their own capital or were able to obtain free land upon arrival, so that there was little resistance until the domestic labour force in the receiving countries became more numerous and better organised, and then more vociferous in opposing further immigration.

Applying the analytical framework of Figure 10.2 to the current world economy suggests that the gains to global efficiency from removing all restrictions to labour movement would be large. Estimates range from an early and influential calculation that global GDP would be doubled (Hamilton and Whalley, 1984) down to a cautious estimate of a ten percent increase in GDP (Moses and Letnes, 2004). Even the low estimate is much greater than any estimates of the gains from removing all restrictions on the movement of goods.[1]

Labour migration is, however, a more complex phenomenon than goods trade. The decision to migrate involves more than simply changing work in order to obtain a higher wage. Emigrants leave

---

[1]The principal source of the large range is the assumptions about inherent productivity differences between workers currently in high productivity locations and workers currently in low productivity locations. Hatton (2007) reviews the literature, presenting evidence in support of the view that Moses and Lettner assume implausibly large efficiency edges for rich-country labour and hence underestimate the gains from mobility.

family, friends and a known culture behind, in order to move to a country where jobs may be plentiful but other workers resentful. There are many externalities. The sending country may have publicly funded training a young adult who has many working years ahead, and fear the consequences of a brain drain or of losing its most dynamic young people.[2] The receiving country may worry that migrants gain access to social services paid for out of past incomes of domestic workers. Both claims may be overstated, but they can be fanned by xenophobia and concerns about immigrants changing the social structure.

International movement of other factors can be analysed with the beaker diagram. International capital mobility in response to differences in the value of the marginal productivity of capital will increase global output. Capitalists in the sending country will benefit, while other factors will lose, and capitalists in the capital-receiving country will lose while other factors gain. Again this explains broad patterns of pre-1914 capital flows from Europe to the Americas and Australasia, as institutions were developed to reduce the risk to European investors of lending to farmers and railway builders thousands of kilometres away across oceans. More recently we see concerns among workers in high-income countries as firms invest overseas or opposition by local capitalists to foreign investment in poor countries, both of which may be wrapped up in nationalist sentiments about exporting jobs or about exploiting national resources to earn profits for foreigners.

International capital movements can also reflect intertemporal choice. If Australia is relatively efficient at producing future goods and Japan has a relatively high preference for future goods (i.e. a low

---

[2]There is a large literature on self-selection among immigrants of differing abilities, largely based on the models of Roy (1951) and Borjas (1987). Empirically, Chiswick (1978) showed that emigrants are more dynamic and better trained than their compatriots; based on US evidence, Borjas challenged this conclusion, while Chiquiar and Hanson (2005) provide evidence in support of Chiswick.

discount rate), then there are gains from Japan exporting present goods to Australia (i.e. lending) in return for promised delivery of future goods. The relative price of present and future goods $(1/(1+r)$, where r is the interest rate) will be determined by the shapes of the production possibility frontiers and community indifference curves with present and future goods on the axes of a diagram like Figure 4.7.[3] When countries receive a windfall gain, such as a sudden and unexpected change in their terms of trade, they may have insufficient good domestic investment projects to generate future goods and choose to lend to countries better able to produce future goods. The oil-exporting countries did this after 1973, lending to Brazil, Korea and other economies with growth potential, but there is a risk if the lender is unfamiliar with conditions in the borrowing country; loans to Korea in the 1970s were repaid on time, but loans to Brazil and Mexico were never fully repaid because the investments were less productive than expected. The modern counterparts are the oil funds of countries benefiting from the tenfold increase in the price of oil between 1998 and 2008 or the sovereign wealth funds of other countries, such as China, with rapidly increasing foreign exchange earnings.

Capital movements involve acquisition of assets, and the balancing of risk and return makes these movements generally better suited to financial analysis than to trade theory, even though some international capital flows are based on comparative advantage. Individual lenders may diversify their portfolio across countries to reduce country-specific risk, even when there are no differences in the productive potential of the borrowing countries. Analysis of capital flows is also more tractable in a model that includes money, because the store of value function of money facilitates the running of trade deficits and surpluses, which are the counterpart to capital outflows or inflows. When countries have national monies, exchange rate risk itself is a motive for allocating capital to different currency areas.

---

[3]Krugman and Obstfeld (2006, 170–3) provide a clear exposition of the intertemporal choice model.

Goods Flows and Factor Flows: Substitutes or Complements?

In the neoclassical trade model, goods flows and factor flows are substitutes. If two countries begin to trade, then the export of the good which is intensive in the abundant factor will be associated with a higher price for that good and an increase in the returns to that factor. Alternatively if trade is banned but factors can move freely between two countries, the abundant factor will emigrate and the price of that factor will increase, pushing up the relative price of the good that is intensive in that factor. With perfect competition and no distortions other than the restriction on factor or goods mobility, the two outcomes are identical in their impact on prices (Mundell, 1957).[4]

The empirical evidence on the substitutability of factor movements for goods trade is mixed. Anecdotal evidence of substitutability is provided by the shift in the process by which US tech companies took advantage of the wage differential between US and Indian computer engineers in the late 1990s and early 2000s. With Indian wages no more than a quarter of their US counterparts during the 1990s, US tech companies were keen to hire Indian engineers and the engineers were happy to relocate to Silicon Valley. When immigration to the USA became more restrictive after 2001, the US companies began to import the services of computer engineers resident in India via import of programs or other software. The result was a rapid increase in demand in India for experienced computer engineers, whose annual

---

[4]Income distribution consequences, as predicted by the Stolper–Samuelson theorem, can come from goods or factor movements. The IMF (in its spring 2007 *World Economic Outlook*) estimated that the global labour supply had in effect risen fourfold since 1980 because of the opening up of India, China and other formerly centrally planned economies, and that this had a negative income on the real income of labour in high-income countries. It is hard, however, to separate this from the impact of labour-saving technical change and of institutional change, e.g. the negative impact on wage income was reduced in many OECD countries by narrowing the wedge between labour costs and workers' take-home pay.

salaries had reached $60,000–100,000 by 2007, or not much less than the earnings of comparable engineers in California.

Earlier evidence of substitutability in Europe was the response to the declining competitiveness of the textile industry. In areas of England where the protected industry continued to operate in the 1960s and 1970s, the textile mills were increasingly operated by immigrants. When immigration controls were tightened in the 1980s and 1990s and when goods flows were eased in 2005 with the abolition of the Multifibre Arrangement, textile and clothing imports largely substituted for immigration. On the other hand, a significant part of migration from eastern to western Europe in the early 2000s was into non-traded sectors, such as construction for male immigrants, healthcare or age-care for female immigrants, and retail or hospitality trades for young people of both sexes. The impact of these migration flows on trade is indirect and its direction unclear.

One reason why the empirical evidence is mixed is that there are other reasons for trade besides differences in factor endowments and, more importantly, there are other motives for labour migration besides income differentials. Historical studies, such as the work of Kevin O'Rourke and Jeffrey Williamson on the 19th century Atlantic economy, identify a more complex interaction between trade in goods and movement of factors, with the evidence on balance that the two may be complements rather than substitutes, at least in the short to medium term. Immigrants typically bring goods with them from their home country and their tastes lead to continuing imports of goods from their home country that may be unavailable in their new location. On the supply side, labour and capital flows were a necessary precondition for exploitation of the abundant land in the Americas, which would lead to farm exports. Migrants may serve as trade intermediaries, bringing knowledge of potential markets and distribution channels in their country of origin. The role of such intermediaries is highlighted in modern Southeast Asia by the overseas Chinese and other diasporas that conduct much of the intra-regional trade. Other reasons why factor movements and goods trade may be complements are analysed by James Markusen (1983).

The rise of multinational enterprises and the development of global supply chains may be associated with either substitution or complementarity. **Foreign direct investment** occurs when a firm from one country controls (defined as having sufficient minimum shareholding) a subsidiary in another country.[5] Why do multinational enterprises exist, instead of firms simply exporting their products to other countries? There is no single explanation, but the main arguments are covered in John Dunning's eclectic theory of foreign direct investment, often referred to as the OLI model because it relates the spread of MNEs to ownership and location advantages, and to reasons for internalising transactions. The firm must have some ownership advantage in terms of its product or its production or managerial processes to offset the natural disadvantages of operating in a foreign environment.[6] Early multinational enterprises were driven by the location of resources, whether beaver in the case of the Hudson Bay Company (sometimes claimed to be the oldest MNE) or minerals or oil. More recently, with the rise of subcontracting and

---

[5]Definitions of the percentage necessary for control vary, e.g. the US Department of Commerce uses a ten percent threshold to define FDI in the USA and FDI by US companies. A useful data source is the *World Investment Review* published annually by UNCTAD (the United Nations Conference on Trade and Development), the main statistics are available online at www.unctad.org. Note that, although FDI is generally assumed to involve capital flows, this need not be the case; many subsidiaries expand by reinvesting local profits or by borrowing in host-country capital markets, in both cases increasing the amount of FDI in the host country without any capital inflow.

[6]FDI may involve acquisition of ownership advantages, if a firm purchases a foreign company with some technology or skills that the buyer lacks. The Chinese firm Lenovo, whose home country had a comparative advantage in the production of standard personal computers, purchased IBM's PC business in 2005 for $650 million in cash and $600 million in shares, as well as assuming about $500 million in debt, in order to gain access to IBM's management, marketing and corporate sales force, and after-sales expertise.

global supply chains the location advantage can be based on availability of any input, most commonly a specific skill–level of labour.
Location may also be driven by market access, as when foreign firms
operate in countries with high tariff barriers in order to sell in the protected markets (e.g. the location of Ford, General Motors, Toyota and
Mitsubishi factories in Australia when Australian tariffs on imported
cars were high); such 'tariff-jumping' is a clear example of goods and
capital flows being substitutes. Internalisation occurs because the
multinational enterprise prefers to conduct transactions within the
firm rather than as arms–length transactions, perhaps, because it is
easier to transfer knowledge and prevent technology dissipation (or
theft) within a firm or because it is easier to monitor quality in-
house. The spread of multinational enterprises has been facilitated
by reductions in communications and transport costs, which makes
it easier to monitor subsidiaries, and for managers and specialised
staff to move between locations.

The spread of multinational enterprises has been a source of
concern for many people. Host countries worry about the loss of
sovereignty if MNEs respond to pressures from their home country
government, about the use of artificial pricing of within-firm transactions that are not market-based so that the tax obligation in the host
country is minimised (transfer pricing), and about other concerns
such as the footlooseness referred to in Chapter 7, failure to observe
international standards of safety or environmental protection, or to
train local staff. Examples can be found of all of these phenomena, sometimes with lethal consequences. However, in the 1990s and
2000s host countries have generally become more favourably inclined
towards MNEs, recognising that they are effective transferrers of
technology (not just production techniques, but also managerial and
marketing expertise) as well as of capital. These benefits have been
highlighted by the role of foreign investors in China's rapid export-
led growth since the adoption of an open-door policy at the end of the
1970s; especially in the early years entrepreneurs from Hong Kong

and other new industrialised East Asian economies played a critical role in providing appropriate capital and knowledge of how to produce and export labour-intensive goods, which was the catalyst for China to realise its comparative advantage in labour-intensive manufactures. Today, it is more often in the MNE's home country that concerns are voiced, about jobs being moved offshore, with the distributional consequences predicted by the beaker diagram.

Policy Implications

International factor movements raise many policy issues, and debates about movement of people are often especially controversial.[7] These will not be addressed here. The role of factor movements in the remainder of this book is minimal, because the implications for trade theory and trade policy of the degree of factor mobility are about magnitudes, rather than affecting the fundamental results. Absence of factor mobility highlights the importance of gains from goods trade in order to achieve a superior allocation of global resources. The presence of factor mobility may reduce the potential for goods trade or it may be complementary to goods trade. As in the specific factors model, the less mobile a factor is the more its returns are explained by the Stolper–Samuelson theorem and the more mobile a factor is the less extreme is the impact of any change in relative goods prices.

---

[7]The unwillingness of countries to cede autonomy over immigration or foreign investment to a multilateral agency is reflected in the much weaker role of a body like the International Labour Organisation (ILO) or the UN International Organisation for Migration (IOM) compared to the World Trade Organisation (WTO), and in the failure of negotiations in the late 1990s to reach a Multilateral Agreement on Investment (MAI). Although the intensity of migration policies is difficult to synthesise, Hatton (2007, Table 1) provides some evidence that migration restrictions became more common in the 1980s and 1990s.

Part II
Policy

Chapter 11

The Theory of Trade Policy

Governments have long intervened in international trade. This chapter analyses the consequences of government restrictions on trade. Any restriction will create a wedge between the domestic and world prices that reduces the potential gains from trade. This wedge can be most simply represented as a tax on imports, a *tariff*, and historically this has been the most important instrument of trade policy. The following two chapters will extend the analysis to consider other instruments of trade policy, all of which have the effect of introducing a wedge between domestic and world prices.

Figure 11.1 illustrates the general equilibrium impact of an across-the-board tariff. As in Figure 4.7, the export good is on the vertical axis. With a tariff, the domestic price line DD is steeper than the world price line WW, i.e. the relative price of the import good is higher in domestic than in world markets. Producers respond

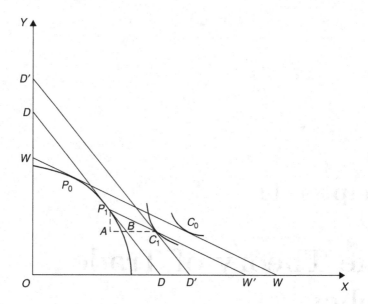

Figure 11.1.   General equilibrium effects of a tariff.

to the new price signal by shifting the output mix towards more of the import-competing good and less of the export good, from P_0 to P_1. From the new output point the economy can still trade along the world price line, although the value of the consumption bundle measured at world prices is now less $(OW'$ instead of $OW)$.[1] Consumers, however, observe the domestic price ratio and will buy less of the import good than they would if they could trade at world prices. As long as the domestic price line is not as steep as the autarchy price line, there will be some trade, but it will be less than

---

[1]GDP should be measured in world prices because they are the country's opportunity cost prices. In practice, GDP is measured with domestic relative prices which overvalue the protected goods. In Figure 11.1 the value of output measured in units of the export good, OD, is higher with protection than with free trade and the value of consumption, OD', is higher still, because units of the import-competing good are being valued higher than WW in terms of the export good, but neither the output-mix above P_1 nor the consumption mix above C_1 is attainable at relative prices which value the import good above the world price.

if consumers were able to maximise their utility along the world price line.[2]

The difference between how many imports consumers receive in exchange for the nation's exports and total imports (i.e. the horizontal distance of the wedge between world and domestic price ratios, BC_1) is the tariff revenue which accrues to the government. The higher the tariff (BC_1/AB), the steeper the domestic price line, the bigger the wedge, and the more gains from trade are foregone.

Figure 11.1 shows that for a small country a tariff is welfare-reducing. Both producers and consumers fail to realise all of the gains from trade open to them because they must exchange goods at the domestic price ratio rather than at the true opportunity cost prices for the country, i.e. the world price ratio. The welfare loss has two components: the loss of output, valued at world prices, from producing less of the export good and the loss of consumer utility from not consuming on the highest feasible indifference curve.

This powerful conclusion needs to be modified for a large country. Imposing a tariff shrinks the trade triangle; $P_1 A C_1$ is smaller than the triangle with hypotenuse $P_0 C_0$. The offer curve shifts closer to the import-axis, leading to an improvement in the terms of trade. In Figure 11.2 (and in Figure 11.1) the world price line becomes flatter, and the large country can achieve a higher indifference curve than the small country could. The positive terms of trade effect will offset some of the costs of a tariff, and might be sufficiently strong for consumption to be on a higher indifference curve than with free trade.[3]

---

[2]A point such as C_1 must exist, because the indifference curve at P_1 is steeper than DD and the indifference curve at C_0 is flatter than DD. At this consumption point, consumers purchase less of the imported good, X, and may purchase less of the export good, Y, because their income has fallen, or more of Y because its relative price has fallen.

[3]In Figure 11.1, as the world price line becomes flatter, so does the domestic price line and the output mix will be somewhere to the left of P_1. The flatter trade line now starts from this point on the PPF, and the consumption point could be on a higher or lower indifference curve than C_0.

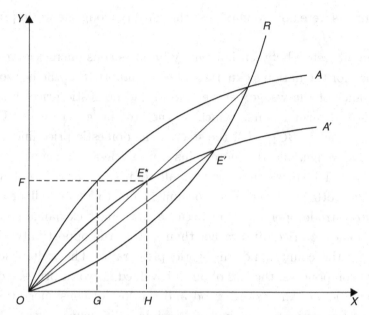

Figure 11.2.   Offer curve analysis of a tariff.
Note: If country A here is the country analysed in Figure 11.1, then $OF = P_1 A$, $GH = BC_1$ and $OG = AB$, and the slop of OE is the same as that of WW and $P_1 W'$. The movement from E^* to E' represents the unambiguously beneficial terms of trade effect on A.

The distributional consequences of a tariff can be analysed in a parallel manner to Chapter 6. If all factors are mobile across sectors, then a tariff by increasing the relative price of the import good increases the real income of the factor of production used intensively in the import-competing activity and reduces the real income of the factor used relatively intensively in the export activity. With specific factors, a tariff increases the real return to the factor specific to the import-competing activity and reduces the real return to factors specific to export activities. Thus, in the short-term we often observe all factors in an import-competing industry uniting to lobby for protection from imports, but in the long term the general pattern is of labour unions being more protectionist in high-income countries and capitalists being more protectionist in labour-abundant countries. The position of landowners depends upon whether land is relatively abundant or scarce, e.g. farmers tend to be free traders in western Canada or Australia and protectionist in western Europe or Japan.

In the general equilibrium model of Figure 11.1, the price wedge could be caused by either a tax on imports or a tax on exports. Both reduce the relative price of the export good in the home market, reduce the level of trade and result in welfare loss for a small country and in an ambiguous welfare outcome for a large country. This result, first pointed out by Abba Lerner, is known as the *Lerner symmetry theorem*.

Partial Equilibrium Analysis of a Tariff

A tariff can also be analysed using the partial equilibrium model of Chapter 5. For an import-competing activity, a tariff of t percent raises the domestic price to $(1 + t).P_w$. In a small economy (Figure 11.3), the higher domestic price induces an increase in domestic production from OQ_1 to OQ_2, a reduction in domestic demand from OQ_4 to OQ_3 and a reduction in imports from Q_1Q_4 to Q_2Q_3. The government receives tariff revenue equal to $t.P_w$ multiplied by Q_2Q_3 (area). There is a loss of consumer surplus (area $a + b + c + d$), and an increase in producer surplus (area a). With equal weight to each unit of all components of the welfare change, the gain to producers and in government revenue is smaller than the loss to consumers. The net welfare loss is equal to the two triangles, $b + d$, sometimes called *Corden triangles*.[4]

If the country is large, then the world price line shifts down as a result of the reduction in import demand (Figure 11.4). The gap between the old world price, P_w, and the new domestic price, $P_d^* = (1 + t).P_w^*$, is smaller than for a small country. The impact on producer and consumer surplus is less in Figure 11.4 than in 11.3, but tariff revenue is larger (it is levied at the same rate, t, but imports are larger because the domestic price is lower $(Q_5Q_6 > Q_2Q_3)$. A

---

[4]The welfare triangles model was pioneered by Max Corden (1957) and Harry Johnson (1960).

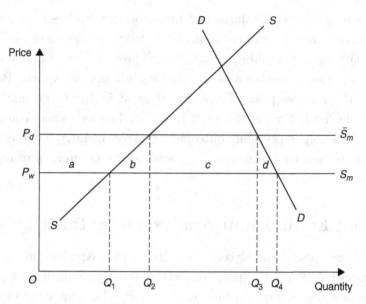

Figure 11.3. Partial equilibrium analysis of a tariff imposed by a small country.
Note: S_m is the import supply curve with no tariff; $\bar{S}_m$ is the import supply curve with a tariff equal to $P_d - P_w$.

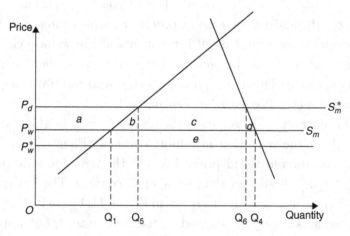

Figure 11.4. Partial equilibrium analysis of a tariff imposed by a large country.
Note: S_m is the import supply curve with no tariff; S_m^* is the import supply curve with a tariff equal to $P_d - P_w^*$ where P_w^* is the world price after imposition of the tariff.

large country suffers less than a small country from imposing a tariff, and may even have a net gain. There is a net gain if the portion of tariff revenue lying below P_w in Figure 11.4 is greater than the two triangles, i.e. if $e > b + d$.

An export tax can be analysed in a similar manner. The tax discourages exports by reducing the price received by producers below the world price. With the lower after-tax price, producer surplus is reduced by area $a + b + c + d$ in Figure 11.5. Consumers gain because producers are willing to sell on the domestic market at a price equal to the world price minus the export tax; consumer surplus increases by area a. The benefits to consumers (a) and the revenue from the tax (c) are less than the cost to producers $(a + b + c + d)$. The net loss consists of a cost of not exporting units for which production costs are below world price (triangle d) and a cost of selling units to domestic consumers who value those units less than their value on the world market (triangle b).

The demand and supply framework is very practical because many trade policy measures are microeconomic policies applying to a

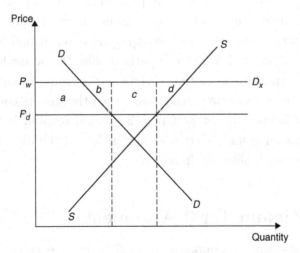

Figure 11.5. Partial equilibrium analysis of an export tax imposed by a small country.
Note: D_x is the export demand curve.

single good, and in most such cases the small country assumption is a good approximation of the policy-adopting country's market power. Moreover, the welfare changes are relatively easy to calculate from observed variables such as output and imports on the basis of demand and supply elasticities that are fairly robust, unlike the costs in general equilibrium analysis, which are defined in terms of production possibility frontiers and community indifference curves. However, it is necessary always to keep in mind the drawbacks of the partial equilibrium approach, which ignores any impact on factor markets and on the trade balance. Especially when many microeconomic trade measures are introduced at once, the effects on factor markets (and income distribution) and on export activities that were analysed in the previous section may be significant.

Although Figures 11.3 and 11.4 are typically used to estimate net welfare effects, they also highlight the point that all trade policies affect the distribution of income. The general equilibrium analysis emphasises the functional distribution of income, based on the source of people's incomes, and the partial equilibrium analysis emphasises the impact on consumers and on producers. The 'equal weights' assumption underlying the identification of the two triangles as the net welfare loss may or may not be appropriate, but it highlights the fact that interpersonal utility comparisons have to be made. Alternatively, it could be argued that if the areas accruing to gainers are larger than the areas representing costs, then the gainers could compensate the losers and net welfare gains would remain, but appropriate lump-sum transfers are not inevitable and the distributional consequences are politically important.

The Optimum Tariff Argument

When a large country imposes a small tariff, the rectangle e in Figure 11.4 is larger than the two Corden triangles. As the tariff is increased, the net welfare gains increase, until at some point the triangles begin to increase by more than the rectangle and the net welfare gains from a higher tariff start to diminish. The tipping point, where national welfare is maximised, is *the optimum tariff*. A prohibitive tariff is welfare-reducing because it precludes realisation of any of the potential gains from trade. The optimum tariff must be somewhere between zero and the prohibitive tariff. The optimum tariff argument is a logically sound case for a tariff increasing national welfare, but there are two important caveats to its practical applicability.

Realising the benefits from an optimum tariff is confrontational because any terms of trade gain to one country is a loss to another country; terms of trade changes are zero-sum. In a world of several large trading nations, an attempt by one to impose an optimum tariff is likely to produce retaliation by other countries. For a retaliating country some of the welfare loss caused by the initial tariff will be reversed, but the mutual tariff hikes reduce the gains from trade leaving the world and at least one of the countries (and probably both) worse off than before the tariff increases (Johnson, 1954). Once begun a tariff war may be hard to stop, and may degenerate into a broader economic conflict. This was not uncommon in the 1800s and early 1900s. The most famous episode of retaliation followed the US tariff increase in 1930, when retaliatory tariff increases by many countries contributed to the decline in world trade which exacerbated the depression of the 1930s; the value of world imports in million gold dollars declined from 2,735 in January 1930 to 1,839 in January 1931, 1,206 in January 1932 and 992 in January 1933.

The second caveat is that in the 21st century few economies are large in the trade–theoretic sense, and even the largest trading nations would be hard-pressed to benefit significantly from an optimum tariff.[5] There may be a stronger case for the existence of

---

[5]The size of the optimum tariff is inversely related to the elasticity of supply of imports. For a small country facing perfectly elastic supply of imports the optimum tariff is zero, but even for a large country the optimum tariff may be small if import supply is highly price elastic.

an optimum export tax for countries with market power in a natural resource; oil exporters succeeded in benefiting from their market power in the 1970s, but the success was short-lived as new sources of oil supply were brought on-line, oil importers reduced their demand and oil prices plummeted in the 1980s. US cotton in the years before 1860 is sometimes cited as a case where an optimum export tax existed; Doug Irwin (2003) estimated that the USA, which supplied 80% of the world market at the time, faced inelastic demand and the optimum export tax was in the order of 45–55%, but the net welfare gains would have been small (about 0.3% of US GDP or 1% of the output of the South). Attempts to benefit from market power have typically led to the development of substitutes (such as artificial rubber in the early 20th century), shifts in consumption (attempts to increase the price of bananas shifted demand to other fruits) or emergence of alternative sources of supply (e.g. to compete with Sri Lankan tea or Ghanaian cocoa). Such market-driven responses suggest that exercise of market power may be self-defeating, but the timeframe matters. OPEC countries benefiting from higher oil prices in the decade after 1973 may have been rudely shocked when oil prices started to tumble after 1981, but if they had used the cartel profits of the previous eight years wisely, then the exercise of market power left them better off than if they had continued to act as passive exporters.[6]

---

[6]Because oil has few close substitutes and discovery and exploitation of new oilfields takes time, the lag before demand and supply adjusted was fairly long, but the adjustments had a long-term impact as new fields in Alaska, the North Sea and elsewhere came online and people bought more fuel-efficient cars or firms shifted to other sources of energy. Oil prices collapsed between 1981 and 1986 and remained low for another dozen years, only picking up after a floor was reached in 1998. Diminished attention to fuel efficiency, low returns to finding new oilfields and rapidly increasing demand from large newly industrialising countries led to rapid increases in the price of oil in the early 2000s, but it was 2007 before they regained their 1981 level measured in constant US dollars.

The Distortions Approach to Trade Policy

The most common argument in favour of trade restrictions is to correct a domestic market failure, i.e. a situation where market prices do not reflect social costs or benefits. For example, a tariff can increase employment in an industry that is concentrated in a depressed region or it can reduce consumption of an undesirable good, or a tariff can provide revenue for the state to provide public goods. In each of these cases the tariff may improve national welfare.

The argument against using trade policy to achieve any of these goals is that it does too much. Using trade policy to increase employment in a protected industry does so at the cost of consumers of that industry's products, which is inefficient and unfair if the increased employment is a national or regional policy goal. In Figure 11.3 increasing output from OQ_1 to OQ_2 can be achieved by a tariff or by an equivalent subsidy (i.e. P_d-P_w per unit of domestic output). The subsidy costs the government P_d-P_w multiplied by OQ_2 (area $a + b$) and increases producer surplus by area a, for a net cost equal to triangle b. This is the minimum cost, at market prices, of promoting the extra employment. The subsidy is superior to a tariff because the tariff has a net cost of $b + d$.[7]

Similarly, reducing consumption from OQ_4 to OQ_3 can be achieved by a tariff or by a sales tax of equivalent size. The sales

---

[7] As in all of these welfare analysis the equal weights assumption is invoked. The choice between a policy that raises government revenue through a tariff and one that requires government spending through a subsidy should be symmetrical, unless raising public revenue is costly. For most governments today, the tariff revenues or subsidy expenditures involved in the policy decisions under consideration are trivial relative to the total government budget. Even in the late 1800s Canada used subsidies to support a major infant industry, steel. A more important asymmetry argument may concern perceptions, insofar as a protected industry may not want to appear as the direct beneficiary of public spending, even though it is the net welfare costs in Figure 11.1 that should matter most for public policy decisions.

tax reduces consumer surplus by $a + b + c + d$ and raises government revenue of $a + b + c$ for a net cost of triangle d. This is the inevitable cost of depriving consumers of the units $Q_3 Q_4$ which they value more than their cost at the world price but less than the domestic price, P_d. Using trade policy incurs the additional cost, triangle b, of having some units $(Q_1 Q_2)$ supplied by domestic firms rather than being obtained at lower cost by trading and importing.

The general point is that, when a distortion exists, the best solution is the one that tackles the distortion as close to its origin as possible. If more output or jobs are desired, then the best policy is to subsidise production or employment. If less consumption of alcohol, narcotics, pornography, guns or whatever is desired, then a general tax on the good is preferable to a tax on imports, and probably even better is a public education scheme to encourage people to voluntarily reduce consumption. Only in the coincidental case where it is desired to reduce consumption and increase output by amounts consistent with the same trade barrier (e.g. in Figure 11.3 by $Q_3 Q_4$ and $Q_1 Q_2$) will a tariff be ideal, and even then it could be replicated by a sales tax and subsidy.

The argument about using trade taxes to raise revenue is similar insofar as they may be justified if there is no better way of raising government revenue, and government spending has higher social value at the margin than an equivalent amount of private spending. At low levels of national income and public spending this is likely to be true (Greenaway, 1984). Many poor countries rely on trade taxes because they are relatively cheap to collect, especially if the border is easily monitored. The same pattern applied historically in today's high income countries; in earlier times their governments relied on trade taxes for revenue, but as bureaucratic capabilities improved these were replaced by less distortionary sales and income taxes. Today, trade taxes account for a trivial share of most high- and middle-income countries' public revenues.

Trade Policy with Imperfect Competition

Imperfectly competitive markets provide other situations where trade policy may improve the situation, but are not necessarily the best policy. Compared to other distortions arguments, the added complication is the absence of any global regulator, which could enforce a competition policy in world markets. In the rare cases of natural monopolies international agreements have been reached, e.g. the Universal Postal Union, established in 1874, sets the rules for international mail (although the monopoly has been eroded in recent decades by courier services) and arguably the United Nations is the international provider of peacekeeping services, but countries have been reluctant to yield national sovereignty and have preferred to rely on national policy responses.

A simple and clear case for policy intervention arises when a good is supplied by a single foreign firm. In Figure 11.6, a profit-maximising monopolist with constant costs, OA, supplies quantity OQ_0 at which marginal revenue is equal to marginal cost; the foreign firm charges a price P_0, and makes a profit equal to AP_0EH. By imposing an import tax of AB per unit, the government shifts the monopolist's average and marginal cost from OA to OB, and its profit-maximising output is now OQ_1 for which it charges a price P_1; the firm's profit is reduced to BP_1FC. The country is better off because tariff revenue $ABCJ$ is greater than the lost consumer surplus P_0P_1FE (Svedberg, 1979). The source of the national welfare gain is the transfer of part of the monopoly profit to the state budget via the tariff.

A sales tax is not the best way to deal with a monopoly because the problem is of undersupply and the tax reduces supply still further. A superior policy would be a profits tax set as close as possible to the no-intervention profit level, AP_0EH; such a lump-sum tax would leave output and consumer surplus unchanged but transfer monopoly rent to the public purse. An even better policy would be to set a

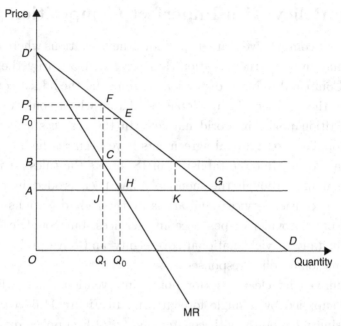

Figure 11.6. An import duty on a good supplied by a single foreign firm.
Note: The tariff shown here is levied on the cost price, and *ad valorem* tariff of AB/AO would have the same effect as the specific duty AB. If the tariff were related to the selling price, then an *ad valorem* duty of AB/AO percent would be preferred to the specific duty AB, because it would yield more tariff revenue on the same imported quantity. This could be shown by representing the specific duty as a parallel downward shift in $D'D$ so that it passes through K and the monopolist's profit-maximising supply is $\frac{1}{2}AK(= BC = OQ_1)$, and the *ad valorem* tariff as a counterclockwise pivot of $D'D$ from the D origin passing through K so that the profit-maximising supply is still $\frac{1}{2}AK$ but the tariff component of the price, OP_1, is bigger.

price ceiling as close as possible to OA, forcing the monopolist to set price equal to marginal cost. This will not only yield the maximum national benefit, increasing consumer surplus by area AP_0EG, but it would also be a net global welfare improvement; the loss of monopoly profits by the foreign firm is less than the gain in consumer surplus, by the triangle HEG, and there is no possibility to realise a greater net gain.

In sum, if a country is being supplied by a foreign monopolist, then a trade tax would reduce the monopoly profits to the importing country's net benefit, although a profit tax or a price ceiling is likely to be superior. This is, however, a moot point as it is difficult to think of any global market with a single supplier and no prospective entrant to limit abuse of monopoly power.

In the more plausible situation of a global oligopoly, governments may be able to use *strategic trade policies* to shift excess profits (i.e. returns over and above what equally risky use of capital elsewhere in the economy could earn) from foreign to home firms by influencing the firms' strategic interaction.[8] James Brander and Barbara Spencer developed a simple duopoly model to illustrate this possibility. Two firms located in different countries could compete in the world market, but the market can only support one profitable firm and the profitability of either firm thus depends upon the other firm's decision about whether to produce or not. With no government intervention, it could be chance which firm enters the industry and is profitable. First-mover advantage should be decisive, unless there is a coordination failure and both firms start production with mistaken beliefs about market size or their rival's action.[9]

The scope for government intervention can be illustrated by a numerical example. Suppose each firm could make excess profits of 100 units if they had a monopoly. If both firms produce, each will make 5 units loss. There is also the option of not producing and making zero profits. For simplicity, ignore the impact on consumers,

---

[8]The terminology may be confusing. Trade policy is sometimes advocated to support strategic industries, which may mean that they have perceived positive externalities (i.e. it is a distortions argument and a subsidy is superior) or they may be held back by being a latecomer where external economies of scale are strong as in Figure 9.2.

[9]This appears to be what happened in the market for three-engine large passenger jets during the 1970s when Lockheed and McDonnell Douglas entered the market with similar planes (L1011 and DC10). The L1011 failed to break even, and Lockheed ceased producing civilian aircraft in 1984. McDonnell Douglas remained in the commercial aircraft business, but was taken over by Boeing in 1997.

who are spread across the world so that changes in their well-being are a minor consideration to the two countries' governments. If one government offers its home firm a subsidy of more than five units, then that firm will be profitable whether or not the other firm produces. With the knowledge that its competitor will definitely produce, the unsupported firm will not produce. The country with the subsidised firm is better off because, although there is a transfer from the government to the firm, the subsidy is less than the excess profits that now accrue to the firm.

The significance of the subsidy in the Brander–Spencer example is that it is a credible commitment, which changes the strategic interaction between the two firms and determines the outcome. Although this is a simple example, it can be generalised to any oligopoly situation where the strategic interaction between firms can be shifted to produce a different outcome. However, implementation is likely to require more information about the firms than any government possesses and mistakes are probable. Firms have an incentive to overstate the required subsidy, and release information about costs or strategic interaction which will favour their interests rather than the national interest. The firms are unlikely to be identical; in the above example, if the firm which receives the subsidy happens to be the less efficient firm, then the outcome may be inferior for the subsidising country and will be globally suboptimal.

The strategic trade policy argument has been criticised as a theoretical curiosity, which has given governments a justification for assisting undeserving domestic producers. This is an empirical argument, and the evidence is difficult to interpret (Pomfret, 1992). The Brander–Spencer example is often illustrated by competition between Boeing and Airbus in large civilian jet aircraft, which is the most obvious example of a global duopoly. Even the Airbus–Boeing case is unclear because, although the subsidies to Airbus were substantial, there is disagreement about the extent to which Boeing benefited from US government support, mainly in the form of military

orders which helped to cover the fixed cost of aircraft design and
launch, and the outcome was further complicated because Boeing
was disadvantaged by US dollar appreciation in the first half of the
1980s when the B757 faced the A310. In fact, both Boeing and Airbus remained in production, possibly at a cost to both US and EU
taxpayers which outweighed the benefits from shifting profits. The
beneficiaries were airlines in third countries, who paid a lower price
for their aircraft than they would have done had there been a single global supplier or an unsubsidised duopoly, and hence airline
passengers.

Concorde provides a cautionary tale about the perils of strategic
trade policy. The scale of British and French government assistance
ensured that the supersonic plane entered the market and led to
Boeing's abandonment of a competing supersonic aircraft when US
government assistance was cut back. Concorde enjoyed a monopoly in
the supersonic large commercial jet market, but it was a commercial
disaster because insufficient passengers would pay fares high enough
to cover even the marginal costs of operation. The outcome was a
net economic cost to the subsidising countries and to the then state-
owned airlines, British Airways and Air France, who were obliged to
operate the planes at a loss.

Another imperfect competition situation where there may be a
justification for policy intervention arises when a firm can segment
markets and charge different prices. Discriminatory pricing in the
domestic market is often perceived as unfair or anti-competitive and
is outlawed by many national competition policies, although some
exceptions are tolerated or considered desirable (e.g. discounts for
students or pensioners). Figure 11.7 illustrates price discrimination
in an international trade setting. A firm which operates as a monopolist in the domestic market, but faces perfect competition in the world
market, maximises profits by equating marginal cost and marginal
revenue, in this case equal to the world price P_w, and by allocating
sales between home and export markets so that marginal revenue

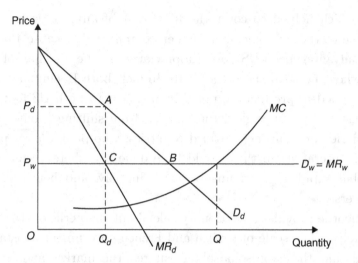

Figure 11.7. Price discrimination by an exporting firm with a domestic monopoly.

is equalised in the two markets. The firm's output OQ is divided between Q_dQ units sold in the world market at the world price and OQ_d units sold in the home market at the higher price P_d. The **discriminatory pricing** allows the firm to earn monopoly profits in the home market, as long as domestic consumers are unable to purchase at P_w whether due to trade barriers or to devices like warranties and after-sales services that are only available in the country of purchase. There is a welfare loss to the home country, because the lost consumer surplus from not being able to buy at the world price $(P_d.ABP_w)$ is greater than the monopoly profit $(P_d.ACP_w)$.[10]

---

[10]The situation where an exporter with monopoly power charges foreigners a higher price than it charges in its domestic market is more likely to be harmful to the importing country. The main example of such behaviour is in energy markets, e.g. many oil-producing countries have domestic prices below the world market price. The price for natural gas in Russia is about 15–20% of the price at which the gas is sold to Germany (and many domestic consumers simply do not pay — in 2005 the Russian national gas company, Gazprom, reported two billion US dollars worth of unpaid bills). However, oil and gas importers seem to be more concerned about security of supply than about the discriminatory pricing.

When international trade is involved, the most plausible situation is that portrayed in Figure 11.7, where home country consumers suffer and consumers in countries where the price is P_w should be happy to be paying less. Nevertheless, one of the most pervasive trade policy instruments today is *antidumping duties* imposed by the importing country against exporters who are charging less in their export markets than in their home markets. Preventing such discriminatory behaviour may be justified if the discriminatory behaviour is predatory, intended to drive domestic firms out of business by undercutting them on price and then once the foreign firm is the sole provider it will raise prices to earn monopoly profits at the expense of consumers in the home country (as in Figure 11.6). This is, however, an uncommon situation because it requires the predator not only to absorb short-term losses during the price war but also for barriers to entry or re-entry to be sufficiently high that the monopoly will not be contested when prices are subsequently increased.[11] In practice, the main attractions of antidumping duties seem to be for the protected firms rather than being in the public interest and this argument will be addressed in the next two chapters.

Conclusions

Trade policies can achieve desirable public objectives, but among economists there is a strong consensus that free trade is the best policy. The optimal tariff argument is valid if no retaliation occurs, but the risk is substantial that if retaliation does occur then it

---

[11]Strategic interaction between firms may lead to discriminatory pricing with ambiguous welfare consequences; in a symmetrical global duopoly, reciprocal dumping may be privately profitable, in which case the cross-hauling is wasteful but the increased competition in each country's home market is welfare-enhancing (Brander and Krugman, 1983). Falvey and Nelson (2006) survey the literature and conclude that "dumping can be associated with just about any effect on welfare" and that "only a very small share of antidumping duties could be associated with predation".

could degenerate into a destructive trade war. All economies have cases where social costs and benefits do not match private costs and benefits and in many such situations imposing a trade barrier might be better than doing nothing, but trade policies introduce new distortions and a policy which tackles the divergence between private and social costs as close to the source of the original distortion as possible would be superior. Trade taxes can raise public revenue, but other taxes are less distortionary. With imperfect competition, it may be possible to design policies which shift excess profits to domestic producers and thus increase national welfare, but this assumes omniscience on the part of policymakers and there are incentives for producers to misstate costs, elasticities and strategic interaction in order to increase their profits even when it may not be in the public interest.

A division can be made between arguments for restrictive trade policies based on domestic distortions, where a superior policy would tackle the distortion closer to its source, and arguments based on international market imperfections, where policies may be national-welfare-improving in theory but are likely to be confrontational or misdirected in practice. A presumption in favour of free trade policies recognises the pervasiveness of gains from trade, and is not an endorsement of laissez faire economic policies. The distortions approach explicitly recognises the existence of market failures in need of correction, but indicates that trade policy is not the appropriate instrument.

A second lesson from the theory of trade policy which has not been stressed so far, but is clear from the analysis, is that trade policies always have distributional consequences. The analytics are straightforward because they represent reversal of the distributional effects of free trade as captured in the Stolper–Samuelson theorem or the specific factors model. A trade barrier benefits the factor used relatively intensively in the import-competing activity and hurts factors used relatively intensively in export activities.[12] Factors specific to import-competing sectors benefit from trade restrictions and factors specific to export activities lose. The partial equilibrium model highlights the conflicting interests of producers and consumers, and also that the welfare transfers (notably area a in Figure 11.3) may be much larger than the triangles which capture net gains. The presumption that with compensation of losers there is a net national gain may offer little comfort to potential losers. In the face of distrust of the political system to carry through such compensation, whether a trade barrier is introduced or not may depend upon the relative political influence of those who gain from trade and of those whose wellbeing is threatened by trade.

---

[12]More precisely, factors used intensively in the activity whose relative price increases benefit. In a large country the terms of trade effect could conceivably be sufficiently strong that a tariff lowers the domestic relative price of the import and the factor used intensively in the export sector is the gainer (Metzler, 1949). This implies that demand for the country's export is highly inelastic, and the Metzler paradox has few if any proven examples.

Chapter 12

The Political Economy of Trade Policy

The theory of trade policy reaches strong policy conclusions about the desirability of free trade for a small country, and even for a large country attempts to take advantage of market power through an optimum tariff are likely to be self-defeating. To a large extent, these conclusions are reflected in actual policy decisions, as trade barriers have been substantially reduced worldwide since the 1940s, but they still beg the questions of why trade barriers have often been high and why trade policy debates remain contentious. The answer largely lies in the distributional impact of trade and of trade barriers. Those who benefit from a trade restriction have an incentive to seek protection, and legislators may respond to such pressure group politics.

The losers from trade are owners of the scarce factor, such as the landowners in Ricardo's England. Thus, labour unions in high-income countries and capitalists in low-income countries tend to be suspicious of trade liberalisation. At the microeconomic level, owners and workers often join together in calls for protection, as the specific factors model predicts: if all factors working in a particular activity have some degree of specificity, then they may unite to protect that activity's producer surplus. In this they may be pitted against consumers of their output or against exporters who see the general equilibrium consequences of protection, but consumers may be less well-organised than producers and exporters may not be as aware of the trade policy consequences (or may not yet exist if it is potential exports that are being excluded by protection). There may also be a loss-aversion bias insofar as the negative weight that people place on a loss of income is often greater than the positive weight placed on an equal-sized increase in income.

This chapter examines the domestic forces behind the determination of trade policies. Trade policy decisions seldom happen in a vacuum. They largely involve revision of existing policies when it is hard to draw general conclusions about the patterns of trade barriers. For this reason the analysis will start with some historic cases, when major trade policy changes occurred and the patterns were clear. One reason why the evidence on why trade barriers exist is less clear in recent years is that they have become subject to stronger international agreements, to be dealt with in Chapter 14. Another reason is that the domestic conflicts are settled in the political arena by trade–offs and by providing adjustment assistance to those who will lose from policies which will yield net national benefits, so that the outcome may be manifested in non-trade measures rather than in trade barriers.

Vested Interests and Trade Policy Formation

A pioneering study on the political economy of trade policy was Charles Kindleberger's (1951) study of how western European countries reacted to falling grain prices in the last quarter of the 19th century. Falling transport costs, farm mechanisation and the end of the Crimean and US Civil Wars led to increased supply of North American and Russian grain in western Europe during the 1870s. The imported grain brought gains from trade for all western European countries, but their policy responses differed.

Great Britain stuck to the free trade policies adopted in the first half of the century; although farmers demanded protection, industrial interests who appreciated the impact of cheap grain on their workers' real wages dominated Parliament. In Denmark farmers' influence was stronger, but they had already begun a shift towards livestock farming and they used cheaper grains to accelerate the structural change, i.e. farmers took advantage of the new relative prices rather than trying to resist the change. In France, the 1789 revolution had created an agricultural sector based on small farms and a political system with universal male suffrage, so that farmers both felt the impact of competing imports and had sufficient political influence to obtain high protective tariffs very soon after imports started to push down grain prices. In Germany, a similar outcome for farmers was obtained by a different route; the large landowners of eastern Germany were not powerful enough to push through protection against the opposition of non-agricultural producers in western Germany, but they were able to form a political alliance with heavy industry (i.e. producers with little concern about the impact of lower food prices on real wages) to introduce trade barriers on imports of grain and some capital–intensive goods — the rye-steel alliance.[1] In Italy and Austria, although the grain-farming sector was large, political institutions were less responsive to economic demands; trade barriers

---

[1] A similar alliance lay behind the high US tariff of 1824 analysed in the next paragraph. Congressmen from protectionist states in the North united with Congressmen from the West who wanted public funding for infrastructure investment, but the alliance was destroyed when President Jackson vetoed the spending bills and free-trade states (notably South Carolina) refused to cooperate in collecting customs duties (Irwin, 2008). US tariffs remained lower until after the Civil War, when loss of political influence by the free-trade South and temporarily dominant power of the North led to the USA having the most protectionist tariffs in its history during the 1870s.

were only introduced after a lengthy time lag, and in the meantime falling grain prices led to emigration rather than structural change. These varying outcomes were important and had long-term effects, as Italian migrants had lasting impact on US or Argentinean society, the increased influence of large landowners and heavy industry provided a fertile field for militarism and anti-democratic tendencies in Germany in the first third of the 20th century, and the farm lobby remained powerful in France throughout the 20th century.

Kindleberger's study is important in illustrating the importance of institutions in determining trade policy outcomes. Another influential concept in understanding trade policy formation is the *logic of collective action* (Olson, 1965). A trade barrier is a public good in the sense that all producers in an industry benefit whether or not they contributed to the lobbying required to obtain the protection. Any individual producer has an incentive to under-contribute to lobbying costs in the hope that other producers' efforts will be sufficient to influence policy. Successful free-riding is less possible and trade barriers are more likely if the affected producers are few and relatively easy to organise. Jonathan Pincus (1975) tested these hypotheses against the structure of the first serious US tariff, the 1824 Tariff Act, and he found that industries with few producers or that were geographically concentrated (i.e. located in a few counties in each state where they operated) obtained higher tariffs. Subsequent tariff changes are harder to analyse because they do not start from scratch, but Elmer Schattschneider (1935) provided a classic description of how vested interests successfully lobbied for protecting their own industries after it became clear that the USA was going to implement a substantial general tariff increase in 1930.[2]

---

[2] A letter signed by 1,028 US economists, including all of the leading academic economists, requested the President to veto the bill, but in vain. The letter and associated documents were reproduced in *Econ Journal Watch 4(3)*, September 2007, 345–358. Economists who were working on the political economy of trade barriers in the USA produced a variety of interest group models in the 1980s and early 1990s, of which the most influential has been the protection-for-sale approach of Grossman and Helpman (1994).

In the USA, interest group politics is especially powerful because individual members of Congress have substantial independence from party discipline, represent geographical constituencies, and are responsive to offers of campaign contributions. In a Westminster system with strong parties and no separation between legislative and executive branches of government, import-competing producers may lobby their representative for protection, but the representative then has to convince the party leadership of the desirability of protection, so that responses to individual pressure groups are less likely. However, when a major shift in trade policy is promised after a change of government it can be implemented quickly and drastically, as when Britain abandoned free trade in 1931 or when Australia and New Zealand abandoned their high tariff policies in the 1980s.[3]

Another interest group who may play a role in trade policy formulation and implementation is the bureaucracy. This is most apparent in highly interventionist regimes where allocation of import quotas or other valuable trading rights can be a source of income for corrupt administrators, who will resist reform of the system. Even in less extreme cases the bureaucracy may be a force for interventionist trade policies, because they increase the administrators' influence and status. Customs departments tend to see their role in terms of controlling illicit trade rather than facilitating compliance with the law with minimal interference in legitimate trade. Where government offices are industry specific, the bureaucrats often identify

---

[3]Dictatorships can change policies even more rapidly. China's dramatic switch from autarchy to an open door policy in 1979 is often contrasted to India's slow shift from a protectionist to a more open trade regime in the final decades of the 20th century (despite its Westminster system). There is a robust negative correlation between democratic government and average tariff. Kono (2006) estimates that in the early 2000s a switch from dictatorship to democracy was associated *ceteris paribus* with a seven percentage point decline in tariffs (from 22% to 15% at the mean), but there is an offsetting tendency towards less transparent trade barriers which Kono calls optimal obfuscation.

with "their" industry's needs, most obviously in the way that Agriculture Ministries in high-income countries tend to favour protection for import-competing farmers.

In the high-income countries a few industries have been particularly successful in obtaining protection from imports: agriculture, clothing, steel, and cars. These do not fit well with the pressure group approach to trade policy insofar as some are concentrated (steel and cars) but some are not (farming and clothing). A common feature of these protected activities is that they are declining industries. Whether an industry is declining or growing is important because success in obtaining protection that increases producer surplus provides a signal to new entrants, who will erode the incumbent firms' profits. In a sunset industry, or an industry with high barriers to entry such as automobiles, such erosion of the benefits from protection is much less likely.

Multinational enterprises may provide a counterweight to protectionist pressures. When many countries had high trade barriers, MNEs operated subsidiaries in the protected market in order to jump the tariff barrier and still be able to exploit their firm-specific advantages. In such a situation the MNE might lobby against trade liberalisation if it would reduce the value of their fixed investment. Such motivation for establishing foreign subsidiaries has diminished as countries worldwide have reduced trade barriers. Today MNEs are more likely to operate subsidiaries as part of a global value chain, in which case they want to minimise obstacles to moving components and finished goods across national borders.[4]

The institutional setting can change over time. In Western Europe the shift of trade policy authority from national capitals to Brussels was initially associated with reduced pressure group influence in the 1960s, but as lobby groups established a presence in Brussels and gained better understanding of EU decision-making

---

[4]In the MNE literature the two types are referred to as horizontal and vertical investment (Markusen, 2002).

their influence revived. In the USA since 1934, in reaction to the unconstrained exercise of pressure group politics in determining the 1930 tariff, the President has on occasion been given time-bound authority to negotiate trade liberalisation, so-called fast-track authorisation, although trade negotiations are seldom quick; the shift in authority is important because the President has a national mandate rather than being responsible to a geographical area in which an industry requesting protection from imports may be locally important. Most important of all since 1947 has been the steady increase in the authority of international trade law as a constraint on national autonomy; the reasons for and consequences of this will be analysed in Chapter 14. As with the transfer of negotiating authority to the US President, the willingness of countries to abide by WTO rules is a sign of governments' willingness to have their hands tied in order to withstand pressure from narrow vested interests whose aims may not be in the public interest.

Evidence on the Impact of Trade Barriers in High-Income Countries

An important development during the second half of the 20th century was the improved collection and availability of trade data and the use of the data to estimate the costs of protection. This work indicated the net costs and the distributional consequences of trade policies, and highlighted the sometimes enormous cost of achieving goals such as employment protection through trade barriers.

The first estimates used the demand and supply diagram (Figure 11.3) to estimate the size of the Corden triangles. This work was disappointing to many trade economists because although trade barriers were still substantial in the 1960s and early 1970s, the partial equilibrium model yielded small estimates of national welfare loss, typically equal to less than a quarter of one percent of GDP in the high-income countries, which seemed to understate the seriousness of the resource misallocation. The partial equilibrium model was more effective as the basis of estimates for individual highly protected sectors, such as clothing or steel, and its policy impact was strongest when it revealed the high cost to consumers of saving a steelworker's or a carmaker's job through trade restrictions.

During the 1980s new empirical techniques tried to capture the general equilibrium impact of trade barriers by constructing computable general equilibrium models, which mimic the entire economy as a set of simultaneous equations. The policy variables can be changed to reflect alternative scenarios and calculate their impact on output and on the income of various groups. The CGE models are an advance over partial equilibrium calculations because they better capture the indirect effects of trade barriers, as in Figure 11.1. However, the results are often difficult to assess because the complexity of the models makes it hard to know whether any particular assumptions or parameter values are driving the results.

The partial equilibrium model remains useful for analysing the impact of a trade barrier affecting a narrowly defined good. Estimates of the cost of protecting US sugar producers provide strong support for the pressure group view of trade policy; the net costs are small compared to an aggregate such as GDP, but the benefits to each of the small number of sugar producers are very large, while for individual sugar consumers the loss of consumer surplus is small, but added over all consumers it is large.[5] The sugar producers are concentrated

---

[5]In 2004 refined sugar sold in the USA for 23.5 cents per pound, when the world price was 10.9 cents. Domestic production was just under 18 billion pounds. The US International Trade Commission (*The Economic Effects of Significant US Import Restraints*, June 2004) estimated that the price wedge reduced consumer surplus by about $2.5 billion, increased producer surplus by $1.8 billion, and increased the revenues of foreign suppliers by $0.4 billion, leaving a net misallocation cost (the Corden triangles) of $0.3 billion. Note that the small magnitude of the triangles relative to the changes in consumer and producer surplus highlights that the consumer and producer surplus estimates are not very sensitive to the choice of elasticities of supply and demand to be used. Reporting is lax, but the labour involved in growing and harvesting sugar in the USA is 40–60,000

in a few states and their political representatives are responsive to their needs, while nobody finds it worth lobbying for lower sugar prices and the opportunity to save a few dollars a year in spending on sugar will never turn this into a national election issue.[6] Similar stories from many countries could be cited for other widely consumed goods with geographically concentrated producers. The costs of these tariff peaks are often lost in more aggregative calculations which take an average tariff over a group of import-competing goods.

In recent years there have been attempts to broaden the search for costs of trade barriers or benefits from trade liberalisation. In Chapter 9, estimates of the gains from lower costs, increased variety and sorting firms by efficiency were mentioned. A more dramatic empirical story has been the success of low-income countries which pursued outward-oriented development strategies and achieved growth rates far higher than anticipated. The search for explanations for the large developmental benefits from openness will be addressed in Chapter 16.

Adjustment Assistance

Trade policy debates have historically been vitriolic as participants could clearly see the potential threat or benefit from imports. The

---

people; the increased producer surplus amounts to about $40,000 per worker, and per landowner it is in the millions of dollars. Virtually everybody in the USA consumes sugar, so the reduced consumer surplus involves an average annual cost of about $8 per person.

[6] A potentially more effective counter-lobby is the sugar-using companies, but they have been ineffective in changing US trade policy towards sugar and their primary responses in the early 2000s were closure or relocation to Mexico or Canada. The US Department of Commerce International Trade Administration (*Employment Changes in US Food Manufacturing: The Impact of Sugar Prices* — undated, downloaded December 2007) estimates that jobs in sugar-containing products fell by 10,000 between 1997 and 2002, and that for every sugar-producing job saved by trade barriers nearly three manufacturing jobs were lost. Hershey Foods, for example, closed factories in Pennsylvania, Colorado and California, relocating 500 jobs to new factories in Canada where the price of sugar was half that in the USA.

general shift towards less restrictive policies, since 1945 in the high income countries and since the 1970s in middle-income countries, can be attributed to clearer recognition of the general interest and reduced pandering to vested interests. It could also be ascribed, particularly in the high-income countries, to recognition of the costs of trade liberalisation to specific groups and attempts to compensate such groups.

In the USA, adjustment assistance dates from the 1962 Trade Expansion Act and to the Manpower Development and Training Act of the same year, both of which during the 1960s focused on the economically disadvantaged as part of the war on poverty. The 1974 Trade Act boosted adjustment assistance by providing up to a year of income supplements to workers adversely affected by trade. In the 1980s and especially in the 1990s, the emphasis shifted to permanent job losses, which often meant people with established work histories who were not economically disadvantaged. The 2002 Trade Act further expanded eligibility and introduced a pilot wage insurance scheme. Even then, the annual spending on trade adjustment assistance was not huge, about a billion dollars in assistance and a billion dollars on retraining, compared to gains from trade estimated at up to a trillion dollars a year (Lalonde, 2007, 5).

Most of these measures were introduced to broaden support for trade liberalisation, although there have been some negative consequences. It is unfair that workers displaced by trade policy changes receive assistance while workers displaced by other forces, such as technical change or changing tastes, do not, and it is often difficult to identify the principal source of displacement. Identifying job loss with trade policy changes, when the evidence points to other determinants of job loss being more significant, has had a negative political consequence in the form of increased resistance to trade policy change.

In recent decades there have been increased concerns in high-income countries about potential job losses of relatively well-to-do middle-aged workers, who in earlier decades anticipated that once they had a job they would keep it until retirement. Although it is still true that the probability of job loss declines with length of time in a job, the rate of job destruction has increased and the costs in terms of lost income are high.[7] Moreover, the awareness of this potential for such a mid-career crisis resonates with a large group of younger people as they set off on careers where they acquire a mix of transferable and company- or industry-specific skills.

---

[7] In the USA the probability of job loss falls to 3% after three years in the same job, but the probability of significant income loss increases with length of job tenure. Workers losing their job after ten years suffer an average income cut of over 15% in their next job, while for workers who have been in a job for twenty years the salary cut exceeds 30%. For a 40–50 year-old worker suffering such income cuts, assistance during the relatively short period between jobs is nothing compared to the reduced income over the rest of their working life. Lalonde (2007, 20) advocates the extension of wage insurance, not as an anti-poverty program, but to address "a substantial market failure that affects middle-aged, middle-class workers and their willingness to embrace beneficial economic policies."

Chapter 13

Instruments of Trade Policy

Tariffs or export taxes are the simplest trade barriers to analyse because they involve only the wedge between domestic and world prices. Other trade barriers not directly based on price can have equivalent effect if they create the same wedge, but non-tariff barriers often involve additional costs. The conditions for equivalence to hold, and plausible circumstances when it will not hold, can be most clearly shown for quantitative restrictions on trade. Other non-tariff barriers may be explicitly aimed at non-trade outcomes, e.g. safety and health standards, while indirectly providing barriers to trade, and an important policy issue is identifying when the trade effects are acceptable or not acceptable consequences. Finally, the chapter examines procedural measures, such as countervailing or antidumping duties, which are the most contentious trade policy instruments today.

Tariffs

Tariffs may be levied as a fixed amount (e.g. a *specific tariff* of 20 cents per shirt) or as a percentage (e.g. an *ad valorem tariff* equal to 20% of the shirt's value). In the 19th century most tariffs were specific because specific tariffs were harder to evade, e.g. by under-declaring the shirt's value. In the 20th century the pattern was to switch to *ad valorem* tariffs because their incidence is not eroded by inflation and they are progressive; rich consumers buying expensive shirts pay more import duty than poor consumers buying cheap shirts.

The *tariff structure* is important because the welfare costs of a tariff rise more than proportionately to an increase in the tariff rate. In the partial equilibrium analysis of the net welfare cost of a tariff, (Figure 11.3), the area of the Corden triangles $(b + d)$ is equal to half of the change in imports multiplied by the tariff: $(Q_1Q_2 + Q_3Q_4) \times (P_d - P_w)$. The first expression is equal to $(t.e_S.Q_1 - t.e_D.Q_4)$, where e_S and e_D are the elasticities of supply and demand, and the second expression is equal to $P_w.t$ so that the product involves the square of the tariff rate. Thus, two sets of tariffs with the same average rate have different welfare implications if one country has a uniform tariff and the other has a tariff structure characterised by peaks and troughs; the latter will be more harmful. The summary of the EU's 10,427 tariff lines (in the Appendix) indicates the complexity of modern tariff schedules; the detail of textile tariffs (1,059 separate tariff lines) is likely to hide some high levels of protection for specific sub-branches.

The concept of the *average tariff* is itself difficult for any country which does not have a uniform tariff. Table 13.1 provides an example of three plausible calculations of the average tariff for a vehicle sector with different tariffs on cars, trucks, bicycles and motorbikes. A simple average tariff (20%) overstates the importance of the prohibitive tariff on trucks, which are a less important branch

Table 13.1. Hypothetical tariffs on vehicles.

Tariff (%)	Good	Value of imports	Share of domestic consumption (%)
10	Cars	70,000	60
50	Trucks	0	15
15	Bicycles	20,000	15
5	Motorbikes	10.000	10

of the industry than cars. The import-weighted average tariff (10.5%) understates the importance of the truck tariff because there are no imports. The consumption-weighted tariff (16.25%) may provide a truer picture of protection for the vehicle industry, but domestic consumption of trucks might have been higher without the tariff and consumption of motorbikes may have been lower if they were subject to the same tariff as cars or bikes.

Taking all tariff rates and calculating the simple average (e.g. adding all of the EU rates and dividing by 10,427) is inappropriate because some tariff lines are more important than others. Weighting by import values is biased downwards, because goods with high tariff rates will be undercounted relative to their weight in a tariff-free world; in the extreme case, a prohibitive tariff will have zero weight. Weighting tariff lines by the share of the good in domestic consumption is a better guide to their economic importance for the importing country, but this is still likely to be biased downwards, because a high tariff raises the domestic price and reduces domestic consumption (but by less than it reduces imports of the good). Conceptually these methods (simple average, import-weighted, consumption-weighted) go from less to more appropriate, but operationally they go from easy to hard to calculate, because consumption is seldom reported by the same categorical classification as trade.[1]

---

[1] Anderson and Neary (2005) analyse how to combine tariffs and NTBs into summary measures of the restrictiveness of trade policies. A fundamental conclusion is that the ideal measure varies, depending upon its intended use; to measure

The structure of tariffs by the stage of production affects the incidence of tariffs. A producer's profits are affected by tariffs on inputs as well as by the tariff on the firm's output. Suppose that with no tariffs on the output or input, a jar of instant coffee sells for $10 and the only inputs are the coffee beans, which cost $9. Imposing a 10% tariff on imports of instant coffee increases the domestic price to $11 and increases value-added from $1 to $2. The increase in value-added might mean that domestic producers can receive twice as much in wages or profits than they could have done without the tariff, or they can be only half as efficient as potential suppliers of imports and still compete. The protection offered to value-added is what matters when gauging the resource allocation implications of trade policy.

The *effective rate of protection* (ERP) is measured by the difference between actual value-added and the free trade value-added:

$$\text{ERP} = (\text{VA}_{\text{actual}} - \text{VA}_{\text{free trade}})/\text{VA}_{\text{free trade}}.$$

Alternatively the free trade value–added can be written as $1 - \Sigma a_i$ where a_i is the share of the ith input in the good's value at world prices and the actual value–added can be written as $(1 + t_o) - \Sigma a_i (1 + t_i)$, where t_o and t_i are the tariff rates on the output and on the ith input. The effective rate of protection is:

$$\text{ERP} = [(1 + t_o) - \Sigma a_i(1 + t_i) - (1 - \Sigma a_i)]/(1 - \Sigma a_i)$$
$$= (t_o - \Sigma t_i.a_i)/(1 - \Sigma a_i).$$

Thus, the effective rate of protection is higher when the tariff on the output is high, tariffs on inputs are low and the share of inputs in total value is high. In the instant coffee example, the ERP is 100%.

---

the costs of protection to the importing country the trade barriers should be weighted by their marginal impact on social welfare, whereas to measure the impact on world trade the weights should be import elasticities (Kee, Nicita and Olarreaga, forthcoming).

Considering the effective rate of protection rather than the nominal tariff is important because it gives a better indication of the impact of the whole tariff regime. In most countries tariff rates tend to cascade: they are low on primary products, higher on intermediate goods and highest on final goods. This means that effective rates of protection are often higher than nominal rates of protection. One implication, which has been important in trade negotiations, is that primary product producers are discouraged from processing their raw materials; the disincentive is especially large for goods like instant coffee or rubber tyres where value-added is small and an innocuous looking tariff on the finished product represents a high ERP.

Export Taxes and Export Subsidies

Export taxes or subsidies operate on prices and can be analysed in a similar way to a tariff. In the partial equilibrium diagram, an *export tax* creates a wedge between the domestic and world prices, which lowers the equilibrium output and increases domestic demand and reduces exports (Figure 11.5). Consumers benefit from the lower domestic price, but the gain in consumer surplus and the revenue from the export tax sum to less than the loss of producer surplus. The net welfare cost can be divided into a demand-side cost, because some units are being sold to domestic buyers who value them less than the world price for which could have been sold, and a supply-side cost, because some exports which would earn more than the cost of production are not produced due to the lower net price received by producers.

An *export subsidy* is slightly different insofar as it encourages more trade than would take place in the absence of any intervention. The higher net price received for exporting encourages an increase in total supply and a shift of sales from the domestic market to the world market. Domestic consumers lose because they have to pay more to obtain goods which are worth more than the world price to suppliers. Suppliers gain because their net revenues increase and they expand production by exporting units which cost more to produce than the world price but less than the world price plus the subsidy. The cost to the government of providing the subsidy plus the loss in consumer surplus is larger than the increase in producer surplus. The net welfare loss arises because the subsidy on the added exports is greater than the value of those extra exports; on the demand side the net value of added exports is equal to the difference between what domestic consumers would pay and the world price and on the supply side the net value is equal to the difference between the world price and the costs of production, and in both cases the net value is negative.

Export subsidies have not been uncommon. A government may subsidise exports because it believes there are externalities from exporting, perhaps in the form of learning effects or other benefits to the economy as a whole. This view was especially popular when export-led growth theories were fashionable in Western Europe in the 1960s or later among countries hoping to emulate the high-performing Asian economies. Another reason for export subsidies is to dispose of surplus output as a result of domestic policies, such as agricultural price support programs. This has been especially controversial because competing exporters are disadvantaged and even the country receiving subsidised imports may be unhappy because of the threat to its import-competing producers.

Export taxes have been much less frequent among high-income countries, and in the USA they are illegal. The politics of this are straightforward, given that producers lose and consumers gain from export taxes (just as import subsidies are rare in high-income countries). Export taxes are more common in low- and middle-income countries where governments may use export taxes, perhaps in the form of compulsory surrender of foreign exchange earnings at an exchange rate below the market rate. The tax may be welfare-improving, if other policies have created distortions in, for example, forex markets, but removing the core distortion would be preferable. Export taxes may also be a source of government revenue or used as an optimal export tax. This has been especially common in countries relying on primary product exports such as cotton or cocoa and is typically administered by requiring growers to sell to a state-run marketing organisation which pays farmers a price below the world price. Such arrangements could be analysed as a simple tax on output if the primary product is sold overwhelmingly for export; if the tax rate is high, its long-term effects are likely to be negative as it discourages new planting and encourages smuggling.[2] Concerns over politically sensitive domestic prices can also stimulate imposition of an export tax.[3]

Quantitative Restrictions

A quantitative restriction on imports, or an *import quota*, can be analysed with exactly the same diagrams that were used to analyse a tariff. Figure 11.3 provides the partial equilibrium analysis of a quota set at Q_2Q_3. At the world price there is excess demand because domestic supply OQ_1 plus import supply Q_2Q_3 is less than domestic demand OQ_4. The domestic price will be bid up until the market clears at price P_d. Compared to the pre-quota situation, consumer surplus has been reduced by area $a + b + c + d$ and producer surplus increased by area a. Area c is the *quota rent* accruing to

---

[2]Such arrangements for cocoa in Ghana substantially reduced the country's position in world markets during the 1970s and 1980s and were associated with development of cocoa production in neighbouring Côte d'Ivoire. More recently, low farmgate prices for cotton in Uzbekistan and Turkmenistan since the early 1990s discouraged effort, encouraged smuggling and impoverished farmers (Anderson, forthcoming).

[3]In 2007–2008, as world grain prices rose rapidly due to bad harvests in Australia, Canada, the EU and other parts of the world, major wheat-exporting countries Kazakhstan and Russia both introduced a 40% tax on wheat exports and several other countries (e.g. Argentina and China) imposed restrictions on wheat exports. The goal was to limit increases in the politically sensitive domestic price of bread.

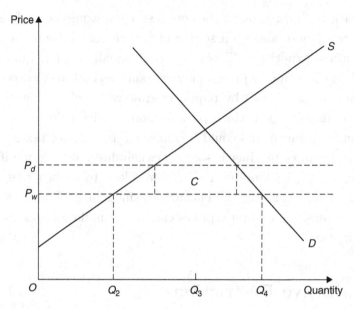

Figure 13.1. An import quota.
Note: The rectangle C, equal to Q_2Q_3 multiplied by $P_d - P_w$, measures the rent on import licences.

importers who hold the import rights and can buy imports at the world price and sell at the domestic price (Figure 13.1). If the quota rights are auctioned, then potential importers should be willing to bid for them until the price reaches $P_d - P_w$. With a competitive auction, the import quota Q_2Q_3 is equivalent to a tariff $P_d - P_w$ in its impact on prices, quantities and welfare.

Equivalence between the quota and tariff is, however, a best-case scenario. Auctioning import rights is atypical and more often they are allocated in a resource-using way, at a minimum requiring would-be importers to fill in forms indicating their need for the import or requiring would-be importers to spend time and money entertaining the officials responsible for issuing import licences. Simple criteria such as first-come first-served waste resources because they encourage 'greyhound effects,' i.e. there is a race to obtain imports sooner than they are really needed in order to avoid risking that quota rights will no longer be available when needed, and inventory costs are increased. Allocating licences for imported inputs on the basis of size or output share encourages firms to operate at above optimal scale in order to earn quota rents. Any resource-using procedure introduces a deadweight loss, while any side-payments for import licences are a welfare transfer.[4] The fundamental dilemma is that it is privately profitable but socially wasteful to use resources to gain import licences, and dissipation of resources may be even greater than area c if would-be importers spend up to the value of the potential quota rent to themselves but some fail to win the competition.

There are a number of deviations from perfect competition in which a tariff and a quota are not equivalent. The most straightforward case is that of a domestic monopoly. With a tariff, the domestic price is set by competing imports which for a small country are available in perfectly elastic supply at a price equal to the world price plus the tariff (P^* in Figure 13.2). A quota set at the quantity imported under that tariff, MQ in Figure 13.2, does not have an equivalent effect. Because the quota limits the amount of import competition the domestic firm does not face a price ceiling as with the tariff, but above the world price it faces an effective demand curve equal to domestic demand minus the import quota (the solid line $DQMD'$). A domestic monopolist maximises profits by setting the marginal revenue associated with the effective demand curve equal to marginal cost and charging price P_m. The monopolist's price will be higher than the world price plus the 'equivalent' tariff, and output and national welfare will be lower than with the equivalent tariff. Welfare is lower because the increase in monopoly profits is smaller

---

[4]Some deadweight loss is almost inevitable. An auction requires would-be importers to prepare their bids and anybody making an unsuccessful bid has wasted their time. When Australia and New Zealand auctioned import licences during the 1980s, the governments failed to capture all of the quota rents due to price uncertainty (McAfee *et al.*, 1999); if the world price fell then the high-bidder might not actually buy the licence, and if world prices increased the high-bidder might resell the licences at a profit.

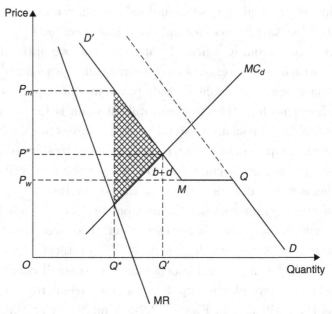

Figure 13.2.   An import quota with domestic monopoly.
Note: The quota MQ is the level of imports associated with a tariff that raises
the domestic price from P_w to P^*. The monopolist maximises profits by reducing
output to OQ^*; with total supply $OQ^* + MQ$ the domestic market price is P_m.
In addition to the net cost of the 'equivalent' tariff $(b+d)$, there is the added cost
of monopoly (the shaded triangle) due to output being reduced by Q^*Q'.

than the reduction in consumer surplus, also the lower output is suboptimal because the cost of producing these units is below the world
price. The sum of these two effects is the shaded area in Figure 13.2,
which measures the gap between opportunity costs and consumer
valuation of the reduced domestic output (relative to output with
the 'equivalent' tariff). Thus a monopolist, and many oligopolists,
prefer quantitative rather than price restrictions on imports because
they leave domestic firms with some flexibility in setting quantity
and domestic price.

Thirdly, a quota and tariff are not dynamically equivalent.
If demand or supply curves shift or the world price changes, then
equivalence ceases to hold. In a normal combination of circumstances

for import-competing industries, such as rising domestic demand, increasing costs and perhaps a falling world price, an import quota has an ever-increasing equivalent tariff. Given that trade policies are not continuously adjusted, import-competing firms often prefer a quota to a tariff because it provides a relatively higher level of protection over time.

Although firms may prefer quota protection to tariff protection, an import quota is generally inferior to a tariff from the national perspective. There is likely to be welfare loss from the allocation of import rights and possibly adverse distributional consequences if quota rents accrue to presidential cronies or corrupt officials rather than going to the public treasury. If the domestic market is imperfectly competitive, a quota is inferior to a tariff because it has inferior pro-competitive properties, as well as having probably undesirable distributional effects in increasing monopoly profits and quota-holders' rent. Finally, the dynamic non-equivalence properties, while attractive to firms because they grant increasing protection, are inferior for the nation for precisely the same reason. In sum, a tariff and a quota may be equivalent, but this is unlikely in practice and in cases of non-equivalence a quota is inferior.

During the 1970s and 1980s *voluntary export restraint agreements* (VERs) were a popular quantitative restriction. In 1981, for example, the USA negotiated a VER with Japan by which Japan agreed to limit the export of cars to the USA to 1.68 million a year. A VER has all the characteristics of an import quota apart from that the exporting country decides how the quota rent should be allocated. For the importing country the net welfare loss is maximised because all of area c in Figure 11.3 is lost. Moreover, because a VER only applies to one supplier, it is likely to be a porous form of protection as alternative suppliers take the place of the restricted exports. In cars this was not an immediate threat to the VER because in 1981 Japanese producers had a large competitive edge, but by the mid-1980s Hyundai of Korea was ready to enter the US markets.

Other ways were found to undermine the protective intention of the
VER, as Japanese carmakers started to build assembly plant in the
USA and to market vans, which were not covered by the VER, as an
alternative to cars, calling them sport utility vehicles. The VER was
abandoned in the late 1980s in part because of these shortcomings
from the perspective of the USA and US carmakers, but most of all
because on a big-ticket consumer item car-buyers started to complain
about the extra $1,000 or more which they were paying for cars as a
result of the quotas.

The most pervasive and long-lasting VERs were those imposed
by high-income countries on imports of textiles and clothing from
low-wage countries. These VERs started as limits on cotton textiles
in the 1950s and were gradually extended to cover other fibres until
they were unified in 1975 as the Multifibre Arrangement (MFA).
As with the car VERs, the MFA was scarcely a voluntary affair
because the importing countries made it clear that, if the exporters
did not agree to VERs, they would unilaterally impose import quotas;
for the importers setting import quotas was less attractive because
they would be illegal under world trade law, and so they bought
the exporters off by offering them the quota rent in return for the
fig-leaf of legality provided by a VER.[5] The MFA expanded continuously to cover more and more countries and more and more fibres,
because the limits of substitutability are almost infinite in clothing production; many fibres can be used and any low-wage country
can develop a clothing industry, especially if established low-wage
producers are constrained by quota limits. The MFA was finally ter-
minated as part of the Uruguay Round of trade negotiations and the
last VERs ended on 1st January 2005, creating a chaotic situation

---

[5]The trivial weight placed on the quota rent by the importing countries which
negotiated VERs during this period is indicative of how insignificant the revenue
aspects of trade policy had become for high-income countries by the final quarter
of the 20th century. In the case of US sugar, area *c*, worth about $400 million,
goes to foreign suppliers, which may be viewed as aid but is larger than the two
triangles.

because after three decades of irrational quantitative limits on trade, it was unclear where exactly comparative advantage lay. Some poor countries certainly lost out from the ending of the MFA because they could no longer compete with more efficient suppliers once the limits on their competitors' exports were lifted, but overall the MFA had been the most costly trade barrier imposed on manufactured exports by poor countries and its demise was long overdue.

Other Non-tariff Barriers to Trade

Customs valuation procedures can act as a trade barrier similar to a tariff. Thus, if an imported good valued at $100 faces a 10% tariff the duty is $10. If the customs authorities have the right to question the valuation and say the good is really worth $150 and hence must pay $15 in duty, then the valuation procedure has the same effect as increasing the tariff to 15%. Discretionary customs valuation has other side-effects in that it can increase the uncertainty of trading and increase the likelihood of corruption among customs officials. Any rules that increase the frequency of physical inspection of imported goods will be associated with longer delays at the border and increased time costs, which may require firms to hold larger inventories. Such trade costs will be dealt with in Chapter 17.

Local content requirements are often imposed on foreign-owned firms, who may be required to have a certain percentage of the value of their output produced domestically or to source a minimum percentage of intermediate inputs locally. Such requirements, if they are binding (i.e. if they make the producer use more domestic inputs than they would have done without the local content requirement), are an implicit tax on imported inputs and, although it may be difficult to quantify precisely, this creates a wedge between domestic and world prices. The wedge will have familiar consequences, increasing the surplus accruing to domestic intermediate goods producers and increasing the costs to the users of the intermediate goods, with a net efficiency loss. By distorting the import choice facing a firm in what may be a discontinuous way (e.g. if there are few options for satisfying the minimum local content level), local content requirements may have added negative consequences for the technical efficiency and competitiveness of firms subject to these requirements.

Government procurement may be biased in favour of domestic suppliers. The economic analysis is identical to the previous chapter's analysis of distorting private sector decisions between domestic goods and imports. For some government purchases, especially by its military forces, there may be a national security argument for maintaining self-sufficiency, but this should be assessed both to confirm that any specific purchase would involve a national security risk if it were made dependent on foreign supply and also to measure the cost of buying domestically when the security benefit is marginal. Although the principle that the government should buy from the least-cost supplier whether domestic or foreign may be clear, implementation may be problematic because many government purchases are one-off and access to the tendering process may favour domestic bidders if potential foreign bidders are unaware that a school or a power station is to be built. There is a related case against the common practice of tying of foreign aid to the purchase of goods and services supplied by the donor country; if the donor is not the least-cost supplier of the tied goods or services, then tying reduces the value of aid to the recipient, increases the producer surplus of the supplier of the goods and services and involves net welfare loss due to the misallocation of resources towards activities in which the donor country does not have a comparative advantage in world markets.[6]

---

[6]Trade issues associated with public procurement are difficult to isolate from more general concerns about non-transparency and lack of due diligence in spending taxpayers' money. Some trade–distorting practices may be justified by arguments about imperfect competition; the US requirement that travel on government money should be on US-owned airlines could be related to profit-shifting trade policies in an oligopolistic global industry, although it is doubtful whether that was the motive or is the consequence of the requirement.

Health, safety and other technical standards often act as *non-tariff barriers to trade* (*NTBs*). Simply requiring labelling of ingredients or health warnings in the national language increases the costs to exporters of supplying countries with different languages to their own. The difficulty in this area is that standards are desirable, and it is hard to separate out their trade–damaging consequences from their beneficial consequences. A useful rule of thumb is to minimise the trade consequences of such NTBs, for example by standardisation of health and safety norms and agreement on eliminating trivial or blatantly protectionist requirements.[7] Even this may be difficult because of sunk costs (e.g. trade costs would be reduced if all countries had the same electricity voltage but the cost of countries changing from 120 or 240 volts would be huge) or of differing national preferences in terms of the degree to which citizens need to be protected from danger (reflected, for example, in differing laws on the labelling of cigarette packets or wine bottles to indicate the dangers from tobacco or alcohol).

Nevertheless, the standard-setting process is often captured by producers, who benefit from shielding their home market from competition. Especially in the area of food and drink, NTBs may be presented as crucial for cultural survival or public health even when their original justification is long past its use by date; the German beer purity law of 1516 was only dropped in 1987 under the EU pressure and Australia's restrictions on cheeses made from unpasteurised

---

[7]The most extreme examples are from the 1930s when countries wanting to get around bilateral trade agreements on tariffs introduced protection by other means. Razor blades imported into France had to have the name of the country of origin stamped on every blade. Britain required imported eggs to be individually labelled in letters not less than two millimetres high. Argentina required paper products such as envelopes to be individually marked with the country of origin, but made an exception for confetti. Japan got around importing countries' labelling requirements about origin, by determining that exports could be labelled by their town of origin and many exports were shipped from the town of Usa. Such blatant use of NTBs or avoiding the spirit of other countries' policies underlined the cost of not having an international body to set the rules and monitor their observance.

milk kept Roquefort cheese out of the market until 2005, although neither NTB was relevant to protecting modern consumers (Belgian beer drinkers or French cheese-eaters were not notably less healthy than their German or Australian counterparts). Australian quarantine measures in particular have been attacked for over-stringent risk assessment bans on imports of fruits, vegetables, wood and other natural products even when the safety of the import has been established beyond reasonable doubt (e.g. New Zealand apples and Philippines pineapples and bananas are banned because they failed to pass Australian-conducted risk assessment tests whose results are disputed by the exporting countries).

Anti-dumping and Countervailing Duties

A particular type of tariff protection occurs when a government imposes a tariff in order to offset another country's policies. Anti-dumping duties are imposed when an imported good is being sold at a price below that in its home market or at less than its average cost. Countervailing duties are imposed to offset a subsidy given to the producer of the imported good. In both cases, the duties are seen as responses to unfair trade practices and their level is determined administratively in order to be proportionate to the size of the price differential or subsidy which is being countered. The role of a quasi-judicial procedure adds to the complexity of such policies and increases their protectionist impact and net costs.[8]

Anti-dumping duties (*ADs*) have a long history dating back to Canadian legislation in 1904. Anti-dumping legislation was

---

[8]Finger, Hall and Nelson (1982) argue that in the USA the complexity is deliberate because the goal of including administered protection measures in the 1974 Trade Act was not so much protection as to handle complaints about import competition from politically low-profile industries, which pass through a low-track administrative process, while more high-profile industries such as cars or steel were dealt with by more overtly political responses such as voluntary export restraint agreements.

enacted in Japan in 1920, in Australia, the United Kingdom, New Zealand and the United States in 1921. ADs were, however, seldom used in the 1920s and 1930s because most countries had high tariffs, and it was only as tariff rates fell in the second half of the 20th century that resort to ADs became more frequent. In particular, countries joining the WTO after 1995 or substantially reducing their tariffs have become more active in using ADs (Feinberg and Reynolds, 2007; Vandenbussche and Zanardi, 2008). Vandenbussche and Zanardi (2006) argue that the new heavy users of ADs were the main targets of earlier ADs actions and that they now target the old heavy-users, i.e. the discretionary and discriminatory nature of ADs makes them suited to retaliation.[9]

ADs legislation typically requires establishment of less-than-fair-value pricing and of injury to domestic producers, which are sometimes verified by different agencies (as in the USA and Canada) and sometimes by a single agency (as in the EU or Australia). An implication is that the proceedings send signals which can lead to early settlement as the exporter realises that ADs are becoming inevitable and 'voluntarily' reduces the supply of imports or increases their price. The discretion about moving to the final stage allows the importing country to recognise such prophylactic actions by the exporter and contributes to the high number of ADs proceedings which are withdrawn. This flexibility defines ADs proceedings more than the technical requirements of establishing injury or calculating the margin of dumping, although the latter also has substantial element of discretion.

---

[9]The traditional tough users, ranked by AD initiations per year 1980–2000, are the USA, Australia, the EU, Canada and New Zealand; ranked by initiations relative to the value of imports Australia, New Zealand and Canada would be far ahead of the EU and US. The new tough users, with the year in which they adopted an AD law, are Mexico (1986), India (1985), Brazil (1987), Turkey (1989) and Taiwan (1984), although the data in Vandenbussche and Zanardi (2008, Table 2) suggest that China (1997) and Egypt (1998) were tougher than Taiwan in the few years after they adopted their ADs laws.

The technical requirements vary from country to country, but 'injury' is usually defined as reduced revenues for import-competing producers which is easy to prove because it will be the proximate result of almost any trade.[10] The price comparison is more difficult because the importing country's government agency may not have direct information on the exporter's home market price, especially in cases involving heterogeneous goods or exports from non-market economies, and may rely on facts presented by the import-competing firms. Another source of bias in AD proceedings is differing familiarity with and access to the quasi-legal proceedings; especially when exporters are from a poor country or the import market is minor to them, the exporters may have limited understanding of the AD procedures or fail to allocate resources needed to obtain effective legal representation.

An especially insidious abuse of AD proceedings concerns their application to non-market economies. In a landmark case in the 1970s against golf carts imported from Poland, the USA determined that prices in Poland, at that time a centrally planned economy, were too artificial to provide a true picture of domestic costs, and used data from a similar country to construct what the domestic price would have been had Poland had a market economy; a positive finding resulted and ADs were imposed.[11] This procedure, which has been widely adopted, is fraught with potential for selecting as a comparator, a country whose prices result in a low constructed price and high ADs. After central planning was abandoned in eastern Europe and the Soviet Union at the end of the 1980s, the economies in transition from central planning found it difficult to shed the 'non-market economy' label even after accession to the WTO. In 2006–2007 the

---

[10]In the USA, whose AD implementation has served as a benchmark for many other countries' AD policies, the great majority of AD and CVD cases in the 1980s involved a fall in revenues of less than ten percent (Kelly and Morkre, 1998).
[11]The initial calculations, using the cost structure of a Canadian manufacturer, led to ADs being imposed in 1975, but in 1976 using Spanish prices the duties were revoked, highlighting the sensitivity to the choice of surrogate country.

EU conducted AD investigations into imports of certain shoe imports from China and Vietnam, and decided that because they were non-market economies — which would be a huge surprise to the many small and medium-sized shoemakers in the two countries — the 'domestic' prices had to be constructed using Brazilian prices as a proxy; the result was a nine-month investigation in which twenty eurocrats made the calculations and determined that the appropriate ADs were about 20%.

Countervailing duties (CVDs) are far less common, typically accounting for less than a tenth of the number of cases as ADs. CVD cases involve many of the same issues as AD cases, with considerable discretion in calculating the value of a subsidy per unit exported, and hence the height of the appropriate countervailing duty. When Japan imposed a 27% CVD on imports of DRAM chips from Korea in January 2006, Korea took its objections to the WTO whose panel found that the duties were unjustified, but they remained in place while Japan took steps to recalculate the height of the CVDs; even after a Korean appeal to the WTO, the CVDs were still in place at the end of 2007, thus granting at a minimum two-years' temporary protection to Japanese import-competing producers.

A large but difficult to measure cost of ADs and CVDs is their negative impact on trade due to increased uncertainty. A producer considering entering a new export market will think twice about destinations where AD or CVD proceedings are easy to initiate, expensive to oppose and biased in favour of reaching positive findings.[12] Although there is widespread international agreement about

---

[12]In some industries, notably steel, there is little uncertainty because protection, whether through ADs, CVDs or other safeguard measures, is usually provided in the USA and EU. Steel demand is cyclical and during recessions it is relatively easy to find examples of price cuts which can be compared to higher 'normal' prices in an exporter's home market, but once in place ADs can become more than short-term measures. In the early 2000s, faced by low profits in the steel industry, the USA imposed a range of temporary duties on steel imports (Devreux *et al.*, 2006, Vol. 2, 193–233); of the duties introduced in 2002–2004 twenty were

the pernicious effects of procedural protection on exporters, domestic changes sometimes worsen the situation. In the USA, the Byrd Amendment in 2000 revised AD proceedings so that, if a positive finding were reached, the revenue from the ADs would go to the firms who had initiated the complaint; this not only increased the incentive to initiate AD proceedings but also discouraged free-riding, because any firm which did not contribute to the lobbying and legal costs would not receive a share of the revenue (Reynolds, 2006).[13]

ADs, and to a lesser degree CVDs, are today the most harmful explicit trade policy instruments and yet difficult to dismantle. Earlier studies which were comforted by the small number of initiations that led to imposition of ADs (e.g. Finger, Hall and Nelson, 1982) or which estimated a small impact on trade flows (in the range of 2–5% according to Hindley and Messerlin, 1986) appeared to have downplayed the chilling effects of the threat of AD–action and of a reputation as a tough AD–user. Using a gravity model and the natural experiment of new tough users emerging in the 1990s, Vandenbussche and Zanardi (2006) estimated that the impact on these countries' trade was to depress imports by 6.7%. Application of ADs and CVDs is only dependent upon cost to producers from the actions of a foreign firm or government; because consumers' interests are ignored, there

---

discontinued in 2004–2007, mostly involving minor product lines or small suppliers, while seventeen duties against major suppliers were all continued despite the domestic industry's strong profits in 2006–2007, with the steel lobby claiming that if the duties were not continued than dumping would resume. Among other consequences, the EU used trade diversion due to high US duties to justify their own administrative protection of steel producers. The American Institute for International Steel, an advocacy group for US steel users, claimed that the US steel industry received a total of $17 billion in subsidies over the 2001–2007 period (*Wall Street Journal*, 12 November 2007).

[13]The distributed revenues in 2001–2003 were between $230 and 330 million per year, mostly related to findings about softwood lumber, steel, bearings and candles. In 2002, confirmed after the appeal in 2003, the WTO ruled the Amendment illegal. It was repealed in 2006, effective October 2007.

is a bias towards finding injury and introducing a trade barrier. AD actions are popular among producers because the process favours them and the quasi-legal process is most favourable for those who can afford good lawyers.[14] Moreover, the process is non-transparent and there is no upper bound to the duties that can be imposed. The net welfare effects are likely to be higher than for normal tariffs because ADs tend to be higher, ADs are discriminatory and likely to divert trade (see Chapter 15), and the legal proceedings use real resources.

Conclusions

The variety of policies affecting international trade is infinite. In general equilibrium any policy which impacts on the production possibility frontier or on public or private tastes will affect the trade triangle. Even focusing on the most direct tariff and non-tariff barriers introduces a variety of policy-specific consequences. Nevertheless, general conclusions can be drawn: all trade barriers increase the relative price of imported goods to export goods above the true opportunity cost prices for a small country (i.e. world prices) and encourage greater domestic supply of import-competing goods and

---

[14]The spread of outsourcing and emergence of global value chains, however, may pit producers against each other. When the German firm Osram tried to initiate AD proceedings against light bulb imports from China in 2007, it was opposed by the Dutch manufacturer Philips. Most of Osram's bulbs are manufactured within the EU whereas Philips produces large quantities in China and wants to be able to organise its production and marketing without worrying about barriers to international flows of light bulbs. A report by the Swedish government's National Board of Trade (Kommerskollegium, 2007) argued that EU anti-dumping actions against shoe imports from China and Vietnam hurt the European economy because over half of the value-added of these shoes went to EU producers in the value chain.

lower domestic consumption of those goods.[15] The price wedge is the source of the presumption against trade barriers being in the national interest, and the previous chapter's analysis of the net costs of the wedge is valid for all trade barriers.

In general, non-tariff barriers to trade (NTBs) have additional costs. This is most easily shown for quantitative restrictions on imports, which may be equivalent to a tariff but the conditions for equivalence are unlikely to hold and when these conditions are absent quantitative restrictions reduce national welfare by more than the 'equivalent' tariff. Quantitative restrictions are especially harmful when the domestic industry is a monopoly or oligopoly and when import licences are allocated in a manner which encourages costly rent-seeking. Health and safety standards and similar NTBs are difficult to analyse on anything but a case-by-case basis because there was often a public interest motive for their introduction, but this benefit (and the manner in which it is realised) should be weighed against the costs of being a barrier to trade.

Trade policy debates often involve dubious semantics. In international negotiations, countries refer to reductions in their own trade barriers as 'concessions' to their trading partners, although the main benefit is typically to the country itself. Supporters of NTBs such as military spending, local content requirements or antidumping duties often play on public sentiment by appealing to national security, culture or fairness, but it is important to identify the cost of realising desirable ends and the extent to which NTBs merely shield domestic suppliers from foreign competition. The vocabulary of anti-dumping and countervailing duties is especially obnoxious with its reference to 'fair' trade policies, the negative connotation of 'dumping', and the

---

[15]Trade barriers also increase the relative price of non-traded goods. However, there is a conceptual problem in establishing a category of intrinsically 'non-tradable goods'. With low transport and other trade costs few goods are non-tradable. With prohibitive trade barriers and complete autarchy, production is entirely of non-traded goods.

blaming of the country against whom countervailing is necessary; the process is also hypocritical as high-income countries themselves export at well-below domestic price (e.g. US food aid which is given to poor countries) or complain against countries selling above their domestic price (e.g. EU opposition to Russia charging higher prices on gas exports than to Russian consumers).[16]

---

[16]These last examples illustrate the difficulty of generalising about the welfare effects of price discrimination, which is the main result in Chapter 15. Assessment of the effects of price discrimination is often complicated by differing perceptions of deserving and non-deserving groups (i.e. the one dollar one vote for aggregating welfare effects is not accepted). Food aid, for example, can help starving people in poor countries, but it hurts farmers in those countries and the depressing effect on world prices as well as the implications for donor–country farmers and public finances mean that the overall effects are hard to sort out.

Chapter 14

International Trade Law and Multilateral Trade Negotiations

Long distance trade existed for millennia without a formal legal basis, but as with any market it will function better within a framework of agreed and enforceable rules of conduct and with an accepted means of exchange. With the emergence of modern nations, states began to negotiate formal agreements to regulate their bilateral trade. In the 19th century the gold standard emerged as a widely accepted payments system, although actual payments were usually in a currency which was 'as good as gold' (such as the British pound) rather than gold itself. This system worked reasonably well in the relative prosperity of the decades before 1914, although lengthy trade wars were

not uncommon.[1] Tensions did mount, however, as leading trading
nations began to compete for markets, and economic competition
turned into world war in 1914. Attempts to restore a global trading
system based on moderate trade barriers and fixed exchange rates
between 1919 and 1939 were unsuccessful. Countries were unwilling
to cede autonomy over trade and monetary policies and in the 1930s
increasingly adopted trade policies for national motives (e.g. to com-
bat unemployment or to create spheres of influence) that increased
international tensions. Key policymakers in the USA and UK saw
the lack of an appropriate international economic system as a con-
tributing force to the outbreak of world war, and as something to be
put right in the post-war era.

The post-1945 system was designed to set rules for zero-sum competitive situations (e.g. on when countries could devalue their currencies) and to address market failures. In 1944 at Bretton Woods,
agreement was reached on establishing the International Monetary
Fund to oversee exchange rate and other international monetary
arrangements and the International Bank for Reconstruction and
Development (subsequently rebadged as the World Bank) to provide
financing for reconstruction and development. A third institution,
the International Trade Organisation, was intended to complement
the two Bretton Woods institutions but negotiations on the ITO's
Charter dragged on and, although a draft was agreed in Havana in
1948, it became clear that the US Congress would not ratify the
terms. The fundamental issue was the unwillingness of the USA, and

---

[1]Trade wars occurred, for example, between France and Italy (1888–1898),
Switzerland and France (1893–1895), Germany and Russia (1893–1894), Germany
and Spain (1892–1906) and Germany and Canada (1897–1910). The length of
the trade wars often reflected that they were easier to start than to end. The
Germany-Canada war was triggered by Canada's adoption of preferential tariff
rates on imports from within the British Empire; Germany's actions failed to
reverse Canada's policy and Germany acknowledged this by not reacting to similar measures introduced by Australia and South Africa, but in the absence of
any climb-down by Canada, Germany could not dismantle its counter-measures
against Canada without loss of face, so the trade war dragged on for over a decade.

many other countries, to surrender their trade policy autonomy to a supranational institution.

Nevertheless, the US Administration was keen to reduce the high tariffs of the 1930s and wanted a contractual framework within which to do this. In 1947 twenty three countries, including all of the major trading nations, signed the General Agreement on Tariffs and Trade (GATT), which contained the provisional ITO trade rules (Curzon, 1965; Irwin, Mavroidis and Sykes, 2008). Article I of the GATT, stated that all signatories should treat the trade of all other signatories as well as that of the most-favoured nation. The ***unconditional MFN principle*** established that the basis for the GATT system should be non-discrimination. Among the other Articles some exceptions to this principle were allowed, but they were not expected to be a substantial feature of the global economy. In addition, the GATT Articles set out rules aimed at making trade policy as transparent and efficient as possible. If imports were to be restricted, it should be by tariffs, and other measures such as customs valuation procedures should not be used as substitutes for formal trade restrictions. Each country agreed to bind its tariff rates, guaranteeing that they would not be raised in future above the bound rate, which was a prerequisite for any reciprocal agreements to reduce tariffs.

A small secretariat administered the GATT, unlike the large bureaucracies soon established at the IMF and World Bank. Another distinctive feature of the GATT was that signatories took decisions by consensus, rather than by weighted voting. Both the absence of a large supranational authority and the consensual decision-making reflected governments' sensitivity about sovereignty over trade policy. Yet, in a series of rounds of multilateral trade negotiations, progress was made in reducing the level of tariffs. This bargaining process and its outcomes will be analysed in the next section.

Several theories can explain the establishment and success of the GATT. Law is a public good and the problem for the international trading system in the 1919–1939 period was that major trading

nations did not recognise that it was in their own interest to contribute to the provision of this public good. In the post-1945 global
economy, the USA had an unmatched importance and its commitment to the GATT was critical to its establishment. The Western
European economies and the British Dominions and a handful of
other independent countries saw the GATT as worth signing in order
to commit the USA to its tariff reductions.

An alternative approach is to see the GATT as a response to
a prisoners' dilemma situation when large countries may try to
impose their optimum tariffs. Without binding commitments that
other countries will not retaliate, it is easy to construct a scenario
where each large country will impose a tariff and the retaliatory
spiral leaves everybody worse off. Such scenarios could capture the
responses to the US 1930 tariff increase or to Germany's attempts in
the 1930s to establish spheres of influence in eastern Europe, both of
which led to outcomes that the initiators had not foreseen and presumably would not have wished for. The GATT was a form of tariff
disarmament in which signatories foreswore first strike in a tariff war.

Whatever the reasons for the GATT's origins and early success,
in the long-run the best measure of its value has been the increasing
number of signatories. In the final GATT round of negotiations, a
key outcome was the establishment of a permanent secretariat, the
World Trade Organisation (WTO), in 1995. The GATT became the
basic document of WTO trade law, and the 128 GATT signatories
became charter members of the WTO. In January 2007, Vietnam
became the 150th WTO member.

Multilateral Trade Negotiations

The early rounds of GATT trade negotiations adopted the principal
supplier approach. A country would identify an important market
for an export and negotiate easier access to that market in return
for giving improved access to its own market for a good important

to the other country. Agreements between these principal suppliers of the two goods would be generalised through the Most-favoured Nation (MFN) principle. Such product-by-product trade liberalisation helped to establish a climate of reduced trade barriers during the 1950s, but not all GATT signatories participated in every round of negotiations (Table 14.1) and it was a slow route to a general reduction in trade barriers.

The Kennedy Round (1964–1967) saw the first attempt to reach agreement on across-the-board tariff reductions. Although it was the longest round of negotiations so far, it was successful in bringing down tariffs substantially. The major weakness of GATT at this time was that membership was not universal. It included all of the major trading nations and they generally (but not always and not contractually) extended MFN treatment to non-signatories. However, most developing countries were not signatories and even those that were, such as India or most of the South American countries, largely ignored GATT in the 1960s. One consequence was that goods of most interest to exporters in developing countries tended to be ignored, most blatantly in the exclusion of agriculture and of textiles and clothing from the reductions in trade barriers.

The exclusion of agriculture reflected the power of farm lobbies in the high-income countries and absence of strong countervailing

Table 14.1.   Rounds of GATT/WTO Trade Negotiations.

Dates	Round	Number of participants
1947	Geneva Round	23
1949	Annecy Round	13
1951	Torquay Round	38
1956	Geneva Round	26
1960–1961	Dillon Round	26
1964–1967	Kennedy Round	62
1973–1979	Tokyo Round	102
1986–1994	Uruguay Round	123
2001–	Doha Development Agenda	

forces. The initial request to exclude agriculture came from the USA in 1955, but when six Western European countries formed a customs union in the 1960s the Common Agricultural Policy that they introduced was even more restrictive, and Japan, Korea and some of the smaller European countries have the highest protection levels for farmers.[2] The textiles and clothing restrictions, dating from a US decision to negotiate a VER with Japan on cotton textiles in 1955 and expanding into the *Multifibre Arrangement* (MFA), illustrated the problems that arise from partial protection in a sector where the potential for substitution, among fibres and among low-wage supplier, is huge. Restricting imports from Japan led to growth in imports from Hong Kong and then from other low-wage suppliers. The 1961 Short-term Cotton Agreement and 1962 Long-term Cotton Agreement allowed GATT signatories to negotiate bilateral quotas with all low-wage suppliers of cotton textiles and clothing. The restrictions on cotton imports led consumers to turn to other materials, and in 1974 the MFA extended the Long-term Cotton Agreement to include wool and synthetic fibres. Exporters were promised high growth rates of quotas, but over the 1970s and 1980s quotas became tighter and covered more items; by the 1980s the MFA was the high income countries' most costly trade barrier.[3] In sum, the MFA led to global resource misallocation; the losers were consumers and efficient

---

[2] The OECD's producer support estimates (PSEs, measuring the total impact on farmers' revenues relative to what they would have had at world prices) for 2004 include for the EU 33%, Japan 56%, USA 18%, Korea 63%, Turkey 30%, Switzerland 68%, Iceland 69%, Norway 68%, Australia 4%, and New Zealand 3%.

[3] Some high-income countries benefited, e.g. in the EU clothing manufacturers in Italy were protected from external competition. As the MFA quotas evolved historically without regard to changes in comparative advantage, it became impossible to know which low-wage countries benefited relative to a MFA-free world. Although the MFA imposed large costs on developing countries as a whole, many exporters became sceptical about reform because they feared loss of quota rents. Among its many distortions the MFA encouraged suppliers to fill binding quotas with higher quality clothing items, so that among the suffering consumers in high-income countries the poorest consumers suffered most.

suppliers, but there were many beneficiaries who resisted reform of the system. The MFA gave a lesson to rich country governments of the danger of starting down a protectionist path; restricting cotton from Japan eventually led to restrictions on all textiles and clothing from all low-wage countries.[4]

The Tokyo Round (1973–1979) continued the process of across-the-board tariff reduction, to the extent that GATT signatories' tariffs on most manufactured goods other than textiles and clothing were reduced to under ten percent. The Tokyo Round also began to address the more difficult issues associated with non-tariff barriers to trade (NTBs), which tend to be less transparent and less easily measured than tariffs. NTBs could be used as substitutes for tariffs and hence the logical accompaniment to reduced tariffs was agreement on when NTBs were permissible (for example, on health or safety or environmental grounds) and when they should be outlawed as (inferior) surrogates for tariffs. Although there was general agreement that NTBs had to be on the GATT negotiating agenda, little was achieved in the Tokyo Round. The urgency of addressing the issue was highlighted in the 1980s by the proliferation of measures such as VERs which went against the spirit of GATT but were not illegal.

The final round of GATT multilateral trade negotiations was the Uruguay Round (1986–1994). This was the most contentious round because it continued the process of bringing non-tariff barriers into the GATT and also it included more countries than ever before, which made the consensus rule more onerous. However, as in previous rounds a small group of countries took the lead in the negotiations, in this case the USA, EU, Japan and Canada. After several near-breakdowns the negotiations were completed in 1994.

The Final Act of the Uruguay Round included agreement to create a World Trade Organisation (WTO). Tariff reductions brought

---

[4]The lesson was learned when steel companies in the USA and EU pushed for VERs. Although the importing countries did negotiate VERs, they were careful not to let them escalate into a Multimetals Arrangement.

the average tariff for OECD countries down from 6% to 4% and for developing countries the average tariff fell from 15% to 12%. The two major exempt sectors were brought under normal trade rules; for agriculture the agreement entailed standstill or reduction in export subsidies and price supports and tarrification of NTBs (which indicated how high the equivalent tariffs were as the bound tariffs for 2000 included for wheat EU 82%, USA 4%, Japan 152%, and for sugar EU 152%, USA 91%, Japan 58%), and for textiles and clothing the Multifibre Arrangement was to be phased out by 1st January 2005. On other non-tariff barriers and contingent protection, there was a pledge not to use VERs, but little progress on AD duties. Finally, the negotiations dealt with other areas, which were not part of the 'single undertaking' (i.e. implementation was not mandatory): a General Agreement on Trade in Services (GATS) was adopted, and codes on trade–related investment measures (TRIMs)[5] and trade–related intellectual property rights (TRIPs)[6] — the last one was controversial because a specialised agency of the United Nations, the World Intellectual Property Organisation, already exists to address these issues.[7] Although these last agreements were weak, they were

---

[5]The TRIMs agreement prohibits making approval of foreign investment contingent on compliance with laws or regulations that favour domestic producers. Violations are not defined, but are illustrated by a list of inadmissible practices.
[6]The TRIPs agreement attempts to establish minimum levels of protection that governments grant to the intellectual property of other WTO members, following the principles of nondiscrimination and transparency and with the added goal that intellectual property protection should contribute to technical innovation and technology transfer.
[7]Developing countries tend to prefer the UN as a forum because in the General Assembly motions are adopted on a one-country, one-vote basis. However, the Generalised System of Preferences (GSP), which was pushed through the UN system before being accepted as an exception to the GATT non-discrimination principle in 1971, ended up delivering little to the developing countries because GSP schemes were designed by the importing countries. The GATT/WTO system, with its consensus approach to decision-making, has a *status quo* bias, but anything that is adopted after a round of negotiations has a contractual nature that cannot be unilaterally amended in the way that importer-determined GSP schemes could be.

a first step in establishing principles such as non-discrimination (or 'national treatment') in these areas.

The GATT era was one of great trade liberalisation, and the GATT framework facilitated this process. By the 1990s tariffs had become minor obstacles to trade. The incidence of major NTBs, such as import quotas, VERs and customs valuation procedures, had been greatly reduced either as a result of their inclusion in the original Agreement or by clarification in multilateral rounds, even if other NTBs partially took their place. Most of all the GATT had provided a set of rules for world trade, which were accepted by all of the major trading nations and by a growing number of low- and middle-income countries. However, although GATT imposed obligations on contracting parties, its rules were poorly enforceable and there was a lingering sense that the big countries would disregard the rules if it really suited them. The potential for such conflict was heightened by the inclusion in the Uruguay Round Final Act of agriculture and textiles and clothing, sectors known for the power of domestic vested interests in the USA, EU, Japan, and other high income countries, and a key element of the WTO was an enhanced dispute settlement mechanism intended to make enforcement accessible to all.

The World Trade Organisation

Newspaper headlines focus on public protests against the global trading system and the WTO, as at Seattle in 1999 and subsequently at Genoa in 2001 and Cancun in 2003, or on the slow progress of the current round of multilateral a trade negotiations, the Doha Development Round. Yet the WTO has been a magnet for countries around the world. When Ukraine joined in 2008 it became the 152nd member; only Russia, Kazakhstan, Iran, Iraq, Afghanistan, Algeria and some smaller countries remained non-members, and for all of them accession negotiations are under way, so that the WTO is

a global organisation.[8] Moreover, unlike in GATT, large low- and
middle-income countries such as Brazil, China, India and South
Africa are playing an active role in the current round, rather than
treating it as irrelevant to them. The reasons for poorer countries'
changed attitudes towards international trade will be analysed in
Chapter 16, but a question that needs to be addressed here is why
do so many countries, and not just the original couple of dozen GATT
signatories, see WTO membership as beneficial?

The main benefit from the existence of the WTO is that it provides a set of rules about acceptable and unacceptable trade policies
and practices which reduce the uncertainty of trading internationally.
The benefits from a rules-based international trading system are, as
with other sets of standards, **network benefits**. The more countries
that observe a common set of rules, the more useful the rules are likely
to be. The network benefits of a rules-based trading system increase
with the number of countries that agrees to abide by the rules, but
with an additional country the added benefits accrue to others rather
than to the new member itself. Indeed, if a new member was already
benefiting from MFN treatment in the markets of existing WTO
members, then they would notice little or no difference, even though
the systemic benefits are increased by expanding WTO coverage.

The potential benefits from the WTO *dispute resolution
mechanism* and a *seat at the WTO negotiating table* are
greater now than they were during the GATT era (1947–1994) when
the system was biased in favour of the major trading nations, both
in the coverage of trade liberalisation (agriculture and textiles and
clothing were largely outside the system) and in effective recourse

---

[8]A list of members and the current state of accession negotiations can be found
on the WTO website www.wto.org. Tonga became the 151st member in 2007
and Ukraine's accession negotiations were concluded in 2008, leaving twenty-nine
accession negotiations still in progress. It is harder to find a list of countries not
interested in joining the WTO; Turkmenistan was the largest country that had
not applied before 2008.

against countries breaking GATT rules. Most complaints from 1948 to 1994 involved rich countries, but one aspiration of the shift to the more formal WTO was that the dispute resolution process should be open to all. In the very first case brought before the WTO dispute resolution mechanism, Venezuela complained that the 1990 US Clean Air Act discriminated against foreign refined petroleum; the complaint was successful, and the USA agreed in 1996 to amend the Act to remove the discriminatory clauses.

The GATT rounds of multilateral trade negotiations were dominated by the USA, EU, Japan and Canada, but a feature of the Doha Round has been the much greater involvement of middle- and low-income countries either individually or as the Group of 20. A striking example of the higher profile of developing country interests and potential benefits is cotton, where Brazil's case against the USA was the first dispute in which a developing country successfully challenged an OECD country's farm subsidy program in the WTO. Cotton is a symbolic commodity because concerns raised by four poor West African cotton-producing countries about US and EU farm policies were central in turning the Doha Round into the Doha Development Agenda.

The WTO can provide an **anchor for market-friendly reforms**. Even during the negotiations phase, countries such as China, Russia or Kazakhstan have reformed their economies by passing WTO-consistent legislation during this period. For small countries, WTO commitments were an important policy anchor or a necessary staging-post to a firmer anchor (e.g. for the Baltic countries WTO accession was a necessary step towards EU accession). WTO accession is important because it is contractual and because openness is a frequent concomitant of successful reform, but WTO membership is not a sufficient anchor, and many GATT/WTO members have slid into non-reform.[9] Emphasising the 'anchor' property

---

[9]The terminology may be misleading here. A policy 'anchor' focuses on the need to constrain a country so that it sticks to its reforming path, whereas the main

of WTO accession may be double-edged if the WTO is 'blamed' for difficult reforms, or the WTO may be the subject of blame by association, if WTO accession provides no immediate and visible benefits but coincides with an economic downturn.

There are real *costs to WTO accession*, which are often ignored by economists. It is, however, important to distinguish between pseudo-costs and real costs. The reduced sovereignty in the area of trade policy formation is a minor consideration if WTO rules enforce best practice for a small open economy. For the original GATT signatories this is a lesson learned over decades, and explains the strength of the system even when enforcement appears weak. Although existing WTO members generally impose stricter terms on new members' tariff bindings than they themselves observe, setting high tariffs is not in the self-interest of a small open economy. The shift away from trade taxes as a source of government revenue is desirable under almost all imaginable conditions.[10] Thus, loss of 'policy space' by developing countries' governments who observe WTO rules is of little significance.[11] The real costs of WTO accession are the institutional requirements for negotiating and implementing non-mandatory codes, which for small poor countries are substantial in their demands on scarce human capital. The issue is controversial

---

contribution of the GATT/WTO system may have been to facilitate reforms by providing a framework of a credible guarantee of more or less stable access to the major foreign markets.

[10]In extreme cases of very poor trade-tax-dependent countries there may be a good case for foreign aid to compensate for the revenue loss associated with tariff reduction.

[11]Dani Rodrik (2007) argues that the loss of policy space is damaging for policymakers wishing to pursue heterodox policies such as those used by India or South Korea. However, India is a long-term GATT/WTO member and Korea's policies were generally GATT-compatible, so it is unclear what policy space, if any, is threatened by WTO membership. Moreover, India's long-term economic performance has been disappointing and, while South Korea pursued more interventionist policies than other high-performing Asian economies, it was also the least successful of the original Gang of Four, with lower income levels than Hong Kong, Singapore or Taiwan and greater exposure to financial instability in 1997.

because some codes may be inappropriate for developing countries (e.g. TRIPS and health).[12]

The first round of multilateral trade negotiation since the founding of the WTO was delayed by protests in Seattle in 1999, but launched in Qatar in November 2001. The **Doha Development Round** tackles unfinished business, in particular agriculture and high tariffs on manufactures in some of the large middle-income countries, but it also addresses the so-called (because they were introduced at a ministerial meeting in Singapore) 'Singapore' issues: public procurement, trade facilitation, investment, competition policy. Many of these new issues are not traditional trade policy issues, because they do not concern border measures. The emphasis on behind-the-border obstacles to trade draws on evidence such as that assembled by Anderson and van Wincoop (2004) about the nature of trade costs, to be discussed in Chapter 17. *Trade facilitation* has become the term describing policies to reduce these trade costs.

---

[12]While there are good arguments for granting pharmaceutical companies patent protection so that they can be rewarded for developing new drugs, sick people in poor countries should not be denied access to drugs whose marginal costs of production are low but whose price is high due to a patent-protected monopoly. The policy challenge is to design subsidies, perhaps financed by foreign aid, for patients in poor countries while preventing arbitragers from exporting the cheap drugs into high-income countries.

Chapter 15

Discriminatory Trade Policies and Regionalism

For several years in the mid-2000s the WTO website contained a paper with the opening sentence — which sounded like a warning — "Regional Trade Agreements (RTAs) are a major and perhaps irreversible feature of the multilateral trading system" (Crawford and Fiorentino, 2005). The website also featured a dramatic graph illustrating this phenomenon by the number of RTAs notified to GATT/WTO (Chart 15.1). It is surprising because the WTO stands for non-discriminatory trade policies and with few exceptions discriminatory trade policies, such as RTAs, are illegal, or at least contrary to the spirit of the GATT/WTO.

Article I of the GATT, which is also the basis for world trade law under the WTO, requires all WTO members to treat any other member as the most-favoured nation. This strong commitment to non-discrimination was pushed by the USA in 1947, in part because

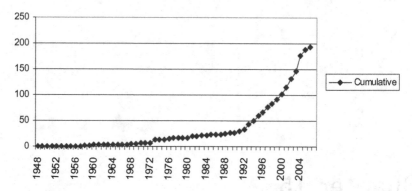

Chart 15.1.   Number of RTAs notified to GATT/WTO 1948–2006.
Source: Crawford and Fiorentino (2005) as updated in Pomfret (2007), based on data on the WTO website www.wto.org
Note: in 2008 the website introduced a more complex diagram differentiating between notified RTAs (380 at the end of 2007) and 'active' RTAs (about 200) without full explanation of the increase in registered notifications or of criteria for identifying an RTA as active.

attempts to create trade blocs in Europe were viewed as having contributed to the political breakdown that led to war in 1939 and also because the USA viewed special treatment for colonies (imperial preferences, of which the most important in 1947 were within the British Empire) as both wrong in principle and against US interests (especially with respect to access to Canada, one of its largest markets). In practice, neither of these concerns has been very relevant to trade policy since 1947. The European empires soon disappeared and Britain's imperial preferences lapsed when it negotiated membership in the European Communities in 1972.

A clause in the GATT, Article XXIV, permitted customs unions or free trade areas under certain conditions. In 1947 this was seen as potentially applying only to special cases like San Marino and Italy or Monaco and France and not especially important for the global system. However, following the successful creation of a customs union among six Western European countries during the 1960s, which was a step towards the European Union, customs unions, free trade areas and other discriminatory trading arrangements have been a recurring feature of the global economy. Such arrangements are often seen as a threat to the multilateralism embodied in the GATT and underlying the current WTO-based international trading system.

Preferential trading arrangements proliferated in three waves.[1] Following the signing of the Treaty of Rome in 1957 and creation of the European Economic Community, of which the customs union established during the 1960s was the prime feature, many country groupings in Africa and Latin America were established as free trade areas, customs unions or economic communities. Although some survived on paper, none was a practical success; two of the temporarily most successful, the Central American Common Market (CACM) and the East African Community (EAC), folded under economic pressures and eventually degenerated into open warfare.[2] In the second wave, the USA abandoned its principled opposition to discriminatory trade policies, signing trade agreements with Caribbean countries, Israel and Canada, culminating in the North American Free Trade Area (NAFTA) agreement of 1993 with Canada and Mexico. Also in the 1980s the European Communities created the Single Market (the EC92 program) and Australia and New Zealand signed the Closer Economic Relations (CER) agreement. This wave was characterised by 'deep integration' as the participants, who generally had low tariffs on one another's imports, brought non-tariff barriers and other areas into the regional agreement. The third wave began

---

[1]As in other areas of trade policy semantics have been important. The positive-sounding 'preferential trading arrangements' has been a more popular term than 'discriminatory trading arrangements', although any preferential arrangement discriminates negatively against non-preferred trading partners. The WTO uses the term regional trading arrangement, but many of the agreements notified as RTAs involve countries from different regions. The term 'free trade area' is especially abused, being attached to many agreements that leave trade among the signatories far from free.

[2]In the CACM Honduras was dissatisfied with the distribution of perceived benefits even before a 1969 war with El Salvador triggered Honduras' secession from CACM in 1970. In East Africa, discontent over Kenya's perceived lion's share of the benefits and war between Tanzania and Uganda preceded the disbanding of the EAC in 1977.

around the turn of the century and has mainly consisted of bilateral agreements between countries which are not necessarily neighbours, and unlike the previous waves Asian countries were leading participants. Interleaved between these waves, as the desire for discriminatory trade policies weakened, have been major episodes in the strengthening of the multilateral trading system, notably the implementation of the Kennedy Round after 1967 in which tariffs were substantially reduced and completion of the Uruguay Round in 1994 which was followed by the establishment of the WTO.

The attraction and shortcomings of discriminatory trading arrangements can be explained with the help of a few powerful analytical tools. First, it is helpful to draw on a taxonomy of preferential trading arrangements which was set out by Bela Balassa (1961). Define a *free trade area* as a preferential arrangement in which trade among the members is tariff-free, but each member sets its own trade policy towards non-members. A *customs union* is a free trade area plus a common trade policy towards non-members. A common market is a customs union plus free movement of factors of production among members. An economic union is a common market plus common policies, such as macroeconomic policies, competition policies and so forth. No actual arrangement exactly matches these categories (the term 'free trade area' is especially abused), but for analytical purposes it is best to start from clearly defined arrangements.[3]

---

[3]Many see this as a sequence that will be followed, but that is not necessarily so. Brunei and Singapore share a common currency but are not in a customs union. The EU is a customs union with many elements of a common market (but incomplete because, for example, some professional qualifications are not recognised if a person crosses an EU border) and some elements of economic union (e.g. some but not all members have a common monetary policy). Canada is an economic union but provinces have some independence in, say, fiscal policy. In general, integration beyond the free trade area or customs union stage, i.e. *deep integration*, is harder to place in a well-defined taxonomy.

Trade Creation and Trade Diversion

Customs unions were for a long time a controversial and confusing phenomenon in trade theory, because both free traders and protectionists supported them. Free traders supported the freeing of internal trade, while protectionists valued the erecting of a tariff wall around a larger internal market. The crucial analytical insight was developed by Jacob Viner, most clearly in his 1950 book *The Customs Union Issue*, in which he showed that both sides could be right — and both could be wrong.

The key concepts are trade creation and trade diversion. If a trade partner is granted preferential tariff treatment such that their goods sell at less than the tariff-inclusive domestic price, then imports from the preferred partner may increase for two reasons. On the one hand, removal of the tariff may lead to the preferred supplier undercutting and displacing domestic suppliers and the lower cost of imported goods to domestic consumers may induce them to buy more imports; both of these increases in imports from the preferred supplier involve an increase in total trade or **trade creation**. On the other hand, imports from the preferred supplier may displace imports from other countries which were more competitive when all imports were treated equally but are not competitive with tariff-free imports from the preferred supplier; this does not involve any net increase in trade, but rather a change in the source of imports or **trade diversion**.

Preferential trading arrangements increase the welfare of the importing country and of the world when they lead to trade creation. The analysis is similar to that of a general tariff reduction; gains arise from, firstly, replacing domestic production by imports with a lower cost in terms of the resources needed to produce the exports to pay for them and, secondly, from increased consumption when faced with prices closer to true opportunity costs. Preferential trading arrangements reduce the welfare of the world and of the importing country when they lead to trade diversion. There is no change in trade volumes, but production has shifted from the least-cost location to a higher-cost location. For the world the poorer allocation of global resources is obvious. In the importing country consumers gain because they pay lower prices for the diverted imports, but the loss in tariff revenue is greater than the benefit to consumers.

The various impacts on the importing country can be illustrated with a partial equilibrium diagram. In Figure 15.1, the preferred imports sell at a price between the world price, P_w and the tariff-inclusive domestic price, P_d. The preferred supplier sells Q_0Q_3, of which Q_0Q_1 and Q_2Q_3 represent new trade and Q_1Q_2 represents diverted trade. Consumer surplus increases by $a + b + c + d$, producer surplus falls by a, and tariff revenue equal to $c + e$ is lost. The net welfare effect is $b + d - e$, of which the two triangles are the familiar gains from new trade while e is the portion of lost tariff

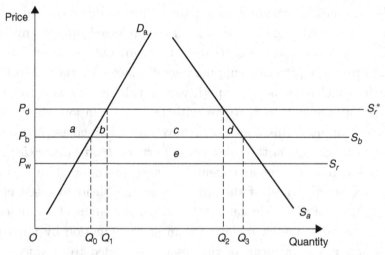

Figure 15.1. Partial equilibrium analysis of discrimination with a perfectly elastic supply of imports.
Note: S_a and D_a are domestic supply and demand curves in A; S_b is the supply of imports from the preferred source B, which is perfectly elastic at a price P_b; S_r is the supply of imports from the rest of the world, and P_w is the world price; S_r^* is the tariff inclusive supply curve, and P_d is the pre-preference domestic price in A.

revenue which is not offset by increased consumer surplus. The net effect can be either positive or negative.

This ambiguous conclusion is an example of the *theory of the second-best*: if there is a reduction in one distortion but other distortions remain in place, then the outcome is not necessarily welfare-improving (Lipsey and Lancaster, 1956–1957). In Figure 15.1 the price distortion caused by a tariff which imposes a wedge between the price of domestic products and the price of imports from the preferred partner is removed, but the wedge between the price of domestic products and the price of imports from non-preferred partners remains and a new distortion is introduced between the price of preferred and non-preferred imports. Without further information, it is impossible to say whether the new distortion is more or less harmful than the one which it displaced.

Ambiguity is not the same as ignorance. Although it is impossible to generalise about customs unions or free trade areas being good or bad, it is possible to analyse individual preferential arrangements and to make some general statements. For example, preferential treatment offered to a country whose price is close to the world price is likely to be more trade–creating and less trade–diverting than similar treatment offered to a country whose price is close to the tariff-inclusive domestic price. Some actual examples will be considered below.

Figure 15.1 illustrates the key concepts, but is unrealistic in its all-or-nothing prediction about the source of imports and in ignoring terms of trade changes. These features follow from the underlying assumptions that the importing country is small and the preferred partner and the rest of the world are both large. An alternative, but more complex diagram, allows all three to be large; in Figure 15.2 all supply curves are upward-sloping.[4] Preferential treatment leads to a shift in the proportion of imports coming from the preferred partner

---

[4]For analysis of Figure 15.2, see Pomfret (2001, 198–200).

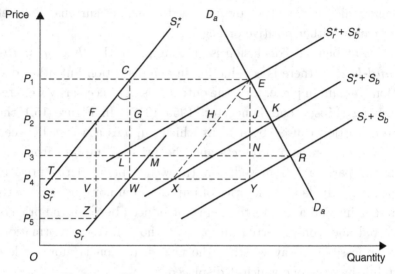

Figure 15.2.   Partial equilibrium analysis of a discriminatory trade barrier with upward-sloping supply curves.
Note: D_a is A's import demand. S_b is the supply of imports from preferred sources, and S_r is the supply of imports from the rest of the world; S_b^* and S_r^* are the same including A's tariff. Assuming no non-tariff barriers or transport costs and no exchange rate changes, E, K and R represent demand-supply equilibria with A's tariff, with free access for B's goods, and without A's tariff, and P_1, P_2 and P_3, are the corresponding prices; P_4 is the price received by exporters to A when A's tariff is in place, and P_5 is the price received by non-preferred exporters to A when B receives preferential access.

and from the rest of the world. The importance of trade creation and trade diversion as determinants of the net welfare effect for the importing country remains. In Figure 15.2 the preferred supplier benefits and the rest of the world loses, both plausible outcomes that are ruled out by the horizontal supply curves in Figure 15.1. The rest of the world loses producer surplus on its exports which no longer exist due to trade diversion and receives a lower price on its remaining exports.

At a more aggregated level, Robert Mundell used a macroeconomic model to illustrate the general equilibrium effects, including the "most important proposition about discriminatory tariff reductions: a tariff reduction in a member country unambiguously improves the terms of trade of the partner country" (Mundell, 1964, 5). The terms of trade effects — positive for the preferred partner, ambiguous for the importing country, and negative for the rest of the world — highlight the potentially confrontational nature of RTAs involving large countries. In the case of the Western European customs union, third parties' concerns were assuaged by active participation in the Kennedy Round and substantial reductions in the common external tariff of the customs union. In many RTAs, the terms of trade effects may be small, but excluded countries fear the negative consequences however uncertain their magnitude.

A more realistic, but analytically more complex, approach would allow for heterogeneous firms. Finite but differing elasticities of substitution between the goods of domestic, preferred and non-preferred countries' firms would prevent all-or-nothing outcomes while introducing differing conditions for preferred country firms and non-preferred countries' firms. However, such disaggregation would not challenge the two core results from the simple models. First, RTAs are from the world of second-best, with ambiguous welfare outcomes for those involved in the RTA, reflecting the balance between trade creation and trade diversion. Second, terms of trade effects of predictable direction but uncertain magnitude create tensions between possible winners and certain losers.

Free Trade Areas versus Customs Unions

On the surface customs unions seem less likely to exist than free trade areas (FTAs), because while both require the members to agree to free trade among themselves, a customs union also requires them to agree on a common trade policy towards third countries. In addition, customs unions typically involve agreement on the use of tariff revenue, because the points of entry for dutiable goods from third countries may not be evenly spread; for example, many German imports enter through the Dutch port of Rotterdam where they pay any EU customs duties, so that without an agreement on tariff revenue the Netherlands would receive a disproportionately large share of the revenue and Germany would receive little revenue. Trade policy and fiscal policy are two areas that nation states have historically guarded very carefully.

FTAs do, however, face a problem of *trade deflection*. If two countries form a FTA there is an incentive for third countries to ship all of their exports to the FTA through the low-tariff member and then trans-ship them to other FTA members duty-free. In response to this, most FTAs have rules of origin to determine whether a good crossing internal borders actually comes from a member country. This necessity for checking goods at internal borders, which can be dismantled in a customs union, adds to the trade costs within a FTA.

More importantly, even if rules of origin are imposed and effective, indirect trade deflection can still undermine policy independence. If goods are reasonably homogeneous, then the low-tariff country can import from outside the FTA, and its producers can supply the other FTA members. This is worthwhile for the internal supplier because prices in other FTA members are higher than in the low-tariff country.[5] Shibata (1967) showed that the outcome is the same as with direct trade deflection: all of the tariff revenue accrues to the low-tariff country and the high-tariff countries are unable to protect their producers because internal trade will grow until prices are equalised. Figure 15.3 illustrates the outcome when two small countries, 'Norway' and 'Sweden,' form an FTA. The welfare-maximising response by all FTA members should be to cut their external tariffs

---

[5] An example of the benefits to the 'internal supplier' in a different context is the natural gas trade between the Commonwealth of Independent States and Western Europe. Russia, although it is the world's largest gas exporter, imports large amounts of gas from Turkmenistan, the world's fourth largest exporter. Russia pays Turkmenistan a lower price than it receives for its gas exports to Europe. The imports allow Russia to export more of its own gas and make a profit on the price differential, while Turkmenistan and Europe cannot deal directly with one another because Turkmenistan's pipeline network ties it to sending almost all of its gas through Russia.

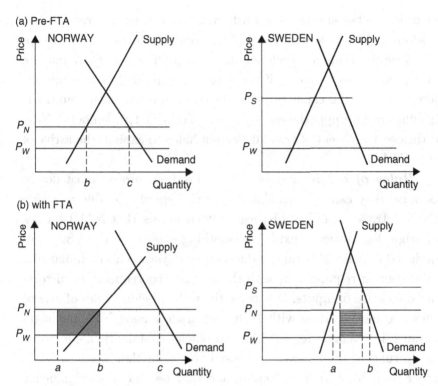

Figure 15.3.   Direct and indirect trade deflection.
Note: Before the FTA both countries have tariffs that raise their domestic prices, P_N in Norway and P_S in Sweden, above the world price, P_W. After forming a FTA, imports from Norway will drive the Swedish price down to P_N. Norwegian demand and supply are unchanged, but part of its output (ab) is now sold in Sweden and a corresponding quantity is imported from outside the FTA. Norwegian consumers and producers are unaffected, but national welfare is increased by the added tariff revenue $(ab(P_N - P_W))$. Swedish consumers benefit by more than the loss to Swedish producers, but the net welfare effect is ambiguous owing to the disappearance of tariff revenue. The extra tariff revenue to Norway must exceed the loss of tariff revenue to Sweden that is not offset by consumer gains (i.e. the shaded area is larger than the stiped area); the FTA as a whole must benefit from the displacement of high-cost internal suppliers by external imports. There is no trade diversion, so the global welfare effect is positive. By lowering its tariff so that $P_S < P_{N'}$ Sweden could ensure that it enjoys a net welfare gain, but that will initiate a race to the bottom in which the equilibrium external tariffs are zero.

in order to become the low-tariff country, but such a race to the bottom and its logical outcome of free trade with respect to all suppliers would terminate preferential trading. Of course, there may be obstacles to this outcome, if transport costs are high, goods are differentiated or the capacity of producers in the low-tariff country is insufficient to supply the entire market of other FTA members.[6] Nevertheless, the threat of trade deflection helps to explain the rarity of true FTAs.

Rules of origin may be a more insidious protectionist device because they can be formulated to assist specific producers inside the free trade area. Anne Krueger (1993) argues that NAFTA rules of origin for Mexican textile and clothing exports to the USA were designed to make Mexican producers use US yarn. This is similar to a local content requirement, with the negative consequence of distorting the choice of inputs. Whatever the reason behind rules of origin, they are incompatible with truly free trade among FTA members because internal trade is subject to official examination. Moreover many rules of origin are more restrictive than they need to be in order to address trade deflection, and they become more significant and more complex as production processes become more fragmented. Complexity not only discourages imports from outside the FTA, but high compliance costs may reduce take-up of preferential tariffs if the preference margin is small.

There is no agreed format for rules of origin. Rules of origin are redundant if a good is entirely made in one country. Otherwise the rules are usually based on one of three criteria: the percentage of value-added where the last substantial transformation took place, a change of tariff classification as an indicator of such a transformation, or a technical test for which the justification is the product-specific requirement of transformation. The first two are the most common, but there are many variations (Estevadeordal and Suominen, 2006). The advantage of a percentage rule is that it can set a standard across

---

[6]Martin Richardson (1995) assumes producer rather than consumer arbitrage and shows that the race to the bottom may stop while external tariffs are still positive.

products, although in practice the percentage is often manipulated to protect favoured producers and it can create unpredictability for traders (e.g. exchange rate fluctuations can change the percentage of value-added taking place in a country). A change of tariff classification rule, which is the basis for EU and NAFTA rules of origin, may be simpler but it involves using the Harmonised System of Tariff Classification (HS) for a purpose for which it was not designed and for which in some cases it may be inappropriate, and the rules of origin can be manipulated by selecting the level of HS aggregation.[7] Apart from the NAFTA textile rules, product-specific technical tests are common in hi-tech industries in which producers' expertise often has to be called upon. However, when the domestic industry plays a role in designing such rules they can become protectionist devices or even give firm-specific advantages which distort global trade flows; the outcome is likely to be rules of origin which encourage trade diversion in favour of internal suppliers rather than trade creation at the expense of domestic suppliers.

The European Union

The European Union is the most important example of a customs union in the world economy and its evolution sheds some light on the

---

[7]The Harmonised System is an international product nomenclature developed by the World Customs Organisation (WCO) to implement the 1974 International Convention on the Simplification and Harmonisation of Customs procedures (the Kyoto Convention, not to be confused with a later Kyoto Convention on climate). Introduced in 1988, the HS comprises about 5,000 commodity groups, each identified by a six-digit code, which are aggregated into just over 1,200 four-digit headings, which in turn are in 96 two-digit chapters; e.g. chapter 22 is alcoholic beverages, 2208 is denatured spirits, and 220840 is rum. Countries can add finer levels of disaggregation but they must be consistent with the detailed definitions of the commodity groups. The system is used by more than 200 countries and economies as a basis for their customs tariffs and for the collection of international trade statistics, and over 98% of the merchandise in international trade is classified in terms of the HS. By strengthening transparency in the definition of goods covered by a tariff the HS contributes to the efficient operation of the GATT/WTO system.

process of regional integration. The origins of the EU lie in the devastated Europe of the late 1940s, following three wars between France and Germany in which territory had been transferred backwards and forwards and millions had been killed. One initiative towards regional integration was the Organisation for European Economic Cooperation (OEEC) which was established in 1948 to promote economic cooperation and trade liberalisation among recipients of Marshall Plan aid from the USA. The OEEC's primary role was in improving payments mechanisms; as the European currencies became convertible in the late 1950s it lost its role and was transformed into the Organisation for Economic Cooperation and Development with a wider membership of high-income countries. A second initiative followed the French government's decision that, rather than benefiting from Germany's temporary weakness in defeat as in 1919, it should try to make future wars less likely by integrating the iron and steel industries which were the basis for military production. In 1951, the European Coal and Steel Community was created. France and Germany were joined by Belgium, Italy, Luxembourg and the Netherlands, but other European countries stayed out because they disliked the idea of a supranational authority administering such important industries. The idea of a federal Europe had many supporters but, after a proposal to form a European Defence Force was defeated in the French Parliament, the emphasis was placed on economic rather than political integration. In 1957, the six European Coal and Steel Community countries signed the *Treaty of Rome* which established the European Communities: an economic community with a customs union and common policies in areas such as transport and atomic energy.

The customs union was completed by 1968. The process was facilitated by political support from the USA for a more unified Western Europe. Concerns among GATT signatories about the negative impact on non-member countries were neutralised by active participation in the Kennedy Round of multilateral trade negotiations, where the European Community negotiated as a single unit and successfully agreed on a package that included substantial reductions in its own common external tariff. The most controversial policy area was agriculture, but following US precedent in the 1950s this sector was kept outside GATT.

The dynamism of the six countries in the customs union encouraged other countries to want to join. In 1961 Greece signed an association agreement which envisaged membership after a 22-year transition period; the agreement was frozen after the 1967 military coup in Greece and unfrozen after the re-establishment of democracy in 1974, and Greece became a member in 1981. Following Greece's association agreement Turkey applied for associate status, which the Six granted slightly more reluctantly, and without a timetable for membership — Turkey is still waiting to join.

The United Kingdom, which had initially responded by forming the European Free Trade Association (EFTA) with six smaller countries, opted to join the customs union, together with Ireland and Denmark, in 1973. The UK had initially chosen not to sign the Treaty of Rome because it disliked the supranational institutions, but the greater dynamism of an organisation which included the three other large Western European economies was too great an attraction. By staying out at the start, the UK had no seat at the table when the common agricultural policy was devised. When the UK joined the customs union, it might have enjoyed some trade creation gains on trade in manufactures but it suffered large net economic losses due to trade diversion in agriculture.

The success of the customs union encouraged the political leaders to move towards closer economic union through monetary union. This ambitious agenda began with a tighter fixed exchange rate regime in 1972, but within weeks the UK, Italy and France had abandoned the fixed exchange rates; France rejoined, but then exited again in 1976, leaving only Germany and some smaller countries behind, and the plan was dead. The large countries placed too much weight on having independent monetary policies for them to accept such an arrangement. Surprisingly, however, the political leaders almost immediately devised a new exchange rate arrangement very similar to the one that had collapsed, and in 1979 eight of the then nine EC member countries joined the European Monetary System. Why the rush back to exchange rate stability? Large exchange rate fluctuations undermined the functioning of the customs union because they distort price signals. They were especially problematic for common policies, notably agriculture. The farm prices which would be supported during each coming year were determined by hard bargaining and, if the delicate balance was disrupted by large bilateral exchange rate changes which revised the gains and losses to farmers, food-buyers or taxpayers in different directions in different member countries, there would be political dissatisfaction and pressure for constant renegotiation.

Failure of the first attempt at monetary union, difficulty integrating Greece and perhaps most of all a troubled world economy, left the European Communities in the doldrums during the early 1980s. There were concerns about further expansion to include Spain and Portugal in 1986, which had been deemed politically unavoidable when those countries like Greece overthrew dictatorships in the mid-1970s. The response to these troubles was the 1986 Single European Act, which envisaged completion of the internal market by 1992 by reducing non-tariff barriers to internal trade, especially when the NTBs took the form of national regulations which were unjustified on health or safety grounds.[8] The process had begun in the 1979 Cassis de Dijon case, when the European Court determined that, as long as the product met French standards and posed no health or safety risk, Germany could not ban sale of the French drink on the grounds that it did not meet German regulations about alcohol

---

[8]The 1992 program also ended the anomalous national import quotas on textiles and clothing, cars, footwear, bicycles and many other goods, which required internal controls to prevent transshipment from less sheltered to more sheltered national markets (i.e. trade deflection).

content. The principle of mutual recognition was a powerful tool for removing NTBs. In tricky cases it was reinforced by harmonisation, a more time-consuming process of producing a single regulation. Despite concerns that bureaucrats were imposing supranational standards on everything from German beer to British sausages, the EC92 process ended up being popular and successful. In 1992 the now twelve member countries signed the Maastricht Treaty changing the name of the regional organisation to the European Union and, among other things, setting out a timetable for establishing monetary union. By the end of the 1990s a common currency, the euro, had been established for financial transactions and in 2002 euro banknotes circulated.

The reinvigoration of the EU was associated with further expansions. As the political situation in eastern Europe changed following the shredding of the iron curtain and dissolution of the Soviet Union, Austria, Finland and Sweden joined the EU in 1995, followed in 2004 by eight eastern European countries together with the two island economies Malta and Cyprus, and then in 2007 by Bulgaria and Romania. However, not all EU members are happy with the enlargements, and some have imposed transitional periods during which EU rights such as on the movement of labour are not fully granted. There is concern about the limits of future expansion in the Balkans and to the east, and most notably the position of Turkey. There are also reservations about the degree of integration, and not all EU members joined the eurozone; the UK, Sweden and Denmark chose to retain their national currencies.

The EU is unique in the past half century for its progress towards deeper and wider integration which has left it somewhere between a RTA and a federal state. The shortcomings of a customs union that does not cover non-tariff barriers or monetary cooperation led to ever deeper integration, which has caused some members to worry about loss of sovereignty and some potential members (Norway, Switzerland and Iceland) have chosen to remain completely outside the process for this reason. The net economic benefits have been positive for most members, but some have clearly experienced greater trade diversion losses than trade creation gains, notably the UK, and the slowest pace in lowering external trade barriers was in sectors where trade diversion was greatest (cars, steel, textiles and clothing, as well as agriculture).[9] Many of these benefits could have also been realised by non-discriminatory trade liberalisation, but an overriding reason for the RTA was political, as it was with the Italian, Canadian, German and Australian customs unions of the 19th and early 20th centuries.

Evidence on Other Discriminatory Trading Arrangements

During the 1960s many countries in Central and South America and in Africa followed the European lead in forming customs unions or free trade areas. Some of these existed on paper only, as gestures of friendship but with no implementation. The ones that were implemented were typically among countries pursuing import-substituting industrialisation strategies and the RTA was seen as a way of securing a larger internal market for domestic industries. Without exception, these RTAs failed to have a lasting economic impact and in two of the most promising, the Central American Common Market and the East African Community, members fought wars against one another (Pomfret, 2001, 297–303). The economic basis for failure was that these RTAs overwhelmingly led to trade diversion rather than trade creation. In the East African Community, for example, Kenya was happy to have a market in Uganda and Tanzania for its fledgling industries, but was not happy to purchase manufactured goods from its partners when imports from elsewhere were superior,

---

[9]The trade diversion bias reflects the political economy of trade policy. Domestic producers will oppose measures leading to trade creation but are indifferent to trade diversion, whereas consumers and taxpayers tend to have less direct influence on policy formation.

while Tanzania and Uganda were dissatisfied that industrial development continued to be concentrated in Kenya. In the EU, free trade in manufactures is trade–creating because the union's most efficient supplier is likely to be at or close to the world price, but this is highly unlikely in groupings of small low-income countries.

The one-way preferential tariff treatment granted by the EU to former colonies was more resilient. The Treaty of Rome provided special associate status for colonies and the 1963 Yaoundé Convention gave former colonies duty-free access to all Six member countries' markets. After the accession of the UK preferential treatment was extended to a wider group of African, Caribbean and Pacific countries in the four Lomé Conventions, which ran from 1975 to 2000 and included special treatment for key agricultural goods and a price stabilisation scheme for minerals exports, covering 77 countries by 2000. For the EU, which had no foreign policy instruments, this was a relatively low-cost way of retaining special ties with former colonies. For a small country, receiving preferential access to a large country's market is a costless benefit. In Figure 15.4 duty-free treatment means that the exporter receives the domestic price P_d instead of the world price P_w; exports increase from OA to OB and producer surplus increases by $\alpha + \beta$. Even if exports are price inelastic, there is a windfall gain from the surplus on existing exports OA. The Yaoundé and Lomé Conventions illustrate Viner's generalisation that preferential trade arrangements between large and small countries are based on political considerations for the large partner and economic considerations for the small partners. As the EU's MFN tariffs fell, the preference margins were eroded and its preferential arrangements with small partners declined in attractiveness, especially as the EU developed alternative foreign policy instruments and the WTO outlawed some of the measures in 2000.[10]

---

[10]In order to make the arrangements consistent with the WTO Article XXIV, the Lomé Conventions were to be replaced by broader Economic Partnership Agreements established after a seven-year transitional arrangement, the Cotonou

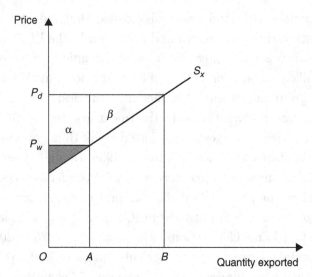

Figure 15.4.   Trade preferences for a small country.
Note: S_X is the preference recipient's export supply curve, P_w is the export price received without the trade preference, and P_d is the price received with the trade preference.

The Generalised System of Preferences (GSP) schemes introduced after 1971 similarly offered a no-cost windfall gain to developing countries, but the benefits turned out to be disappointing. In practice, developing countries benefiting from the GSP schemes found that the gains were limited because if exports of a good increased by too much then quantitative limits on preferential treatment would be imposed, or if there was a general increase in exports the country would be graduated out of GSP. In sum, the rich

Agreement. The EU was also required, after losing a WTO case, to revise the special regime for banana imports from ACP countries, which discriminated against non-ACP suppliers. South Africa signed an RTA with the EU in 2004. The other ACP countries were reluctant to open their markets to EU goods and were concerned about the loss in tariff revenue. Fifteen members of the Caribbean Forum signed a new reciprocal trade agreement with the EU in December 2007 and 20 other ACP countries signed Interim Economic Partnership Agreements, while 32 least developed countries qualify for free access to EU markets for Everything But Arms, and the remaining nine settled for access to EU markets under the EU's GSP scheme.

countries were content to transfer tariff revenue to poor countries (area α), but, if tariff barriers were protecting powerful domestic producers, then they would not allow AB to be large. This illustration of the limitations of non-contractual market access encouraged many developing countries to think about joining the GATT/WTO and lobbying for better MFN treatment on goods of interest to them, such as clothing, although less dynamic developing countries worried about losing preferential access (and area α).

In view of the theoretical ambiguity of the consequences of discriminatory trading arrangements, it might be expected that measurement of their consequences would be more precise than the above descriptions. The major problem is that, unlike measurement of the impact of a non-discriminatory tariff which requires knowledge only of the cross-price relationships between domestic and foreign goods, measurement of the impact of a discriminatory tariff requires knowledge of the cross-price elasticities with relevant non-beneficiaries. When, for example, Greece, Portugal and Spain joined the EU the balance between trade creation and trade diversion depended upon how many EU imports of oranges might be diverted from Morocco or Tunisia, whereas when Austria, Finland and Sweden joined a decade later a different set of competitors was relevant.[11] Multi-region computable general equilibrium models often invoke the Armington assumption, that the substitutability between goods is the same for any pair of countries, which simplifies computation but is clearly unrealistic, and in a way that is critical when dealing with discriminatory trade policies; the results are biased towards overestimating trade creation or trade diversion, depending on the inbuilt assumptions, which limits their value as independent measure.[12]

---

[11]The Finger and Kreinin (1979) export similarity index can give an idea of which third countries are likely to be most affected by a preferential trade policy (Pomfret, 1981), but measuring the size of the impact requires knowledge of cross-price elasticities.

[12]Partial equilibrium models were used in the 1950s and 1960s to measure the consequences of RTAs, but by assuming horizontal supply curves (as in Figure 15.1)

The second and third waves of discriminatory trading arrangements are less easy to analyse with the tools developed in this chapter. The deep integration of the second wave occurred in countries whose tariffs were already low and hence the potential for trade creation or trade diversion was limited. In key respects deep integration is more about reducing the behind-the-border trade costs to be discussed in Chapter 17.

An approach to measuring the impact of any kind of RTA is to examine whether trade flows are different before and after the agreement. This was pioneered in a study by Aitken (1973) of the impact of the Treaty of Rome and of EFTA, which he measured by comparing the share of trade which countries conducted with their fellow RTA members before and after the agreement. This approach, which is commonly used in popular debates, is flawed because many factors influence the direction of trade. In Southeast Asia, for example, intra-ASEAN trade was low in the 1970s and 1980s despite the existence of the RTA, and the share of intra-regional in total trade increased after the mid-1990s with the development of regional value chains which had little to do with the existence of an RTA. As with any policy, the true measure of its impact is a 'with and without' comparison, not a 'before and after' comparison.

Many researchers have used the gravity model to assess the impact of RTAs on bilateral trade flows by including a dummy for the existence of a trade agreement between any pair of countries. This literature has been inconclusive, in part because it suffers from a similar drawback to the trade shares approach; the results depend upon which other control variables are included (e.g. a common border or a shared colonial legacy are closely related to RTA membership). The gravity studies' results also depend upon which RTAs are

---

they excluded realistic consequences (as in Figure 15.2). An influential early assessment of GSP by Baldwin and Murray (1977) tried to avoid the need for cross-price elasticities (or varying export supply curves), but their simplifying assumptions were biased towards finding trade creation (Pomfret, 1986b).

included in a global analysis of trade flows and which are excluded as merely paper agreements; RTAs like the EU and NAFTA are serious agreements, while many agreements were no more than statements of friendship and others were less than preferential (e.g. India and Pakistan were members of the South Asian Association for Regional Cooperation but at times in the 1990s their bilateral trade was on worse than MFN terms). However, if a prior decision is taken to exclude all RTAs that are believed to have had no effect, then the results are hardly a general assessment of the impact of RTAs.

Is Regionalism a Threat to the Multilateral Trading System?

There is an inconclusive theoretical literature about whether preferential trading arrangements are a building block or a stumbling block in constructing a global economy based on multilateral free trade. Kemp and Wan (1976) showed that if FTAs are required not to harm third parties and that FTAs will always be formed whenever there is an opportunity to improve members' welfare, then FTA formation will eventually lead to global free trade. The Kemp–Wan argument assumes that FTAs can be tailor-made to avoid losers or that losers are compensated and that FTAs involve no negotiation costs. If negotiations costs are an obstacle to trade liberalisation in the GATT/WTO framework which requires consensus among over 150 countries, then FTAs may provide a short-cut to global free trade through competitive liberalisation. It may also be easier to negotiate WTO–Plus items such as TRIPS among like-minded countries than within the WTO. On the other hand, negotiating preferential trading arrangements distracts trade policy makers from the multilateral arena and creates vested interests who benefit from the discriminatory trade measures and will oppose general trade liberalisation.[13]

---

[13]The building block imagery is due to Jagdish Bhagwati, who comes down strongly on the stumbling block side of the debate; see, for example, Bhagwati and Panagariya (1996).

Each wave of discriminatory trading arrangements has aroused fears that the multilateral trading system is under threat. The first wave posed a challenge to the nascent GATT system (Patterson, 1966), but proved to be an empty threat because the European customs union took steps to reduce costs to outsiders by lowering its external tariff in the Kennedy Round, the USA supported regional integration in Western Europe and remained true to the non-discrimination principle in its own trade policies, and customs unions and other arrangements among protectionist and nationalist developing countries were doomed because of their high trade diversion content. The second wave led to fears of the world economy splitting into three trade blocs as the USA signed NAFTA and proposed a Free Trade Area of the Americas, the EU created a tighter economic arrangement with special ties to Africa, and Asia was left by default as the third unit. The nightmare was succoured by simple models which showed that three blocs was a plausible outcome of FTA formation and also the worst number for global welfare (Krugman, 1991). Again, however, fears were misplaced as the USA and EU cooperated to bring the Uruguay Round to a conclusion and create the WTO, strengthening the multilateral system. Deep integration has generally turned out to be a good thing because non-members as well as members benefit from, for example, harmonised standards for all EU countries.

In the 1970s and 1990s the multilateral system emerged stronger than ever. Will this happen after the third wave of RTAs? The current wave contains many diverse agreements, the majority of which are bilateral with specific and limited terms. The agreements signed by the USA have rewarded allies, and the economic goals have been narrowly targeted on WTO–Plus items, usually extending TRIPs or TRIMs.[14] Although the agreements go beyond WTO obligations in

---

[14]The political element is illustrated by the differing treatment of New Zealand and Australia. As a critic of US policy, New Zealand has been cold-shouldered, while as a close ally Australia was rewarded with an FTA. The FTA's content was,

some cases, they are often WTO-lite in other areas because the US negotiators do not take on powerful domestic lobbies.

The Asian agreements in the third wave are harder to categorise. The 1978 Asian Crisis was a catalyst because many countries felt that international institutions such as the IMF served the region poorly in its hour of need and therefore regional arrangements were needed. Japan led a push for monetary integration and the 2000 Chiang Mai Initiative created currency swap arrangements among the ten ASEAN countries, China, Japan and South Korea (ASEAN+3), but after that regionalism fizzled out in the monetary area. A second catalyst was the emergence of regional value chains in East Asia; before the 1990s the fast-growing Asian economies mostly traded outside the region, with North America, Western Europe or Australia, but intra-Asian trade began to grow rapidly during the 1990s and this suggested a need for institutional arrangements to facilitate regional trade. The open regionalism of Asia Pacific Economic Cooperation (APEC) was inadequate, and China in particular sought an East Asian solution once it had completed its WTO accession in 2001. The outcome was the 2004 China–ASEAN free trade agreement.

By number, however, most of the agreements negotiated by Asian countries since 2000 have been bilateral and often not with neighbours (i.e. not strictly *regional* trading arrangements) and always with minor impact. The first one, between Japan and Singapore, involved two countries with low tariffs on manufactured goods and no interest in bilateral trade in agricultural goods. The Japan–Thailand agreement's main items were reduced tariffs on car components entering Thailand, mainly bound for Japanese-owned factories, and

---

however, mainly limited to Australia accepting US requests for stricter protection of pharmaceutical companies' patent rights in return for limited improvements in access to US markets for some farm exports. To call the result of such an agreement a free trade area is highly misleading because on most of their bilateral trade Australia and the USA already had low tariffs and goods where trade liberalisation would have made a difference (e.g. allowing Australian sugar into the US market) were excluded.

simplified procedures for work permits for Thais working temporarily in Japan; the agreement was disparagingly referred to by Japanese economists as the Thai cooks' agreement. These agreements are minor examples of deep integration or similar to earlier treaties such as double-taxation agreements, or in the extreme case little more than declarations of bilateral friendship; in all cases the terms FTA or RTA are much too grandiose.[15]

One conclusion is that counting RTAs, as in the WTO's chart at the start of this chapter, is not a meaningful way to measure their significance. Some RTAs are of major importance to the world economy, the EU being the most obvious, but many agreements that are signed are trivial because of the exclusions, or because trade between the signatories is tiny, or because the agreement is never implemented.[16] Are they a threat to the system? Probably not, as long as they are not taken too seriously, and the benefits of non-discriminatory trade continue to be recognised, but there is always a danger that RTAs will arouse discontent in excluded countries and proliferate to the point of undermining the multilateral system.

A common fear about the spread of RTAs is that they are creating a more complex global trading system. Already by the end of the 1960s the European Community's "pyramid of preferences" was seen as a problem because beneficiaries of preferential treatment may not

---

[15]The declaratory nature of trade agreements is most pronounced in the former Soviet Union where over 250 trade agreements have been announced, the overwhelming majority of which were never heard of again after the presidents departed from the summit where they declared bilateral amity.

[16]The post-1990 proliferation of RTAs was driven by the disintegration of the USSR, Yugoslavia and Czechoslovakia each of which was followed by new agreements among the new countries and between the new countries and others. This was a sign of disintegration rather than regional integration. When eight of the eastern European countries joined the EU in 2004 over 60 RTAs among the new members became redundant, but this net reduction is not taken into account in the WTO chart. Since 1995 there is double-counting because many agreements are notified to the WTO under GATT and GATS whereas before 1995 they would only have been notified once. Pomfret (2007) analyses these issues.

realise where they stood in the hierarchy and there were plenty of sources of complaint about unfairness relative to competitors.[17] The term spaghetti bowl was coined to capture this confusion, and when Asian countries jumped on the RTA bandwagon in the 2000s writers on Asian trade talked about the noodle bowl effect.

In itself the proliferation of RTAs may not be so important if they have little impact. Traders can choose not to avail themselves of preferential access if the MFN tariffs are low, and there is evidence within many RTAs of this happening and that the costs of foregone preferential access are minor.[18] More serious misallocation may arise from measures which increase the complexity of RTAs' operation, in particular rules of origin which are more restrictive than they need to be in order to prevent trade deflection and which may be tailor-made to distort or discourage trade as production processes become more complex.

---

[17]The approximate hierarchy in the 1970s was associates (Greece, Turkey) at the top, followed by EFTA countries who had free trade in manufactures with the EC, other Mediterranean countries, the ACP countries, countries eligible for GSP treatment, the handful of countries receiving MFN treatment (USA, Canada, Japan, Australia, New Zealand, Taiwan, South Korea), and finally the centrally planned economies who were treated in an *ad hoc* way. The complexity of arrangements intended to create a hierarchy meant that the ranking was imprecise; a country might receive preferential treatment over its neighbour in one good and inferior treatment in another good.

[18]For example, it is believed that many imports from the country's ASEAN partners enter Singapore at the MFN rate, rather than trying to claim ASEAN preferential treatment. Because Singapore's MFN tariffs are low, and on many items zero, it is scarcely worth the effort to discover if there is a preferential tariff rate and then claim preferential access.

Chapter 16

Trade and Development

One of the most influential criticisms of neoclassical trade theory has been that, although it shows the resource allocation costs of trade barriers, it fails to capture dynamic elements of trade policy. This view was at its peak in the 1940s and 1950s, coinciding with global decolonisation and the coming to power of modernising governments in what became known as the Third World. Without exception, these countries adopted development strategies which shielded their economies from international trade.

Proponents of the dynamic benefits of protectionism cited the success of Germany and the USA in the late 19th and early 20th century when, behind high tariff barriers, they caught up to and overtook Britain as the dominant industrial powers. From a larger set of countries, Kevin O'Rourke (2000) reports a positive correlation between tariffs and growth in the 19th century. Clemens and Williamson (2002) find the same result during the first half of the 20th century, although the relationship changes after 1950. These generalisations have however been disputed by Doug Irwin (2002), who shows that the correlation depends upon a group of fast-growing settler economies (Argentina, Australia and Canada) which were open economies but whose governments used high tariffs for revenue. In sum, the historical evidence on the long-term relationship between trade policy and growth or industrialisation is inconclusive; the sample of developed economies is not large and many other forces influenced those countries' economic growth in the two centuries following the industrial revolution of the late 1700s.

Policymakers in the Third World in the late 1940s and 1950s were strongly influenced by recent events. The decline in commodity prices, which began in 1928 with terrible consequences for some countries (e.g. Cuba's GDP fell by two-thirds after world sugar prices collapsed), convinced many policymakers of the dangers of participating in international markets.[1] The success of the Soviet Union, which unlike capitalist Russia in 1914 had withstood invasion in 1941 and through its industrial strength defeated Germany in World War II and went on in the 1950s to launch the first man in space, encouraged many to believe in the possibility of autarchic development with little attention to the price mechanism. The example of Japan, whose rapid growth with (externally enforced) free trade policies had led it to military victories over China in 1895, Russia in 1905 and Britain in 1941–1942, was written off after its defeat in 1945. Finally,

---

[1] Hans Singer and Raul Prebisch argued that primary product exporters inevitably faced declining terms of trade because the income elasticity of demand for primary products is less than that of manufactures. The opposite case could be made: the relative price of primary products will rise over time because of supply constraints. During the 1950s and 1960s the evidence seemed to support the Singer–Prebisch hypothesis, but the commodity booms of the 1970s reversed the trend. Overall, the empirical evidence is mixed depending on the choice of time period (the early 1950s happened to be years of strong demand for primary products due to the Korean War) and the specific commodities. Over the 20th century, the relative price fell for some commodities (e.g. rubber or wool), increased for some (e.g. tobacco or lamb), and for others showed no clear trend (Kellard and Wohar, 2006).

the popularity of Keynesian macroeconomics in the 1950s and 1960s encouraged distrust of neoclassical economic theory; theorising based on assumptions of market distortions led to a new sub-discipline of development economics.

The universal adoption of import-substitution policies in the Third World provided a convincing experiment on the dynamic consequences of trade policies. The ultimate failure of import-substitution policies strongly supports the analysis in Chapters 11 to 13. The contrasting success stories of a handful of Asian economies which turned to more outward-oriented development strategies from the 1960s onwards reinforced the message that the central conclusions of trade theory are universal and not just applicable to rich countries.

Import-substituting Industrialisation

An old argument for protection is the *infant industry argument*, which states that an industry may need time to establish itself and there may be a net social benefit from protecting the industry through its infancy. The argument is logically sound, although it is sometimes forgotten that the industry eventually becoming competitive is not sufficient justification for infant-industry protection; the discounted stream of future benefits must exceed the initial costs of protection. The infant industry argument is a classic second-best case for protection, and the best policy is that which tackles the distortion as close to its source as possible. A subsidy would be superior to a tariff. Capital market reform is likely to be better still, so that a would-be producer can borrow to cover the initial losses and repay the debt out of the eventual profits. A subsidy or capital market reform would have the added benefit of dealing with infants who never grow up; such industries become adept at lobbying for continuation of their tariff protection for a little longer and given the stickiness in tariffs they often succeed, but governments are less likely to continue paying out subsidies and banks will not keep rolling over loans.

The novelty of the trade policies adopted by Third World countries was that, although they sometimes referred to the need for infant industry protection, their trade policies introduced across-the-board protection for industry rather than tariffs on selected products with potential for becoming internationally competitive. *Import-substituting industrialisation* (ISI) policies had many variants around the common central theme of promoting industrial development by encouraging domestic production of goods which were being imported. In Latin America, apart from post-1959 Cuba, tariffs were high because the economies were based on private enterprise and the price mechanism. Cuba, like China after 1949 and several other countries, adopted the Soviet model of central planning and state ownership in which prices had little relevance. India, whose intellectual influence was great, adopted a middle way of directing investment towards public enterprises but allowing the private sector and market forces to operate; ISI was pursued by mobilising resources through tax policies which were used to finance heavy industry and by an increasingly complex web of regulations, including detailed import licensing and quotas, which protected producers from competition. Iran was open in the sense of having a high export/GDP ratio, but used its oil revenues to finance heavily protected import-competing industries. Turkey did little planning but the state-owned banks directed credit to import-competing industries. In all cases the effective rate of protection for industries, and especially the most capital-intensive industries, was high. Agriculture and export activities were neglected and the relative price structure ensured that resources were directed away from those sectors.

The consequences were illustrated in a series of country case studies.[2] Initially, ISI strategies brought high growth rates because

---

[2]The evidence against ISI was presented most effectively in an OECD project (Little, Scitovsky and Scott, 1970) and in an NBER project coordinated by Anne Krueger and Jagdish Bhagwati, as well as in projects coordinated by Bela Balassa for the World Bank and by Juergen Donges at the Institut für Weltwirtschaft in Kiel, Germany.

they were associated with modernising regimes which managed to better mobilise national resources. Early industrial development might involve relatively easy ISI, in activities with high natural protection due to their bulk/value ratio and mature technology, such as beer or cement, and hence the resource misallocation was not very severe. Once the domestic market for these products had been filled, the strategy entailed moving into more difficult ISI where the resource misallocation costs would be greater. High rates of effective protection led to misallocation, captured in high domestic resource costs of saving a dollar's worth of imports relative to the resources needed to produce a dollar's worth of exports to pay for the imports. The inefficient allocation of scarce capital was reflected in higher incremental capital–output ratios; under normal conditions in a reasonably efficient economy 3–4 dollars' worth of investment generates an additional dollar's worth of GDP, but in India, for example, the incremental capital–output ratio had increased to over ten by the mid-1970s. Because ISI policies, in contrast to developing countries' comparative advantage, encouraged capital-intensive activities, even the high initial growth rates failed to generate much employment. High wage rates in the protected industries encouraged rural-urban migration, and migrants spent time being underemployed while trying to position themselves for the well-paid but scarce jobs in the modern sector; whether in Lagos, Mexico City, Rio de Janeiro, Dhaka or Calcutta, a concomitant of ISI strategies pursued over decades was large urban slums. It should be no surprise that promoting capital–intensive industries in labour-abundant countries led to more unequal income distribution, although cross-country differences in equality also depended on other things beside trade policies. Finally, the measures supporting ISI strategies, with their extensive controls which typically included restrictive import quotas, provided fertile ground for increased corruption.

Despite the mounting evidence against ISI strategies, becoming clear after perhaps 10–15 years in larger economies such as India and sooner in countries with smaller domestic markets, reversing the strategy was everywhere difficult due to the vested interests that had been created. Owners and workers in protected industries opposed change, and often controlled the government or found ready support within the bureaucracy. The symptoms of the failure of ISI varied, with the common underlying thread of resource misallocation. In India, disastrous harvests in the mid-1960s highlighted the neglect of agriculture and absence of export industries whose earnings could finance food imports, but for another quarter of a century the government adopted ineffective piecemeal reforms and subsidised the sheltered industries; only when the costs of supporting sick companies overwhelmed the public budget in the 1980s did the government finally bite the bullet and adopt thoroughgoing reform in 1991. In many Latin American countries, the key symptom of failure was build-up of external debt during the 1970s, followed by the 1982 Debt Crisis. Some countries undertook drastic reform, such as Thailand in 1981–1982 or China in 1978–1979, while others such as Turkey or Brazil went through several cycles of partial reform followed by crises and further partial reforms.

By the end of the 20th century, ISI strategies were discredited almost everywhere, but vestiges of these policies remain strong in many countries. An important lesson was that ignoring trade theory and specialising according to comparative disadvantage had been costly, but the real proof for policymakers came from actual experiences rather than logical arguments, and the costs took decades to become indisputably clear. Another lesson was that although policymakers sometimes have a blank sheet on which to write trade policy, e.g. after independence or after a revolution, under more normal conditions, radical change is difficult because vested interests can see the potential costs to themselves while the potential gainers from trade reform, especially producers in export activities that do not yet exist, are likely to be less influential.

Trade, Economic Growth and Poverty

During the 1970s and 1980s, a consensus emerged that openness was positively associated with growth and economic development. In large part this was a reaction to mounting evidence that the import-substituting industrialisation policies pursued by almost all low- and middle-income countries in the 1950s and 1960s were failing to deliver sustained growth and were having adverse effects on employment and income distribution. At the same time, the handful of newly industrialising economies with outward-oriented trade policies continued to grow rapidly even during the globally depressed decade 1973–1983.[3] Over the last quarter of the century, there was a rising tide of previously closed economies opening up to world trade, including China (1978), Mexico (1986), Eastern Europe (1989), India (1991) and many former Soviet republics (1992), and this was reflected in the growth of WTO membership.

The macroeconometric evidence for a positive relationship between trade and growth during the last half century is strong, although the significance of the relationship continues to be debated.[4] Correlation does not equate with causality. It may be the case

---

[3]The consensus was reflected in the World Bank's *World Development Report* in 1981. A 1975 OECD report coined the phrase *newly industrialising countries*, and the variant of newly industrialising economies (NIEs) quickly became common use. Although the OECD report included some Mediterranean and South American countries, the term NIE was most commonly identified with high-performing East Asian economies: initially Hong Kong, Korea, Singapore and Taiwan, joined by China, Indonesia, Malaysia and Thailand in the 1980s.

[4]Trade openness can be measured by an index of trade policy or by the share of trade in GDP, which are not always related (e.g. Turkmenistan and Uzbekistan have high trade/GDP ratios but illiberal trade policies), but in cross-country regressions both yield positive relationships; Dollar (1992) and Dollar and Kraay (2004) use trade ratios, Sachs and Warner (1995) use a policy index. Rodriguez and Rodrik (2001) criticise the robustness of these measures and results. In the wider literature of cross-country growth regressions, Levine and Renelt (1992) conclude that openness is not a robust determinant of growth, but their extreme bounds test is so strict that almost no explanatory variables are robust; Sala-i-Martin *et al.* (2004) using a less extreme test find that openness is one of the more robust determinants of growth.

that economic growth determines openness, which is unpersuasive (Frankel and Romer, 1999), or that growth and openness are both determined by a common cause, which is more plausible. Some writers argue that good institutions are related to both trade liberalisation and growth, and that when both institutions and openness are included as determinants of growth institutions trump trade.[5] This is an almost insoluble debate because it is hard to identify cases of bad institutions and good trade policies or, even more so, of good institutions and bad trade policies. A reasonable interpretation is that policies and institutions interact, and to seek a single dominant determinant of growth is a chimera. Every high growth economy in recent decades has been open and economies which have remained closed have been among the worst performers, but openness alone is not a good predictor of growth. The implication is that openness is necessary but not sufficient condition for sustained growth.[6]

The transmission mechanisms from trade to growth remain unclear. The resource allocation benefits of trade (the Corden triangles of Figure 11.3) are only a small part. The measured benefits from tariff removal in OECD countries are a small fraction of one percent of GDP and, although higher in more heavily protected low- and middle-income countries, the allocative efficiency gains still seem too small to explain the large differences in growth rates between closed and open economies.[7] Moreover, simply removing trade barriers should, in this analysis have a *level* rather than a *growth* effect,

---

[5]Rodrik *et al.* (2004) claim that 'Institutions Rule'. Others, such as Easterly and Levine (2003) argue that geography is the deep determinant of everything.

[6]Freund and Bolaky (2007) find that trade leads to a higher standard of living conditional on the regulatory environment. Where the structure of economic activity is rigid, the positive trade–growth relationship breaks down. The most important regulations in their tests relate to businesses rather than labour markets, which is consistent with the finding in the heterogeneous firms literature that much of the gains from trade comes from firms becoming exporters.

[7]William Cline (2004, 180) estimated that removing all trade barriers in 1997 would have increased world GDP by $228 billion, or by 0.93 percent; nearly two-fifths of the gains would go to developing countries.

increasing GDP by a certain amount, which would continue to accrue every year and is thus well worth having, but not explaining the sustained high growth rates of outward-oriented economies.

A more convincing growth connection recognises the complexity of the production process and the importance of access to best quality imported inputs. ISI policies which created a domestic steel industry not only led to an inefficient steel industry but imposed a competitive disadvantage on every producer using steel directly or indirectly. Producers in open economies can purchase inputs from the most efficient supplier, which may involve imported inputs as in global value chains or may be from domestic suppliers who are world-class because they have to be so to prosper. More liberal trade policies, encouraging import of intermediate goods or of machinery and equipment, impact positively on the vintage and quality of the capital stock (Grossman and Helpman, 1991).[8] Growth depends not only on increased factor inputs but also on improvements in factor productivity which often occurs through a learning process, whether through learning-by-doing in the production process or learning-by-seeing in the global economy.[9] Finally, corruption opportunities may be more limited in open economies than in closed economies, which tend to be more regulated.

The evidence that protected industries become inefficient is strong. The heterogeneous firm literature (Chapter 9) has also shown a positive relationship between export-orientation and productivity growth, but the causality of this last relationship could go in either

---

[8]Using Indonesian data for all manufacturing firms with twenty or more employees in the years 1991–2001, Amiti and Konings (2007) found that the largest productivity gains from trade liberalisation went to firms using imported inputs and that the gains from lower input tariffs were at least double the gains from lower tariffs on outputs. Kasahara and Rodriguez (2008) find that in Chile use of imported inputs has an immediate beneficial impact on plant-level productivity, whose size varies by sector and estimator but is at least 2.6%.

[9]In a study of 71 developing countries, Coe, Helpman and Hoffmaister (1997) found that growth in productivity is related to the amount of R&D carried out by trade partners, i.e. openness promotes technical diffusion.

direction (i.e. firms with increasing productivity become exporters or exporters become more productive). Other studies have found more new entrants in sectors where trade liberalisation takes place, suggesting some differential entrepreneurial dynamism.

The trade–growth relationship is important for poverty alleviation because the evidence from recent decades is that the decline in absolute poverty has come from increased growth rather than from reduced within-country inequality (Dollar, 2005). In China, for example, in the post-liberalisation period the Gini coefficient increased substantially from 0.32 in 1980 to 0.38 in 1992, but the effect was swamped by per capita income growth of 3.6% per annum, and the number living on less than $2 per day fell by 250 million.[10] Similarly in India in the 1990s, the effect on poverty of a slight increase in inequality was swamped by accelerated growth and, although the magnitudes are disputed, poverty fell dramatically.

The non-growth links from trade to poverty are less clear-cut (Winters, McCulloch and McKay, 2004). Openness can increase instability which may hurt the poor disproportionately, but openness can also be stabilising (e.g. food imports can offset a bad harvest). Trade liberalisation will affect wages and employment opportunities, and will change relative prices. The new opportunities could have intra-household effects, whose welfare interpretation is often unclear or depends upon prior beliefs; if women are induced to enter the formal labour market, for example, drawing them from household production may increase output but be socially destabilising, and for young women having their own earning power may be liberating but disconcerting for their parents or potential husbands. Adjustment costs to opening the economy may fall disproportionately on the poor, but whether this is in fact the outcome is case-specific and

---

[10]The Gini coefficient measures inequality over a range from one, when a single household or individual receives all of the nation's income, to zero, where every individual or household has the same income.

the empirical literature reveals no consistent pattern of pro-poor or anti-poor adjustment costs.

Trade liberalisation affects government revenue, as revenue from trade taxes declines. Whether this hurts the poor depends on whether aggregate tax revenue is allowed to fall, and on the source of replacement revenue. Although falling public revenue may be associated with diminishing services for the poor, the evidence suggests that tax revenue can be maintained in the face of trade liberalisation — and decisions to change the size of the tax take and its use are political rather than economic. In sum, the quantitatively important links from trade to poverty alleviation are through accelerated growth; other links via the income distribution, increased economic insecurity and adjustment costs, or the public budget appear to be relatively minor and their direction is unclear.

Poverty is an individual- or household-specific phenomenon and the impact of trade liberalisation will be mediated by the varying characteristics of households. Thus, poverty specialists have been sceptical of the macroeconometric results and argue that any generalisations need to be modified by country-specific conditions. Martin Ravallion (2004) concludes that there is little evidence from household surveys of trade pulling people out of poverty and claims, for example, that the decline in poverty in China during the 1980s was due to agrarian reform rather than opening the economy, but the household survey data alone do not permit such statements of causality to be made with confidence. One approach to identifying trade–related determinants of poverty alleviation is to estimate the price changes resulting from trade reform, and then to map these changes on to the consumption and income patterns of surveyed households to calculate how the number of households below the poverty line will change. These studies show, for example, that the poorest households in Indonesia were hurt by the trade shock associated with the 1997–1998 Asian Crisis, but they are sensitive to the assumed elasticities, to reporting biases and to the possibility that the effects of a trade policy change may not be transmitted directly to a household.[11] The weakness common to both the cross-country econometric approach and the analysis of household surveys in this context is the absence of a structural model which identifies all links from trade liberalisation to growth and poverty.[12] Also, in reality trade reform is often one of several concurrent shocks to households' position.

To summarise, the empirical evidence for a positive relationship between trade and growth and poverty reduction is strong. Openness appears to be a necessary, but not sufficient, condition for economic growth. The trade–poverty nexus is more controversial. The mainstream view is that trade liberalisation may have positive or negative impacts on inequality, but the positive growth effect will swamp any plausible regressive distributional effect. Poverty specialists question this view, arguing that the trade–growth link is confused with other determinants of economic growth and that poverty correlates are too diverse to support generalisations about a trade–poverty link, implying that poverty alleviation should be addressed by focusing on the determinants of household poverty rather than by relying on a centralised policy reform like trade liberalisation as a panacea. The least controversial way to conclude is to say that trade liberalisation is beneficial, but that it should be accompanied by measures such

---

[11] Deaton (1997) is the classic reference on household survey analysis. In the studies summarised here (e.g. by Levinsohn, Berry and Friedman on Indonesia, Porta on Argentina, Nicita on Mexico), the price changes are estimated from partial equilibrium demand and supply analysis of the major markets for goods and labour; Thomas Hertel and Jeffrey Reimer (2004) survey the literature, which is mainly in World Bank working papers, and point out that these studies find larger impacts on the consumption side, which is surprising because household's income is more sector-specific than their consumption, and suggest that this is due to under-reporting of income, relative to expenditure, in household surveys.

[12] Although they inevitably simplify the structure of the economy, CGE models capture direct and indirect effects and allow us to run alternative scenarios within a rigorous and consistent framework. However, in the huge CGE-based literature on trade and growth, there is relatively little on poverty because the representative agents in CGE models tend to be too average to be poor.

as a social safety net or targeted assistance to vulnerable groups in order to ensure that the benefits include poverty alleviation.

The Political Economy of Reform and Resource Abundance

If trade is so beneficial why is trade reform so difficult? The net benefits from trade reform are small compared to the size of positive and negative effects on specific groups. At least in the short-run, losers from trade reform will be aware of the cost to themselves; if they are politically powerful groups whose wealth and influence derives from protectionist trade policies, then they will be able to obstruct the removal of trade restrictions. On the other hand, the potential beneficiaries may not realise in advance who they are (e.g. future exporters) or feel that the individual benefits are too small to fight for (e.g. consumers). Analysis of the political economy of protectionism has a long history in rich countries (Chapter 12), but the special relevance to poor countries arises when trade reform is likely to be pro-poor; the losers are few but powerful and the potential gainers scattered and politically weak.

In most poor countries the majority of workers are in agriculture and they suffer from ISI policies. The political economy of reform in agriculture is emphasised in the World Bank's multi-country studies (Krueger, Schiff and Valdes, 1991–1992. Anderson, forthcoming). In the African context, where governments have problems collecting sufficient revenue to match their expenditure plans, Bates (1981) and Rodrik (1998) have highlighted export-marketing boards as a particularly insidious obstacle to trade reform. Such state monopolies, which buy crops such as cocoa or cotton from farmers ostensibly for more efficient participation in global markets, provide an opportunity for governments to take short-term fiscal advantage by paying farmers below the world price. The price gap is a tax on farmers but, initially at least, the levy might be opaque if farmers are unsure of what is happening to world prices and of the other costs associated with exporting. However, as the price gap increases farmers have little incentive to increase output and often devote their time to avoiding the official channels.[13] Despite the long-term productivity disadvantages, governments addicted to the revenue from marketing boards and with few alternative sources will continue to squeeze whatever they can from farmers even as the revenue base shrinks.

A recurring theme in the literature on trade and development is the potential, and paradoxical, negative impact of abundant natural resources, or the ***resource curse***. Conversely, resource scarcity may inspire ingenuity or push an economy into activities with greater growth potential; the first industrial revolution occurred in relatively resource–poor Great Britain, and in Asia resource–poor Japan was the first country to establish a modern industrial economy. Sachs and Warner (1995b) sparked the modern literature when they found a negative relationship between resource abundance and economic

---

[13]Ghana is a classic example (Pomfret, 1997, 190–1). In the late 1950s, when Ghana's per capita income was similar to that of South Korea, Ghana produced over 400,000 tons of cocoa a year, and cocoa accounted for over half of Ghana's exports and government revenue. Export taxes on cocoa offered an administratively simple means of gathering significant, and sorely needed, revenue, but export taxes affect the marginal rate of return, farmers made substantial shifts from cocoa to other food crops, and severe exchange rate distortions underlined incentives for smuggling. Ghana has natural advantages for growing cocoa, but increasingly new plantings in the 1970s were adjacent to the long border with the Côte d'Ivoire and sales were in the Ivoirian market where producer prices were some 50% higher than in Ghana. One to two million rural workers migrated from Ghana in the 1970s. The decline in output and farmers' income may be overstated in official Ghanaian data, but government revenue from the cocoa tax was undoubtedly reduced by smuggling. By the 1980s, when an impoverished Ghana finally introduced serious economic reforms, cocoa output had dropped to 200,000 tons. A similarly negative impact of state marketing is occurring in Uzbekistan, the world's second largest cotton exporter; there is little incentive to grow more cotton unless the farm is close to the porous borders with Kazakhstan or the Kyrgyz Republic, where agricultural prices are less repressed and smuggling relatively easy.

growth in cross-country regressions, i.e. on balance resources are a curse rather than a boon.

Three major channels for resource curse outcomes have been identified: earnings volatility, Dutch disease, and rent-seeking leading to institutional degradation. The volatility of resource earnings may lead to poor investment decisions during the boom when finance is plentiful, and a painful adjustment when commodity prices fall; such instability was emphasised in the case studies in a World Bank project (Gelb and associates, 1988).[14] A variant on the intertemporal problem is the **Dutch disease** effect, by which a resource boom makes production of other traded goods uncompetitive (Corden, 1984); this will be harmful to growth if there are shutdown costs which make it hard to reopen production when the boom is over or if there are externalities which make manufacturing or other non-booming-sector activity better for aggregate growth than producing the natural resource.[15] The resource curse is especially associated with point resources, such as oil or minerals, where the geographical concentration of production lends itself to cut-throat competition for resource rents (Isham *et al.*, 2003). The recent empirical literature supports the hypothesis that institutional degradation is the primary cause of the worst resource curse cases.[16] Rent-seeking and

---

[14]The case studies in this project were influenced by recent events. Exporters such as Mexico, Venezuela (oil) or Morocco (phosphates) borrowed heavily during the 1970s expecting to service the debts out of future export earnings, but when commodity prices fell in the 1980s they were unable to service the debts and were forced into short-term austerity measures.

[15]The initial impact of an increase in the quantity of 'land' (or natural resources) reducing the output of goods intensive in other inputs is an example of the Rybczynski Theorem. The Dutch disease is named after an episode in the 1960s when the Netherlands experienced a boom in natural gas exports. The gas boom may have discouraged non-gas exports, but it did not impoverish the Netherlands.

[16]Papyrakis and Gerlagh (2004) obtain a negative coefficient on their natural resource variable (share of minerals in GDP) in a simple conditional convergence growth regression, but the coefficient becomes positive when measures of corruption, openness and schooling are added to the right-hand side. See also Sala-i-Martin and Subramanian (2003), Stevens (2003) and Najman *et al.* (2007).

associated poor governance characterise oil exporters such as Nigeria or Venezuela, but some natural resource exporters (e.g. Norway, Malaysia, Alberta, Alaska) have not suffered from a resource curse and have prospered, suggesting that the resource curse is a conditional relationship, in which the institutional setting is critically important.

Chapter 17

Trade Costs, Trade Facilitation and Trade in Services

The relationship between trade and trade policy has always been influenced by trade costs. Before the 1800s transport costs were a crucial consideration, with trade largely restricted to items of high value relative to their bulk, such as silk, spices or precious stones. European settlement of the Americas was first based on obtaining gold and silver. In North America tobacco and furs were exported to Europe to pay for the settlers' imported goods. In Australia a virtue was made out of distance when the first fleet took convicts to the distant location; imports were provided in return for prison services. Goods with high bulk/value ratios, such as beer or building materials, were seldom if ever traded over long distances.

As transport costs fell during the 19th century more goods were traded. Railways and improved ships reduced costs by land and sea. The introduction of refrigeration on ships extended the intercontinental trade to include meat and butter. The invention of the telegraph and other means of communication made it easier to manage overseas subsidiaries. Against this technological background, and a relatively peaceful century, institutions were developed to facilitate trade, and trade policies came under the control of national governments and became the subject of political debate.

During the first half of the 20th century trade policies were mainly identified with tariffs and quantitative restrictions, although there were many other NTBs. When tariffs were substantially reduced in the 1960s and 1970s, this focussed attention on NTBs which were now relatively more important obstacles to trade.[1] As NTBs were reduced in regional agreements such as the EU and through the WTO, attention began to focus on other trade costs. Placing this in the context of more efficient production chains, Robert Feenstra (1998) highlighted the Barbie Doll, whose production costs amounted to about $1 when it sold in California for $10, a 900% wedge between the producer and consumer price.

Trade costs include all costs incurred in getting a good to a final user other than the marginal cost of producing the good itself, i.e. transport costs (in money and in time), tariffs and NTBs, information costs, contract enforcement costs, financial costs and local distribution costs. Anderson and van Wincoop (2004) estimate that in the high-income countries these costs amount on average to a 170% *ad valorem* barrier to trade. Their breakdown of trade costs is 21% in transport costs, 44% in tariffs, NTBs and other border costs, and 55% in wholesale and retail distribution costs; $1.21 \times 1.44 \times 1.55 = 2.7$ for

---

[1] There is an unsettled empirical debate about the relative importance of the reduction in trade barriers, lower transport costs due to technological innovations, and income growth in explaining the growth of international trade in the second half of the 20th century (Krugman, 1995: Baier and Bergstrand, 2001).

a total markup of 170% over the producer price.[2] Many of these costs are policy-related, and the wedge that is created between the price paid by consumers and the price received by the producer leads to substantial welfare costs, estimated by Anderson and van Wincoop to be worth more than ten percent of income. ***Trade facilitation*** is the process of reducing the policy-related component of the price wedge.

Anderson and van Wincoop assign the 44% border costs to 8% tariffs and NTBs, 7% different languages, 4% different currencies, 6% information and 3% security. Some of these are directly or indirectly policy-related (e.g. retaining an independent national currency is a political decision and language costs can be reduced by an education policy emphasising language teaching or more simply by printing forms in the main traders' languages). In trade policy debates, trade facilitation has generally been treated more narrowly, in terms of reducing the time and cost of crossing borders through simplified procedures, such as a single window where all formalities (immigration, customs, quarantine, etc.) are dealt with or one-stop border crossing points where export/emigration and import/immigration are dealt with instead of passing through a no-man's-land between the two countries' entry and exit points.

Transport costs have a real component, but they are not fixed by the state of transport technology. Limao and Venables (2001) found a large variation in the cost of shipping a standard container from Baltimore to various destinations, part of which is physically determined (for landlocked countries transport costs are on average 55% higher than for a comparable coastal country), but the biggest determinant of price variation is domestic infrastructure.[3] Clark, Dollar

---

[2] Anderson and van Wincoop emphasise that these are rough measures based on a mixture of direct observation and inferences from prices and quantities. Much of the evidence is based on the gravity model, and the composition of trade costs is related to the border effect discussed in Chapter 3.

[3] Low-income countries suffer from higher ocean shipping rates which are partly explained by port efficiency but are also due to low volume and unbalanced cargoes and perhaps shipping companies' monopoly power.

and Micco (2004) found that improving port efficiency from the 25th to the 75th percentile reduces transport costs between the USA and a Latin America country by 12%. Delays due to port congestion, bureaucracy and so forth are costly; Hummels (2001) estimates that each day of travel adds 0.8% to the value of a manufactured good and for the average ocean shipment that is equivalent to a 16% tariff.

Behind-the-border costs — wholesale and retail costs and also local financing arrangements and internal regulations and transport costs — have not usually been considered part of trade policy, but this is changing. The deep integration of the EU and to a lesser extent the CER and NAFTA addressed behind-the-border costs, and the aggressive unilateralism of US trade policy during the Reagan/Bush administrations often targeted behind-the-border costs that were believed to impede US exports. Many of the bilateral trade agreements in the 21st century focus on specific behind-the-border trade costs. Trade facilitation is one of the Singapore issues included in the Doha Development Round of multilateral trade negotiations, and it has also been the subject of agreements within Asia–Pacific Economic Cooperation (APEC) and various regional trading agreements.

A difficulty of negotiations on trade facilitation is that the concept is imprecise and has many elements. ASEAN has made progress in agreeing on common forms, e-documentation and a Single Window, but the extent to which these agreements have reduced trade costs is unclear. APEC adopted a results–based approach with members agreeing to reduce trade costs by 5% over five years, but that has been hard to monitor because it is difficult to measure trade costs.[4] Other organisations such as Central Asia Regional Economic

---

[4]In 2001, at the APEC Shanghai summit, the Committee on Trade and Investment was mandated to reduce transactions costs on trade by 5% by 2006. Starting in 2002, each APEC member was expected to submit annual Trade Facilitation Action Plans (TFAPs), which would achieve the 5% target, and report on their progress. By 2004, 1300 items had been selected in individual countries' TFAPs, mainly in the sub-category of customs procedures, and over half of these had been completed and a further quarter was in progress. APEC's trade facilitation principles emphasise simplification of customs procedures, transparency, and

Cooperation (CAREC) have adopted a corridors approach to trade facilitation, with the goal of reducing trade costs associated with specified transport corridors along which money and time costs can be monitored.

One consequence of the reduction of transport costs, trade barriers and other trade costs is that the set of goods that is internationally traded has expanded.[5] Trade theorists in the 1960s and 1970s often modelled the relative price of traded and non-traded goods, but today it is difficult to think of many non-traded goods. The classic example is haircuts, which are a service rather than a good, and one of the consequences of falling trade costs over recent decades has been to raise the profile of trade in services, as more and more become internationally traded.[6]

Trade in Services

In all economies the service sector tends to increase in importance over time, and in most countries it accounts for over half of GDP. The share of services in world trade is lower, due to the cost of trading services and many barriers to services trade, but it is growing rapidly. Among the difficulties of liberalising services trade are the sector's heterogeneity, the prevalence of regulations, and the frequent need for people to travel in order to provide or consume services.[7] Thus, trade

---

alignment with international standards, but there is a distinctive emphasis on paperless trading and e-commerce and on facilitating and promoting businesspeople's mobility.

[5]Markusen and Venables (2007) model the interaction of factor endowments and trade costs in determining how countries participate in the world economy. As trade costs fall, countries can take greater advantage of differences in factor endowments to trade more goods and fragment production along global value chains, but beyond some point lower trade costs may lead to increased specialisation and greater concentration of an individual country's exports.

[6]Even part of the haircut global value chain is traded as Toni & Guy or Jean Louis David sell their varieties of haircuts in many countries.

[7]The contributions to Mattoo, Stern and Zanini (2008) provide an introduction to various service sectors and the policy issues.

in services has fallen into a no-man's-land between the multilateral trade law for goods and nationally autonomous migration policies.

Trade in services encompasses cross-border trade in road, rail, sea or air transport, foreigners' consumption of tourism, foreigners' provision of construction services, and many services where either the consumer or the producer may travel (e.g. universities may provide education on offshore campuses or enrol foreign students on their home campus or provide distance learning in which neither the teacher nor the student moves). Services such as back-office record-keeping or call-centres may be provided online or by phone without any movement of people. Beyond bazaars at border crossings, trade in goods invariably requires some trade in services, whether transport, financing, insurance or communications. Services are a major part of trade costs, and facilitating trade in services is an important component of reducing trade costs and increasing globalisation.

The gains from specialisation and trade in services are essentially the same as for trade in goods (lower prices and more variety, including a greater quality range), although service sector markets are more likely to contain elements of imperfect competition. Importing services rather than trying to source all services domestically will yield gains from trade. Because many services are inputs into production, trade in services lowers other producers' costs and, much like the cost of protecting steel in countries adopting ISI strategies, autarchic service sectors reduce the competitiveness of many producers of final goods and services.

Unlike trade in goods, restrictions on services trade rarely take the form of taxes on imports, and overwhelmingly take the form of regulations which limit market access. What is traded in services markets is often hard for buyers to evaluate, i.e. many service sectors are characterised by asymmetric information, and governments regulate entry or behaviour. The degree of regulation may vary with respect to the perceived cost of acting on false information; going to an untrained doctor is likely to be more dangerous than going to an untrained car mechanic, but in both cases there may be official certification procedures and punishment for illegally practicing the trade. Such regulation is often considered part of the governments' responsibility.[8] Barriers to entry may, however, be used by the industry to create excess demand for the service and higher wages, e.g. the American Medical Association acts effectively to limit entry and preserve doctors' salaries.[9] Moreover, differing entry requirements can act as barriers to trade in services and shelter incompetence or inefficiency from international competition.

Since 1995 trade in services has been brought into the WTO through the General Agreement on Trade in Services (GATS). GATS is broader than GATT because it includes factor flows in the provision of services, and it is also more flexible. While MFN treatment and transparency are general rules in both GATT and GATS, other GATS rules are subject to specific undertakings by WTO members. These undertakings usually include guarantees of market access and national treatment (i.e. foreign suppliers will be treated the same way as domestic suppliers) in specified sectors or service activities.[10]

One difficulty of reaching international agreements on services trade is that many countries do not even have coherent national policies, e.g. in Canada provincial regulations are more important

---

[8] As Michael Moore (in *Stupid White Men*) observed about the low pay for pilots in US deregulated airlines: "I don't know about you, but I want the people taking me with them to defy nature's most powerful force — gravity — to be happy, content, confident, and well-paid."

[9] The success of such a strategy depends upon the capacity of the industry to segment markets, which may change over time. Although patients generally do not have much flexibility in selecting providers of medical services, with lower transport and information costs an increasing number of Americans travel to Mexico or elsewhere for non-urgent medical treatment.

[10] The necessity of careful specification of included and excluded sectors was illustrated by Antigua's successful complaint to the WTO about restricted access to US markets for online betting. Part of the US defence was that they had meant to exclude gambling from US service sector commitments in 1994, but this was of course no legal defence. The US lost the case in 2005 and again on appeal in 2007 (James, 2007).

than federal policy in regulating the provision of some services. The
EU has been much less successful in establishing a single market for
services than for goods; the Bolkestein proposal that the principles
of mutual recognition and harmonisation, which had been successfully applied to intra-EU goods trade should be applied to services
trade, led to widespread protests and was effectively watered down
by national governments before a much weaker Services Directive
was adopted in 2006.[11]

---

[11]Especially controversial in the original 2004 proposal was the 'country of origin'
principle, under which service providers would be bound by their home-country
standards when supplying a service in another EU country. Consumers' concerns
about erosion of standards of services such as healthcare in western Europe were
seized upon by service sector workers who feared competition from the new member states in eastern Europe — a spectre characterised by the 'Polish plumber.' In
the 2006 Directive, which enters into force in 2010, the freedom to provide services
throughout the EU remains, but member states retain considerable flexibility in
their ability to impose idiosyncratic national rules.

Chapter 18

Globalisation

Governments' attitudes towards the global economy and international trade have changed dramatically in recent decades. This was partly in (over) reaction to global events, but mostly in response to evidence–based understanding of the consequences of trade policies.

In the 1950s and 1960s developing countries, influenced by the disastrous decline in primary product prices in the late 1920s and 1930s and inspired by the success of the Soviet Union in the 1940s and 1950s, adopted import-substituting industrialisation strategies which were the antithesis of specialisation by comparative advantage. The already industrialised countries were more willing to see the disastrous economic conditions of the 1930s as a consequence of trade barriers, and moved cautiously to liberalise trade within GATT. Nevertheless, many countries were reluctant to agree to an International Trade Organisation in the late 1940s and much of the early liberalisation was driven by specific considerations, such as the US decision to reverse to some extent its excessive tariffs of the 1930s,

Canada's desire to encourage this by reciprocal tariff reductions, and six European countries' willingness to reduce their average tariffs as a condition for forming a customs union. Even after the significant tariff reductions which followed the 1964–1967 Kennedy Round, some large sectors (notably agriculture and textiles and clothing) were left out of the process, governments were quick to resort to non-tariff trade barriers when increased imports coincided with recession in the 1970s and early 1980s, and some high income countries (e.g. Australia and New Zealand) did not significantly reduce their trade barriers until the 1980s.

In the 1980s attitudes reversed and the benefits of trade have been more widely appreciated since then. The failings of ISI strategies, although showing different symptoms in different countries, and the success of the high-performing East Asian economies which adopted outward-oriented development strategies provided the evidence against trade barriers and for openness. As would be expected from the pressure group model of trade policy formation, there was substantial opposition to reducing trade barriers from those who would lose producer surplus, but the global trend has been clear.

Acceptance of GATT rules was of little significance to countries pursuing inward-looking policies. With more outward-oriented policies, trade law and market access for exports became important. The establishment of the World Trade Organisation in 1995 was symbolic of the transformation of the GATT system from something imposed by the major trading nations and other high-income countries to a more truly world system. By the early 21st century WTO membership was almost universal, and the main non-members were in the process of negotiating WTO accession. Even more significantly, the low- and middle-income countries, with Brazil, China, India and South Africa in the lead, became actively involved in multilateral trade negotiations during the Doha Development Round.

Ironically the most virulent opposition to the WTO coincided with this move to almost-universal membership. The opposition attained a high profile with demonstrations in Seattle in 1999, and subsequently in Genoa in 2001, Cancun in 2003 and other venues for international trade–related meetings. The demonstrators have mostly been from high-income countries, speaking on behalf of those whose interests they believe to be harmed by trade and by the WTO constraining members' ability to use activist trade policies. Among the issues that have concerned critics of the system are arguments concerning trade and labour, trade and the environment or health, and trade and culture.

Increased manufactured exports from low- and middle-income countries have been a major change in the world economy over the last generation.[1] Compared to rich country standards, workers who produce these goods are paid low wages and may work under poor conditions, and trade union opposition to free trade seizes on these facts. For example, opponents of the NAFTA argued that it would be easier for employers to replace high wage workers in the USA with low wage workers in Mexico (either directly by immigration or indirectly by importing labour-intensive goods). Other critics of the global trading system object to its seeming indifference to workers labouring under dangerous conditions.

Trade theory highlights that, although there are net gains from trade, distributional consequences are important and some groups may be made worse off. For example, it is likely that NAFTA or the 2004/7 enlargement of the EU had, *ceteris paribus*, a negative impact on the wages of unskilled workers in the USA or western Europe, but the magnitude is debated, and whether it is swamped by other determinants of the wage distribution such as technical change, which in recent decades has been biased towards skilled workers, or

---

[1]The high-performing Asian economies led the way in the 1960s and 1970s, but more dramatically global labour supply, according to IMF estimates (in the spring 2007 *World Economic Outlook*), increased fourfold between 1980 and 2005 as India, China and other formerly centrally planned countries entered the world trading system.

institutional changes. If labour markets are flexible or adjustment costs are covered by the state, then the negative impact on wages may be minor compared to the net gains from trade. In any case, rather than foregoing the gains from trade, a better approach is to compensate the losers through the tax and social security system and to lower adjustment costs through active labour market policies such as retraining schemes.

Some WTO critics believe that the competitive advantage of countries specialising in labour-intensive goods comes not just from abundant labour and low wages, but also from lax labour regulations that reduce the non-wage costs to employers. Their policy recommendation is to include labour standards in trade negotiations. However, labour standards imposed by foreign countries are opposed by governments of low- and middle-income countries, because standards set by high income countries may be inappropriate for low income countries and international standards could be used as a protectionist policy for restricting imports from a country deemed not to meet those standards. Disagreements about appropriate labour policies would be better addressed by adoption of the conventions of the International Labour Organisation. The moral force of some of these conventions is more widely accepted than of others, e.g. on the use of child labour or of prison labour, although there may be disagreement about the age when people cease to be children or whether goods produced under duress by political prisoners differ from goods produced by ordinary felons for a wage. ILO conventions are, of course, often breached by countries which have signed them, but a labeling system (e.g. showing that carpets have not been woven by children) can have sufficient credibility to allow consumers to decide whether or not they want to buy the product.

Compared to rich country standards, environmental standards in low- and middle-income countries are often lax and hence provide a competitive edge to producers competing with firms in countries with more globally beneficial labour standards. There may also be concerns about countries with lax environmental standards having a comparative advantage in hazardous activities, such as the disposal of nuclear waste, which from a global perspective should be done under the strictest rules. Some environmental activists want to include environmental standards in trade negotiations, but, as with labour standards, environmental standards imposed by foreign countries are opposed by governments of low- and middle-income countries because standards set by high-income countries may be inappropriate for their countries and their design may be hijacked by import-competing industries as a protectionist device. Such responses are consistent with the distortions approach to policy. In the presence of a market distortion, trade policy may improve the situation, but it is better to implement a policy that tackles the distortion at its root. This may be difficult for products causing global economic harm, but coordinated action through the United Nations or other global fora is likely to be better than the use of unilateral trade threats.

Environmental standards are, even more than labour standards, likely to be hijacked by protectionist interests. The early WTO case brought by Venezuela against the USA concerned a US Clean Act, which was itself desirable on environmental grounds, but which in its implementation treated domestically refined petroleum less restrictively than imported refined petroleum. The WTO dispute panel found that this aspect of the Act was against world trade rules, and the USA complied with the judgment by terminating the discrimination against imports. As with labour standards a less heavy-handed approach to product-specific environmental concerns is through labelling, e.g. to advertise that the tuna in a can was caught with dolphin-friendly nets.[2] Exporters have an incentive to

---

[2] A US ban on tuna imports from Mexico because Mexican fishers' nets were not dolphin-safe was ruled illegal by a 1991 GATT panel. A 1998 WTO panel ruled against a US ban on shrimp imports from India, Malaysia, Pakistan and Thailand because shrimp-fishers' nets were unsafe for sea turtles. However, in the shrimp case the WTO panel did not find the US ban illegal, but it had been introduced without giving reasonable notice to the affected countries. In other

provide information which they think consumers will be interested in knowing, and consumers rather than their governments can decide whether the good should be imported.

Health standards involve similar issues. The line between mandatory requirements and voluntary decision by informed consumers is an unclear one, which depends upon risk assessment as well as ethical concerns about individual versus state responsibility. For food and drugs, countries often have evidence-based approval processes such as through the Food and Drug Administration (FDA) in the USA, which in extreme cases must balance the risk of an unnecessary death against the benefits of a life saved to decide when a potentially life-saving drug's use should be authorised. Premature authorisation can be disastrous as with thalidomide. With food there may be genuine disagreements about what are acceptable and what are dangerous additives or practices, reflected in debates over genetically-modified crops or hormone-induced animal growth. Trade restrictions for quarantine reasons are accepted as valid and in emergency situations may be introduced in contravention to WTO commitments, e.g. when spread of mad cow disease or avian flu threatened. However, such sanitary restrictions are often used as trade barriers even when the health risk is negligible, such as Australian restrictions on importing cheese made from non-pasteurised milk and retention of bans on beef imports long after mad cow disease has been contained (as in French restrictions on beef imports from England or Korean bans on beef imports from the USA in the 2000s). The WTO principle is that governments have the authority to legislate on health, safety or environmental standards, but they should do so in ways that avoid as far a possible discrimination between domestic and foreign suppliers. Thus, when Thailand increased the tax on imported cigarettes in

---

cases, WTO panels have explicitly accepted national environmental policies even if they restrict trade, e.g. a Canadian complaint against a French ban on asbestos products was dismissed by a 2001 WTO panel even though the ban restricted trade.

1990 to protect public health, a GATT panel ruled that although the tax rate on cigarettes was a national issue it must be levied equally on domestic and imported cigarettes.

Another passionately held view is that trade destroys culture. Any economic change leads to changes in everyday life and an argument in importing countries is, if their culture is threatened, should they be able to place restrictions on, for example, Hollywood movies or McDonald's restaurants? This raises questions of individual choice.[3] Should governments establish cultural norms and standards or should people define their culture through the choices that *they* make rather than through standards set by others?

Individual responses are an alternative to public policy in some of these settings.[4] Expressing a view at individual level may involve boycotting goods from obnoxious countries or companies: examples where individual responses reached significant levels in the 1980s and 1990s included boycotts of South African goods before the end of apartheid, and of Nestlé for discouraging breastfeeding of African babies. Conversely, positive discrimination in favour of domestic goods is common and sometimes encouraged by public policy as in 'Buy Australian' campaigns.

Concerned consumers may want to take a more proactive role in supporting poor producers overseas. This desire has been

[3]They may also involve trade–offs of costs and benefits. McDonald's, for example, has been an important source of technology transfer, introducing new management techniques and training to many countries, not to mention the concept of restaurants providing clean toilet facilities (Tschoegl, 2007).

[4]Pressure for using trade policy to influence other countries' labour practices or environmental policies seem to have peaked in the 1990s. Apart from the argument that individuals rather than governments should decide what are unacceptable practices, there is also widespread recognition that trade sanctions have a poor track record in changing government policies (Hufbauer, Schott and Elliott, 1990). Sanctions episodes in the 1990s also highlighted the possibility of adverse humanitarian consequences (comprehensive sanctions against Iraq hurt poor people more than Saddam Hussein) and the uneven distribution of the costs of sanctions enforcement (neighbouring frontline states bore disproportionate costs of sanctions against Serbia).

accommodated by the **Fair Trade Movement,** which aims to guarantee fair prices to poor producers at the end of a long supply chain. Starting with a US coffee importer TransFair USA in 1999, Fair Trade grew rapidly and was estimated to cover $1.4 billion of world trade in 2005. Although the activities of Fair Trade organisations such as Fairtrade Labelling Organisations International (FLO), the International Federation for Alternative Trade, the Network of European World Shops and the European Fair Trade Association may have improved living standards for some participants, there are problems. Fairtrade may provide an incentive for over-supply, e.g. by encouraging producers to grow coffee when market signals are indicating that they should shift to another crop. The focus on cooperatives and small-scale farmers may miss the really poor who work as hired labourers on large farms.[5] Although Fairtrade guarantees a certain payment to the growers' association, there is no guarantee that producers will receive a larger share of the premium prices associated with Fairtrade products; retailers may use the Fairtrade logo as a sign of inelastic demand and charge prices higher than are justified simply by the added costs of paying suppliers more.

Following the rapid growth of Fairtrade products in 2004 and 2005 the movement faced a controversial issue in 2006. How can the movement cooperate with multinationals without a "sell-out"? Is Nestlé *Partners' Blend* Fair Trade Coffee a cheap way for the multinational corporation to gain a good image or is it a sign of corporate acceptance of the Fair Trade idea?

An environmental counterpart to the Fair Trade movement was the growth of organic food sales in the late 20th century. The organic

---

[5]By dealing directly with cooperatives, the Fair Trade organisations may also be encouraging the cooperatives to move into parts of the value chain where they are less efficient than specialised intermediaries. The UK government's Department for International Development provides funding to the accreditor FLO and to the British non-governmental organisation, the Fairtrade Foundation, which raises questions of whether official aid could better be targeted to help those in severe poverty.

movement also grew beyond its small-scale origins, as shops like Whole Foods became major supermarket chains in some large US cities. In the early 2000s "local" seemed to be the new organic, as many consumers in high-income countries, concerned about how their food is being grown, turned away from imported foods to local produce, often sold in farmers' markets or through other fairly direct forms of selling. Among the questions raised by such individual decisions are whether they hurt poor farmers in poor countries and whether they are environmentally harmful (e.g. importing Spanish tomatoes or New Zealand lamb into the UK may save more energy in production than it uses in transport). The prevalence of such responses, however, may reflect a general frustration with the market system, which is efficient at matching demand and supply but is by its nature impersonal and increases insecurity.

Appendix

Appendix. Protection in the European Union, 1999.

Sector	Number of tariff lines	Rate of overall protection
Cereals	21	19.0
Meat	26	76.0
Dairy products	61	110.0
Sugar	7	125.0
Other agriculture	538	20.0
Mining	137	2.3
Food products	1,586	24.5
Beverages	180	8.6
Tobacco	9	47.3
Textiles	1,059	22.1
Apparel	225	30.6
Leather and leather products	102	5.7
Footwear	58	8.9
Wood products	181	2.7
Furniture and fixtures	38	1.8
Paper and paper products	200	3.8
Printing and publishing	41	3.5
Industrial chemicals	1,153	6.0
Other chemicals	423	3.5
Petroleum refineries	62	2.1
Petroleum and coal products	17	2.2

(*Continued*)

Appendix. (*Continued*)

Sector	Number of tariff lines	Rate of overall protection
Rubber products	105	5.5
Plastic products	35	5.9
Pottery, china, etc	25	5.9
Glass and products	137	4.8
Non-metallic products	132	2.4
Iron and steel	521	9.0
Nonferrous metals	255	3.3
Metal products	354	4.5
Office and computing equipment	76	1.0
Other machinery	941	1.8
Radio, TV and communications	321	8.9
Other electrical machinery	358	2.7
Shipbuilding	63	1.6
Railway equipment	40	1.8
Motor vehicles	164	10.3
Motorcycles and bicycles	34	10.4
Aircraft	47	1.7
Other transport equipment	6	1.5
Professional goods	381	2.2
Other industries	308	3.3

Source: Patrick Messerlin: *Measuring the Costs of Protection in Europe: European Commercial Policy in the 2000s* (Washington DC: Institute for International Economics, 2001).

Notes

1. For agricultural sectors, (the first five lines) measures are based on three-year averages of consumer support estimates by the OECD.
2. Within-sector averages smooth out tariff peaks; the degree of heterogeneity of tariff rates is suggested by the number of tariff lines (10,427 in total).
3. Overall protection includes conservative measures of major border non-tariff barriers (quantitative restrictions and antidumping duties), but ignores non-border barriers such as technical standards, public procurement or production subsides.
4. The estimates incorporate all Uruguay Round commitments apart from in textiles and clothing, where the Multifibre Arrangement only ended on the 1 January 2005. They are thus indicative of patterns of EU protection at least until the second half of the first decade of the 21st century.

References

Aitken, Norman: The Effect of the EEC and EFTA on European Trade: A Temporal Cross-Section Analysis, *American Economic Review*, 63, 881–92 (1973).

Amiti, Mary, and Jozef Konings: Trade Liberalization, Intermediate Inputs, and Productivity: Evidence from Indonesia, *American Economic Review*, 97(5), 1611–38 (2007).

Anderson, James, and J. Peter Neary: *Measuring the Restrictiveness of Trade Policy*, Cambridge, MA: MIT Press, (2005).

Anderson, James, and Eric van Wincoop: Trade Costs, *Journal of Economic Literature*, 42(3), 691–751 (2004).

Anderson, Kym, ed.: *Distortions to Agricultural Incentives*, multiple volumes, World Bank: Washington, DC, (forthcoming).

Bagwell, Kyle, and Robert Staiger: *The Economics of the World Trading System*, Cambridge, MA: MIT Press, (2002).

Baier, Scott, and Jeffrey Bergstrand: The Growth of World Trade: Tariffs, Transport Costs, and Income Similarity, *Journal of International Economics*, 53(1), 1–27 (2001).

Balassa, Bela: *The Theory of Economic Integration*, Homewood IL: Richard D. Irwin, (1961).

Baldwin, Richard, and James Harrigan: Zeros, Quality and Space: Trade Theory and Trade Evidence, *National Bureau of Economic Research Working Paper*, 13214, Cambridge, MA, (2007).

Baldwin, Richard, and Frédéric Robert-Nicoud: Trade and Growth with Heterogeneous Firms, *Journal of International Economics*, 74(1), 21–34 (2008).

243

Baldwin, Richard, and Daria Taglioni: Gravity for Dummies and Dummies for Gravity Equations, *National Bureau of Economic Research Working Paper*, 12516, (September 2006).

Baldwin, Robert, and Tracy Murray: MFN Tariff Reductions and Developing Country Benefits under the GSP, *Economic Journal*, 87, 30–46 (1977).

Bates, Robert: *States and Markets in Tropical Africa: The Political Basis of Agricultural Policy*, Berkeley, CA: University of California Press, (1981).

Bernard, Andrew, and Bradford Jensen: Exporters, Jobs, and Wages in U.S. Manufacturing: 1976–1987, *Brookings Papers on Economic Activity: Microeconomics*, 67–119 (1995).

Bernard, Andrew, Bradford Jensen and Peter Schott: Trade Costs, Firms and Productivity, *Journal of Monetary Economics*, 53(5), 917–37 (2006).

Bernard, Andrew, Stephen Redding and Peter Schott: Comparative Advantage and Heterogeneous Firms, *Review of Economic Studies*, 1, 31–66 (2007).

Bernhofen, Daniel, and John Brown: An Empirical Assessment of the Comparative Advantage Gains from Trade: Evidence from Japan, *American Economic Review*, 95(1), 208–25 (2005).

Bhagwati, Jagdish: Immiserizing Growth: A Geometrical Note, *Review of Economic Studies*, 25–6, 201–5 (1958).

Bhagwati, Jagdish, and Arvind Panagariya: Preferential Trading Areas and Multilateralism: Strangers, Friends or Foes? in Jagdish Bhagwati and Arvind Panagariya, eds., *The Economics of Preferential Trade Agreements*, Washington, DC: AEI Press, 1–78 (1996).

Borjas, George: Self-selection and the Earnings of Immigrants, *American Economic Review*, 77(4), 531–53 (1987).

Bowen, Harry, Edward Leamer and Leo Sveikauskas: Multicountry, Multifactor Tests of the Factor Abundance Theory, *American Economic Review*, 77, 791–809 (1987).

Brander, James, and Paul Krugman: A 'Reciprocal Dumping' Model of International Trade, *Journal of International Economics*, 15, 313–21 (1983).

Brander, James, and Barbara Spencer: Export Subsidies and International Market Share Rivalry, *Journal of International Economics*, 16, 83–100 (1985).

Broda, Christian, and David Weinstein: Globalization and the Gains from Variety, *Quarterly Journal of Economics*, 121(2), 541–85 (2006).

Chiquiar, Daniel, and Gordon Hanson: International Migration, Self-selection, and the Distribution of Wages: Evidence from Mexico and the United States, *Journal of Political Economy*, 113, 239–81 (2005).

Clark, Ximena, David Dollar and Alejandro Micco: Port Efficiency, Maritime Transport Costs, and Bilateral Trade, *Journal of Development Economics*, 75, 417–50 (2004).

Clemens, Michael, and Jeffrey Williamson: Why did Tariff-Growth Correlation Reverse after 1950?, *National Bureau of Economic Research Working Paper*, 9181, (September 2002).

Cline, William: *Trade Policy and Global Poverty*, Washington, DC: Center for Global Development, (2004).

Coe, David, Elhanan Helpman and Alexander Hoffmaister: North-South R&D Spillovers, *Economic Journal*, 107(440), 134–49 (1997).

Corden, W. Max: The Calculation of the Cost of Protection, *Economic Record*, 33, 29–51 (1957).

Corden, W. Max: *The Theory of Protection*, Oxford: Clarendon Press, (1971).

Corden W. Max: Booming Sector and Dutch Disease Economics, a Survey, *Oxford Economic Papers*, 36, 825–848 (1984).

Curzon, Gerard: *Multilateral Commercial Diplomacy*, London: Michael Joseph, (1965).

Deardorff, Alan: Weak Links in the Chain of Comparative Advantage, *Journal of International Economics*, 9(2), 197–209 (1979).

Deaton, Angus: *The Analysis of Household Surveys: A Microeconometric Approach to Development Policy*, Baltimore, MD: Johns Hopkins University Press, for the World Bank, (1997).

Devreux, Charan, Robert Lawrence and Michael Watkins: *Case Studies in US Trade Negotiations*, 2 vols., Washington, DC: Institute for International Economics, (2006).

Dollar, David: Outward-oriented Developing Economies Really Do Grow More Rapidly: Evidence from 95 LDCs, 1976–85, *Economic Development and Cultural Change*, 40(3), 523–44 (1992).

Dollar, David: Globalization, Poverty, and Inequality since 1980, *World Bank Research Observer*, 20(2), 145–175 (2005).

Dollar, David, and Aart Kray: Trade, Growth and Poverty, *Economic Journal*, 114(493), F22–49 (2004).

Dunning, John: Towards an Eclectic Theory of International Production: Some Empirical Tests, *Journal of International Business Studies*, 11(1), 9–31 (1980).

Easterly, William, and Ross Levine: Tropics, Germs, and Crops: How Endowments Influence Economic Development, *Journal of Monetary Economics*, 50(1), 3–39 (2003).

Eaton, Jonathan, Marcela Eslava, Maurice Kugler and James Tybout: Export Dynamics in Colombia: Firm-Level Evidence, *J.F. Kennedy*

School of Government Working Paper, RWP07-050, Cambridge, MA: Harvard University (2007).

Eaton, Jonathan, Samuel Kortum and Francis Kramarz: Dissecting Trade: Firms, Industries, and Export Destinations, *American Economic Review, Papers and Proceedings*, 94(2), 150–4 (2004).

Engel, Charles, and John Rogers: How Wide is the Border?, *American Economic Review*, 86(5), 1112–25 (1996).

Estevadeordal, Antoni, and Kati Suominen: Mapping and Measuring Rules of Origin Around the World, in Olivier Cadot, Antoni Estevadeordal, Akiko Suwa-Eisenmann, and Thierry Verdier, eds., *The Origin of Goods: Rules of Origin in Regional Trade Agreements*, Oxford: Oxford University Press, (2006) — earlier drafts circulated as "Rules of Origin: An Analytical World Map and Methodologies for Measurement".

Evans, Carolyn: The Economic Significance of National Border Effects, *American Economic Review*, 93(4), 1291–1312 (2003).

Falvey, Rod, and Doug Nelson: Introduction: Special Issue on 100 Years of Antidumping, *European Journal of Political Economy*, 22, 545–53 (2006).

Feenstra, Robert: Integration of Trade and Disintegration of Production in the Global Economy, *Journal of Economic Perspectives*, 12(4), 31–50 (1998).

Feenstra, Robert: *Advanced International Trade: Theory and Evidence*, Princeton, NJ: Princeton University Press, (2004).

Feenstra, Robert: New Evidence on the Gains from Trade, *Weltwirtschaftliches Archiv, Review of World Economics*, 142(4), 617–41 (2006).

Feenstra, Robert, and Alan Taylor: *International Economics*, New York: Worth Publishers, (2008).

Feinberg, Robert, and Kara Reynolds: Tariff Liberalisation and Increased Administrative Protection: Is There a Quid Pro Quo?, *The World Economy*, 30(6), 948–961 (2007).

Finger, J. Michael, H. Keith Hall and Douglas Nelson: The Political Economy of Administered Protection, *American Economic Review*, 72(3), 452–66 (1982).

Finger, J. Michael, and Mordechai Kreinin: A Measure of 'Export Similarity' and Its Possible Uses, *The Economic Journal*, 89, 905–912 (1979).

Frankel, Jeffrey, and David Romer: Does Trade Cause Growth? *American Economic Review*, 89(3), 379–399 (1999).

Freund, Caroline, and Bineswaree Bolaky: Trade, Regulations, and Income, *Journal of Development Economics*, (2008).

Gelb, Alan, and associates: *Oil Windfalls: Blessing or Curse?*, New York: Oxford University Press, (1988).

Greenaway, David: A Statistical Analysis of Fiscal Dependence on Trade Taxes and Economic Development, *Public Finance*, 39, 70–89 (1984).

Greenaway, David, Alessandra Guariglia and Richard Kneller: Financial Factors and Exporting Decisions, *Journal of International Economics*, 73, 377–95 (2007).

Grennes, Thomas: The Columbian Exchange and the Reversal of Fortune, *Cato Journal*, 27(1), 91–107 (2007).

Grossman, Gene, and Elhanan Helpman: *Innovation and Growth in the Global Economy*, Cambridge, MA: MIT Press, (1991).

Grossman, Gene, and Elhanan Helpman: Protection for Sale, *American Economic Review*, 84(4), 833–50 (1994).

Grossman, Gene, and Esteban Rossi-Hansberg: The Rise of Offshoring: It's Not Wine for Cloth Anymore, in *The New Economic Geography: Effects and Policy Implications*, Federal Reserve Bank of Kansas City Annual Symposium, (2006), (downloaded from http://www.kc.frb.org/PUBLICAT/SYMPOS/2006/sym06prg.htm).

Grubel, Herbert, and Peter Lloyd: *Intra-industry Trade*, London: MacMillan, (1975).

Haberler, Gottfried: *The Theory of International Trade*, London: William Hodge, (1936).

Hallak, Juan Carlos: Product Quality and the Direction of Trade, *Journal of International Economics*, 68(1), 238–65 (2006).

Hamilton, Bob., and John Whalley: Efficiency and Distributional Implications of Global Restrictions on Labor Mobility, *Journal of Development Economics*, 14, 61–75 (1984).

Hatton, Timothy: Should We Have a WTO for International Migration?, *Economic Policy*, 50, 341–83 (2007).

Head, Keith, and Thierry Mayer: Non-Europe; The Magnitude and Causes of Market Fragmentation in the EU, *Weltwirtschaftliches Archiv*, 136(2), 284–314 (2000).

Helpman, Elhanan, Marc Melitz and Yona Rubinstein: Estimating Trade Flows: Trading Partners and Trading Volumes, *National Bureau of Economic Research Working Paper*, 12927, (February 2007).

Hertel, Thomas, and Jeffrey Reimer: Predicting the Poverty Impacts of Trade Reform, *World Bank Policy Research Working Paper*, 3444, (November 2004).

Hindley, Brian, and Patrick Messerlin: *Antidumping Industrial Policy: Legalized Protection in the WTO and What to Do About It?*, Washington, DC: American Enterprise Institute, (1996).

Hiscox, Michael: *International Trade and Political Conflict: Commerce, Coalitions, and Mobility*, Princeton, NJ: Princeton University Press, (2002).

Hufbauer, Gary Clyde, Jeffrey Schott, and Kimberly Ann Elliott: *Economic Sanctions Reconsidered*, revised edition, 2 vols., Washington, DC: Institute for International Economics, (1990).

Hummels, David: Time as a Trade Barrier, (2001), available online at http://www.mgmt.purdue.edu/faculty/hummelsd/research/time3b.pdf

Irwin, Douglas: *Against the Tide: An Intellectual History of Free Trade*, Princeton, NJ: Princeton University Press, (1996).

Irwin, Douglas: Interpreting the Tariff-Growth Correlation in the Late Nineteenth Century, *American Economic Review, Papers and Proceedings*, 92(2), 165–9 (2002).

Irwin, Douglas: The Optimal Tax on Antebellum US Cotton Exports, *Journal of International Economics*, 60, 275–91 (2003).

Irwin, Douglas: Antebellum Tariff Politics: Regional Coalitions and Shifting Economic Interests, *Journal of Law and Economics*, (November 2008).

Irwin, Douglas, Peter Mavroidis and Alan Sykes: *The Genesis of the GATT*, New York: Cambridge University Press, (2008).

Isham, Jonathan, Michael Woolcock, Lant Pritchett and Gwen Busby: The Varieties of Resource Experience: How Natural Resource Export Structures Affect the Political Economy of Economic Growth, *Middlebury College Economics Discussion Paper*, 03-08, Middlebury, VT, (2003).

James, Sallie: Time to Double Down on Online Gambling, *Cato Institute — TCSdaily.com*, (April 13, 2007) (available at www.cato.org/pub_display.php?pub_id=8188)

Johnson, Harry: The Cost of Protection and the Scientific Tariff, *Journal of Political Economy*, 68, 327–45 (1954).

Johnson, Harry: Optimum Tariffs and Retaliation, *Review of Economic Studies*, 21-2, 142–53 (1960).

Jones, Ronald W.: The Structure of Simple General Equilibrium Models, *Journal of Political Economy*, 73, 557–72 (1965).

Jones, Ronald W.: A Three-Factor Model in Theory, Trade and History, in Jagdish Bhagwati, Ronald Jones, Robert Mundell and Jaroslav Vanek eds., *Trade, Balance of Payments, and Growth: Essays in Honor of Charles P. Kindleberger*, Amsterdam: North Holland, 3–21 (1971).

Kasahara, Hiroyuki, and Joel Rodrigue: Does the Use of Imported Intermediaries Increase Productivity? Plant-Level Evidence, *Journal of Development Economics*, (2008).

Kee, Hiau Looi, Alessandro Nicita and Marcelo Olarreaga: Estimating Trade Restrictiveness Indices, *Economic Journal*, (forthcoming).

Kee, Hiau Looi, Alessandro Nicita and Marcelo Olarreaga: Import Demand Elasticities and Trade Distortions, *Review of Economics and Statistics*, (forthcoming).

Kellard, Neil, and Mark Wohar: On the Prevalence of Trends in Primary Commodity Prices, *Journal of Development Economics*, 79(1), 146–67 (2006).

Kelly, Kenneth, and Morris Morkre: Do Unfairly Traded Imports Injure Domestic Industries? *Review of International Economics*, 6(2), 321–32 (1998).

Kemp, Murray: *The Pure Theory of International Trade*, Englewood Cliffs NJ: Prentice Hall, (1964).

Kemp, Murray, and Henry Wan: An Elementary Proposition Concerning the Formation of Customs Unions, *Journal of International Economics*, 6(1), 95–97 (1976).

Kindleberger, Charles: Group Behavior and International Trade, *Journal of Political Economy*, 59, 30–47 (1951).

Kommerskollegium: *Adding Value to the European Economy: How Anti-Dumping Can Damage the Supply Chains of Globalized European Companies — Five Cases from the Shoe Industry*, The National Board of Trade, Stockholm, (2007).

Kono, Daniel: Optimal Obfuscation: Democracy and Trade Policy Transparency, *American Political Science Review*, 100(3), 369–84 (2006).

Krueger, Anne: Factor Endowments and Per Capita Income Differences among Countries, *Economic Journal*, 78, 641–59 (1968).

Krueger, Anne: Free Trade Agreements as Protectionist Devices, *National Bureau of Economic Research Working Paper*, 4342 (1993).

Krueger, Anne, Maurice Schiff and Alberto Valdes, eds.: *The Political Economy of Agricultural Pricing Policies*, Baltimore: The Johns Hopkins University Press, for the World Bank, (1991–1992).

Krugman, Paul: Increasing Returns, Monopolistic Competition and International Trade, *Journal of International Economics*, 9, 469–79 (1979).

Krugman, Paul: Scale Economies, Product Differentiation and the Pattern of Trade, *American Economic Review*, 70, 950–9 (1980).

Krugman, Paul: Is Bilateralism Bad? In E. Helpman and A. Razin eds., *International Trade and Trade Policy*, Cambridge, MA: MIT Press, 19–23 (1991).

Krugman, Paul: Growing World Trade: Causes and Consequences, *Brookings Papers on Economic Activity*, 1, 327–77 (1995).

Krugman, Paul, and Maurice Obstfeld: *International Economics: Theory and Policy*, 7th Edition, Boston, MA: Pearson Addison-Wesley, (2006).

Lalonde, Robert: The Case for Wage Insurance, *Council Special Report No. 30*, Council on Foreign Relations, New York, (September 2007).

Leamer, Edward: *Sources of International Comparative Advantage: Theory and Evidence*, Cambridge, MA: MIT Press, (1984).

Leontief, Wassily: Domestic Production and Foreign Trade: The American Position Re-examined, *Proceedings of the American Philosophical Society*, 37, 332–49 (1953).

Lerner, Abba: Factor Prices and International Trade, *Economica n.s.*, 19, 1–15 (1952).

Levine, Ross, and David Renelt: A Sensitivity Analysis of Cross-Country Growth Regressions, *American Economic Review*, 82(4), 942–63 (1992).

Limao, Nuno, and Anthony Venables: Infrastructure, Geographical Disadvantage, Transport Costs, and Trade, *World Bank Economic Review*, 15(3), 451–779 (2001).

Lipsey, Richard, and Kelvin Lancaster: The General Theory of Second Best, *The Review of Economic Studies*, 24(1), 11–32 (1956–1957).

Little, Ian, Tibor Scitovsky and Maurice Scott: *Industry and Trade in Some Developing Countries*, New York: Oxford University Press, (1970).

McAfee, R. Preston, Wendy Takacs and Daniel Vincent: Tariffying Auctions, *RAND Journal of Economics*, 30(1), 158–79 (1999).

McCallum, John: National Borders Matter: Canada–US Regional Trade Patterns, *American Economic Review*, 85(3), 615–23 (1995).

MacDougall, G.D.A.: British and American Exports: A Study Suggested by the Theory of Comparative Costs, *Economic Journal*, 61, 697–724 (1951).

Markusen, James: Factor Movements and Commodity Trade as Complements, *Journal of International Economics*, 14, 341–56 (1983).

Markusen, James: *Multinational Firms and the Theory of International Trade*, Cambridge, MA: MIT Press, (2002).

Markusen, James, and Anthony Venables: Interacting Factor Endowments and Trade Costs: A Multi-Country, Multi-Good Approach to Trade Theory, *Journal of International Economics*, 73, 333–54 (2007).

Mathews, John, and Dong-Sung Cho: *Tiger Technology: The Creation of a Semiconductor Industry in East Asia*, Cambridge, UK: Cambridge University Press, (2007).

Mattoo, Aaditya, Robert Stern and Gianni Zanini: *A Handbook of International Trade in Services*, London: Oxford University Press, (2008).

Meade James: *The Theory of International Economic Policy; Vol. 1, The Balance of Payments*, London: Oxford University Press, (1951).

Meade James: *A Geometry of International Trade*, London: Allen and Unwin, (1952).

Meade James: *The Theory of International Economic Policy; Vol. 2, Trade and Welfare*, London: Oxford University Press, (1955).

Melitz, Marc: The Impact of Trade on Intra-Industry Reallocations and Aggregate Industry Productivity, *Econometrica*, 71(6), 1695–1725 (2003).

Messerlin, Patrick: *Measuring the Costs of Protection in Europe: European Commercial Policy in the 2000s*, Washington, DC: Institute for International Economics, (2001).

Metzler, Lloyd: International Demand and Domestic Prices, *Journal of Political Economy*, 57, 345–351 (1949).

Moses, Jonathan and Bjørn Letnes: The Economic Costs to International Labor Restrictions: Revisiting the Empirical Discussion, *World Development*, 32, 1609–26 (2004).

Mundell, Robert: International Trade and Factor Mobility, *American Economic Review*, 47(3), 321–35 (1957).

Mundell, Robert: Tariff Preferences and the Terms of Trade, *Manchester School of Economic and Social Studies*, 32, 1–13 (1964).

Najman, Boris, Richard Pomfret and Gael Raballand: *The Economics and Politics of Oil in the Caspian Basin: The Redistribution of Oil Revenues in Azerbaijan and Central Asia*, London: Routledge, (2008).

Ohlin, Bertil: *Interregional and International Trade*, Cambridge, MA: Harvard University Press, (1933).

Olson, Mancur: *The Logic of Collective Action: Public Goods and the Theory of Groups*, Cambridge, MA: Harvard University Press, (1965).

O'Rourke, Kevin: Tariffs and Growth in the Late Nineteenth Century, *Economic Journal*, 110(463), 456–83 (2000).

O'Rourke, Kevin, and Jeffrey Williamson: *Globalization and History: The Evolution of a Nineteenth-Century Atlantic Economy*, Cambridge, MA: MIT Press, (1999).

Papyrakis, Elissaios, and Reyer Gerlagh: The Resource Curse Hypothesis and its Transmission Channels, *Journal of Comparative Economics*, 32(1), 181–93 (2004).

Patterson, Gardener: *Discrimination in International Trade: The Policy Issues, 1945–1965*, Princeton, NJ: Princeton University Press, (1966).

Pearson, Charles: *United States Trade Policy: A Work in Progress*, John Wiley, (2003).

Pincus, Jonathan: Pressure Groups and the Pattern of Tariffs, *Journal of Political Economy*, 83, 757–78 (1975).

Pomfret, Richard: The Impact of EEC Enlargement on Non-member Countries' Exports to the EEC, *The Economic Journal*, 91, 726–9 (1981).

Pomfret, Richard: On the Division of Labour and International Trade: Or, Adam Smith's Explanation of Intra-industry Trade, *Journal of Economic Studies*, 13, 55–62 (1986a).

Pomfret, Richard: The Effects of Trade Preferences for Developing Countries, *Southern Economic Journal*, 53, 18–26 (1986b).

Pomfret, Richard: International Trade Policy with Imperfect Competition, *Princeton Special Papers*, 17, (August 1992).

Pomfret, Richard: *Development Economics*, London: Prentice Hall, (1997).

Pomfret, Richard: *The Economics of Regional Trading Arrangement*, Oxford: Oxford University Press — paperback edition with new preface of book published by Clarendon Press, Oxford, 1997, (2001).

Pomfret, Richard: Is Regionalism an Increasing Feature of the World Economy?, *The World Economy*, 30(6), 923–47 (2007).

Ravallion, Martin: Looking beyond Averages in the Trade and Poverty Debate, *World Bank Policy Research Working Paper*, 3461, (November 2004).

Reynolds, Kara: Subsidizing Rent-seeking: Antidumping Protection and the Byrd Amendment, *Journal of International Economics*, 70(2), 490–502 (2006).

Ricardo, David: *On the Principles of Political Economy and Taxation*, London: John Murray, (1817).

Richardson, Martin: Tariff Revenue Competition in a Free Trade Area, *European Economic Review*, 39, 1429–37 (1995).

Rodrik, Dani: Why is Trade Reform so Difficult in Africa? *Journal of African Economies*, 7, 43–69 (1998).

Rodrik, Dani: *One Economics, Many Recipes: Globalization, Institutions, and Economic Growth*, Princeton, NJ: Princeton University Press, (2007).

Rodrik, Dani and Francisco Rodríguez: Trade Policy and Economic Growth: A Skeptics Guide to the Cross-National Evidence, in Ben Bernanke and Kenneth Rogoff eds., *Macroeconomics Annual 2000*, Cambridge, MA: MIT Press, 261–324 (2005).

Rodrik, Dani, Arvind Subramanian and Francesco Trebbi: Institutions Rule: The Primacy of Institutions over Geography and Integration in Economic Development, *Journal of Economic Growth*, 9(2), 131–65 (2004).

Rose, Andrew: One Money, One Market: Estimating the Effects of Common Currencies on Trade, *Economic Policy*, 30, 9–48 (2000).

Roy, A.D.: Some Thoughts on the Distribution of Earnings, *Oxford Economic Papers*, 3(2), 135–46 (1951).

Rybczynski, T.M.: Factor Endowment and Relative Commodity Prices, Economica, 22, 336–41 (1955).

Sachs, Jeffrey, and Andrew Warner: Economic Reform and the Process of Global Integration, *Brookings Papers on Economic Activity 1*, 96, 1–118 (1995a).

Sachs, Jeffrey, and Andrew Warner: Natural Resource Abundance and Economic Growth, *Harvard Institute of Economic Research Discussion Paper*, 517, Cambridge, MA, (1995b).

Sala-i-Martin, Xavier, Gernot Doppelhofer and Ronald Miller: Determinants of Long-Run Growth: A Bayesian Averaging of Classical Estimates (BACE) Approach, *American Economic Review*, 94(4), 813–835 (2004).

Sala-i-Martin, Xavier, and Arvind Subramanian: Addressing the Natural Resource Curse: An Illustration from Nigeria, *IMF Working Paper*, WP/03/139, International Monetary Fund, Washington, DC, (July 2003).

Samuelson, Paul: The Gains from International Trade, *Canadian Journal of Economics and Political Science*, 5, 195–205 (1939).

Samuelson, Paul: International Trade and the Equalization of Factor Prices, *Economic Journal*, 58, 163–84 (1948).

Samuelson, Paul: International Factor Price Equalization Once Again, *Economic Journal*, 59, 181–97 (1949).

Samuelson, Paul: The Gains from International Trade Once Again, *Economic Journal*, 72, 820–9 (1962).

Samuelson, Paul: Ohlin was Right, *Swedish Journal of Economics*, 73, 365–84 (1971).

Schattschneider, Elmer Eric: *Politics, Pressures, and the Tariff: A Study of Free Private Enterprise in Pressure Politics, as shown in the 1929-1930 Revision of the Tariff*, New York: Prentice Hall, (1935).

Schott, Peter: Across–Product versus Within-Product Specialization in International Trade, *Quarterly Journal of Economics*, 119(2), 646–77 (2004).

Schott, Peter: The Relative Sophistication of Chinese Exports, *Economic Policy*, 23(53), 5–49, (2008).

Shibata, H.: "The Theory of Economic Unions: A Comparative Analysis of Customs Unions, Free Trade Areas, and Tax Unions" in Carl Shoup ed., *Fiscal Harmonization in Common Markets, Theory*, Vol. 1, 145–264 New York: Columbia University Press, (1967).

Smith, Adam: *An Inquiry into the Nature and Causes of the Wealth of Nations*, Strahan and Cadell: London – ed. Edwin Cannan, 1904, London: Methuen and Co., (1776).

Stevens, Paul: Resource Impact — Curse or Blessing? A Literature Survey, *Journal of Energy Literature*, 9(1), 3–42 (2003).

Stolper, Wolfgang, and Paul Samuelson: Protection and Real Wages, *Review of Economic Studies*, 9, 58–73 (1941).

Svedberg, Peter: Optimal Tariff Policy on Imports from Multinationals, *The Economic Record*, 55(148), 64–7 (1979).

Trefler, Daniel: The Case of the Missing Trade and Other Mysteries, *American Economic Review*, 85(6), 1029–46 (1995).

Trefler, Daniel: The Long and Short of the Canada–US Free Trade Agreement, *American Economic Review*, 94(4), 870–95 (2004).

Tschoegl, Adrian: McDonald's – Much Maligned, but an Engine of Economic Development, *Global Economy Journal*, 7(4), Article 5, Berkeley: Electronic Press, (2007).

Utton, Michael: *International Competition Policy: Maintaining Open Markets in the Global Economy*, Cheltenham, UK: Edward Elgar (2006).

Vandenbussche, Hylke, and Maurizio Zanardi: The Global Chilling Effects of Antidumping Proliferation, *CEPR Discussion Paper*, 5597, London, UK: Centre for Economic Policy Research (2006).

Vandenbussche, Hylke, and Maurizio Zanardi: What Explains the Proliferation of Antidumping Laws? *Economic Policy*, 23 (53), 93–138 (2008).

Vanek, Jaroslav: The Natural Resource Content of Foreign Trade, 1870–1955, and the Relative Abundance of Natural Resources in the United States, *Review of Economics and Statistics*, 41, 146–53 (1959).

Vernon, Raymond: International Investment and International Trade in the Product Cycle, *Quarterly Journal of Economics*, 80, 190–207 (1966).

Vernon, Raymond: The Product Cycle Hypothesis in a New International Environment, *Oxford Bulletin of Economics and Statistics*, 41, 255–67 (1979).

Viner, Jacob: *The Customs Union Issue*, New York: Carnegie Endowment for International Peace, (1950).

Wagner, Joachim: Exports and Productivity: A Survey of the Evidence from Firm-Level Data, *The World Economy*, 30(1), 60–82 (2007).

Winters, Alan, Neil McCulloch and Andrew McKay: Trade Liberalization and Poverty: The Evidence So Far, *Journal of Economic Literature*, 42(1), 72–115 (2004).

Index